The Big Book of

SOCIAL MEDIA

Case Studies, Stories, Perspectives

Robert Fine

Yorkshire Publishing

The Big Book of Social Media: Case Studies, Stories, Perspectives
ISBN: 978-0-88144-159-8
Copyright © 2010 by Robert Fine. *All rights reserved.*

Published by
Yorkshire Publishing
9731 East 54th Street
Tulsa, OK 74146
www.yorkshirepublishing.com

Dedicated to my wife, Theresa

Table of Contents

The Media

Government

Employment

Nonprofits

The Artists

Global Perspectives

Moving Forward

Foreword

If we could take a journey back in time just five years, and imagine how technology might change our lives, we might have predicted more sophisticated smartphones, more content available anytime and anywhere, smaller computers, even the iPad. What I suspect most amateur futurists could not have imagined, was the remarkable adoption of social media across all parts of our society. Five years ago, Facebook was a closed network restricted mostly to high school and college students. Twitter had not yet even been imagined. Today, 500 million people have Facebook accounts and some 150 million have Twitter accounts.

These and other social media platforms have changed the way we communicate with our friends, family, and co-workers. In 140-character bursts on Twitter or longer posts on Facebook, social media platforms have changed the way Americans trade in information. As you will find in the essays that follow in this book, from political campaigns to marketing campaigns – social media is now at the heart of the movement of information in this country. And without a doubt, these social media platforms have changed my business – the news business – forever.

When an 8.0 magnitude earthquake hit Haiti, it was Twitter that initially helped us learn about the overwhelming devastation. When democracy protestors in Iran were unable to get their message out, they turned to Twitter. The first image of Captain Sully's downed USAirways jet: did it come from CNN? Associated Press? Reuters? No. It came from Janis Krums, a twitterer who happened to be a passenger on a nearby ferry on the Hudson River.

The moment CNN breaks news, do more people get the news from CNN on TV or do more people learn about the news because they are one of 3.5 million (and growing) who follow CNN Breaking News (twitter.com/cnnbrk) or one of over 20 million who follow other CNN Twitter accounts? I can't tell you that I know the answer, but I *can* tell you that because CNN wants to make sure that you get your news from CNN, we need to make that news available on all devices, on all platforms. When someone clicks the Facebook icon on a story they read on the CNN Political Ticker, that click begins the process of sharing our story with countless other readers and users who may never have thought to connect with CNN that day.

Today, when a political journalist finishes writing a story, the next step that reporter often takes is to tweet it out. We have gone from an era when journalists reported the news to an era in which journalists now promote the news they report. It's all about content distribution via whatever mechanism possible. Even the most old school journalists have realized the value of selling their wares through the world of social media. Put simply, Twitter is helping to revolutionize the news business.

When I joined CNN in 1991, we often discussed how cable news had created the twenty-four hour news cycle and how that had changed journalism and politics forever. In a remarkably short period of time, Twitter has helped journalism move from the "24 hour" news cycle to what I like to call the "1 minute ago" news cycle. The incredible shrinking news cycle has forced governments and politicians to be on alert every minute of every day to respond to an opponent, respond to a news report, or simply respond to an errant tweet. The upside is that misinformation is corrected immediately. The downside is that technology has now forced our leaders to provide instant responses to every issue, when sometimes we might all be better off if those leaders took the time to contemplate a decision or a position.

As a sign of how important social media is to modern journalism, just note what applications are open on computers in newsrooms across the country. Twitter is almost always there, helping editors and reporters watch for news on their beats. They are looking for everything from natural disasters to breaking political news to the next jetliner landing in the Hudson River.

The "1 minute ago" news cycle is here to stay. Whether Americans get their news from television, a Web site, Facebook, Twitter, or from the next great social media phenomenon, we will continue to have access to more news and at a faster and faster pace. The book you're holding in your hand is a window into how social media has already begun to change our lives from politics to entertainment to travel to shopping. Some of those changes are dramatic. Some are subtle. When the history of the early part of the 21st century is written, I have no doubt that the advent of social media will be seen as revolutionary. The only question is whether by then, we'll still be speaking to each other 140 characters at a time.

Sam Feist is the political director and vice president of Washington Programming for CNN Worldwide. Feist oversees political news coverage and political programming, including CNN's daily Washington newscast, *The Situation Room with Wolf Blitzer,* and CNN's Sunday interview program, *State of the Union.* In March of 2010, he launched CNN's new 7pm political program *John King USA.* Feist also oversees production of presidential addresses, presidential debates, primary nights, conventions and election nights for both CNN and CNN.com. Feist and his team won an Emmy award for their coverage of the 2006 Midterm elections and won the 2009 Peabody Award for coverage of the 2008 presidential campaign. In June of 2009, he was featured in Washingtonian Magazine's top fifty Washington journalists issue.

Sam has a policy that he'll only follow 125 people on Twitter and the moment someone tweets what they're eating or the score of a game, he'll probably drop them. You can find him on Twitter @SamFeistCNN.

Preface

What you hold in your hand is the culmination of a journey that started for me back on April 14th, 2009; the day after my thirty-eighth birthday; the day I received the first layoff of my life. I had spent nine years traveling the world through a job I loved, and now I was one of the countless Americans facing unemployment in a diminishing economy.

At that time, I had already been using Twitter for a few months and had begun to learn about social media and the amazing things happening on social networks. I felt there was a need for a low-cost conference focused on social media that went beyond the basics of creating a Facebook page. On June 9th, 2009 I held the first "Cool Social Conference" in Washington, DC. The following seven months were a whirlwind that produced eighteen conferences around North America and one conference held in Dubai. The year culminated in December with a two-day conference focused on government and social media.

What began as a bleak year turned into an amazing journey through which I met countless interesting people, many that I now call close friends. In addition to the connections I made, I learned something new every day. Though I will not claim to be a social media guru, I find that I learn best when I'm exposed to thoughts, ideas and perspectives that are out of my comfort zone and force me to think outside of the box. I've collected together the very best cases studies, stories and perspectives that I've come across in the last eighteen months and hope they will inspire you to generate your own new ideas. In turn, I hope you will help inspire those that follow you by sharing your own stories with us.

I need to thank a number of people who have been instrumental and helpful starting back in April 2009 and through the final stages of publishing this book. Thanks to Kent Fowler for helping me get that first conference off the ground in Washington, DC. Thanks to Brant Beaupre for your continuous design support over the last eighteen months. Thanks to Neal Schaffer for that discussion in the parking lot of the Orange County conference on November 5th, 2009 and providing the idea to do a book. Thanks to Beverly Macy for being a very supportive social media friend. Thanks to both Todd Rutherford and Lily Bomar of Yorkshire Publishing for taking a chance on me and providing me great support. Thanks to Sam Feist for your belief in the book and appreciated contribution. Thanks to Alison Smith for the great opportunity with InsideNGO and your continuing support. Thanks to Cathy Scott for your last minute offer of help. Thanks to Nicole Krug for joining me on this future ride. Thanks to Grant Hibbs for always believing in me through thick and thin, no matter what, over many, many years. Futhermore, thanks to all forty-two contributing authors for your fantastic case studies, stories and perspectives for helping to make the best social media book on the planet.

I invite you, to join our on-going discussion at http://TheBestofSocial.com. Here you'll find opportunities to ask the authors questions, interact in live webinars, find a supportive resource to continue learning, and a place to tell your own story.

I also invite you to feel free to contact me with any questions, concerns, gripes or seething anger. I can be found at:

Bob Fine
bobfine@gmail.com
@bobfine
http://www.facebook.com/robertjfine
http://www.linkedin.com/in/bobfine
http://www.TheBestofSocial.com
http://www.bobfine.com
+1-202-684-6207

Introduction

Introduction

The Start of a Great Shift

By

Mirna Bard

"How can you squander even one more day not taking advantage of the greatest shifts of our generation? How dare you settle for less when the world has made it so easy for you to be remarkable?" – Seth Godin

Gone are the days when it was a must for corporations to work months and months with an agency to develop an extensive advertising plan that would be pushed in front of their target audience with an overly-expensive media campaign. Gone are the days when entrepreneurs or small business owners placed their business on hold because they didn't have any marketing funds to reach prospects.

Gone are the days when we turned to the media to cover the happening stories. Gone are the days when we waited for popular authors to publish content for us. Gone are the days of one-way communication.

We have entered a forceful era that experts are saying is more powerful than the industrial revolution. It is a new generation where business is no longer in charge because consumers are calling the shots. It's a time where consumers have access to vast amounts of online information from a broad range of resources, and they expect to gather the information they need without being interrupted by unwanted marketing messages. It's a time where marketers no longer have to be subservient to the media to get their message out.

It is a period of new media, two-way dialogue, and attraction marketing. Genuine relationships are being built that have added a new meaning to listening, learning, and engaging. The greatest universal shift of our time has been created; it is the age of the social web—a collection of online communities, tools, and applications that enable us to connect with people socially and share stories, interests, and experiences. Search engines, blogs, and wikis—as well as many social networking sites, including Facebook, Twitter, Flickr, YouTube, and LinkedIn—have helped us connect with people across the world in ways we never thought possible.

At a glance, the most recent social web stats are staggering. However, what is even more astonishing is that the number we share today may not be completely accurate split seconds later due to the rapid growth of this extraordinary period. Thus, these stats are being shared only to give you a broad look at what has been happening online.

- Internet usage has hit a major milestone, surpassing 1.2 billion users per month and growing.

- Google is the top Web site in the world, providing more than three-quarters of a billion search results per day.

- Three of the most popular brands online are social media related—Facebook, YouTube, and Wikipedia.

- Facebook has 500 million users, and is the second most popular site after Google. If it were a country, it would be the third largest one.

- Twitter has 150 million users with millions of tweets happening every minute.

- There are over nine hundred thousand new blog articles everyday; enough to fill the NY Times for nineteen years.

- The world spends 110 billion minutes per day on social media sites and blogs.

- Members of social networking sites spend 1.5x more time online than the average Internet user.

- Thus far in 2010, there was a 24 percent increase of people visiting social media sites over last year.

- High school and college students spend 60 percent less time than their parents watching TV and 600 percent more time online.

The era of the social web is a major transformation that has opened the door to limitless opportunities and changed the face of communication forever. This powerful change has eternally altered the way we communicate, live, and do business. Until the last several years, the social web was a thrilling novelty, with no solid business application. Today, the web is truly the greatest tool available to individual marketers and organizations. It has allowed us to manage brand reputation, sway public perception, and establish thought leadership by creating and publishing our own content that showcases our knowledge and expertise.

The social web has also redefined the rules of customer engagement by offering a new low-cost avenue for communicating, educating, entertaining, and collaborating at a much deeper level than traditional marketing and advertising vehicles. It has enabled us to enhance traditional marketing campaigns by using cost-effective pull tactics to create visibility for our businesses and connect with our audiences—customers, prospects, media, partners, employees, and co-workers. More importantly, the social web has given us the possibility to put our finger on the pulse of our customers, which is absolutely priceless.

Social media is currently being used by businesses of all sizes: from someone operating their business from the back of their truck or garage; to the local dry cleaner or restaurant around the corner; to the world-known brand or not-for-profit. The world's most admired companies—Dell, Cisco, Starbucks, and Ford—are realizing the power of this dramatic shift and are rapidly adapting to this new epoch.

Many of the world's business leaders, celebrities, and politicians are not only starting to create social media profiles online, they're also looking more and more at how social media tools can expand their brands and build community. They have begun to listen and learn from the online conversation, as well as communicate authentically with their target audience in ways they are not typically accustomed to. According to a recent study presented at a Pivot Conference (in partnership with Extra Mile Research) entitled, "Marketers' Current and Future Use of Social Media", 63% of marketers are already investing in social media marketing, and of the 37% that are not currently investing in social media marketing, 62% are planning to invest, including 46% who plan to do so within one year[1].

If you are at all skeptical of the online world and if it can work for your business, then you have picked up the right book. We are here to tell you that with some careful planning, commitment and consistency, utilizing the social web will work for any business and individual. This timely book is a collection of forty-two fascinating social media case studies from different authors who share the stories of organizations, entrepreneurs, and individuals who have tremendously succeeded on the social web. These businesses have embraced and leveraged tools of the online world to achieve objectives and maximize results.

We hope these interesting and beneficial case studies here will not only motivate you to start dipping into the online world, but guide you to start applying some of these lessons for the creation of your own strategies, so you or your business grows and thrives online.

But before you move on to the next chapters, I want to share with you more reasons on why creating strong online visibility has become a necessity for business. I will also offer some essential information you need to consider before jumping on the social bandwagon. This information will help you assess whether your organization is ready for the social web, and is vital to succeeding online.

So, let's get started.

---

[1] Eagle, Scott. Acceptance of Social Media Marketers. August 31st, 2010. http://www.mediapost.com/publications/?art_aid=134612&fa=Articles.showArticle

Taking the Social Plunge

If you are struggling with social media because you have to relearn the marketing game, you are not alone. While many companies have woken up to this new reality and social media best practices have emerged, some organizations still lack a basic understanding of the various aspects of the social web and they remain disconnected, disinterested, and constantly struggling with how to best engage their audience.

This struggle is not surprising since social media has only gained significance throughout worldwide popular culture within the last several years, and since it is a relatively new concept, understanding the ins and outs of the social media landscape may not come as second nature to many people. But is it only the newness and lack of knowledge of social media that is holding many businesses back? Not entirely. Lack of strategy and fear also play a significant role.

Many companies are entering into the social web in an ungainly manner. They are failing to acknowledge that successful online marketing takes research, proactive brainstorming, strategy, careful organization, genuine transparency, engagement, and the elimination of fear.

The companies who decide to avoid social media fear the technicalities that come with it, such as privacy issues, the time dedication that is required, brand-haters who leave negative comments online, and the inability to measure ROI as perfectly as they would like. If these are the same concerns you have, then you need to open your mind and understand that: social media is not about technology, it's about relationships; there are ways that privacy can be controlled; it is only a time-wasting distraction when there is lack of planning; brand-haters will talk about you whether they are on social media sites or not; and there are many ways to measure the impact of social media.

We're still in somewhat of a burgeoning period of social media and you're not going to understand everything about everything right away. It's a learning process for all of us, yet it's an exciting process. So don't be afraid to have a voice on the social web. The benefits of using social media outweigh the consequences, and if you use social media properly, it will become an irreplaceable asset to you or your business because it offers some extremely unique opportunities to connect directly with people and consumers.

Whatever fear is keeping you from conversing with your customers and including your voice in what's happening on the social web, it's time to get over it. Your customers don't care why you're afraid. All they see is that you don't care enough to listen and talk to them. The new generation doesn't just prefer to use social media, they require it. Today's generation communicates with one another using social tools and texting, not e-mail and snail mail.

Consumers and business buyers are looking for more personalized relationships and two-way dialogue with companies they want to spend their dollars with. We live in a world now in which buyers want to make up their minds about what they need. They seek and find the information they need to make their jobs easier and their lives better. They have the option of seeking their own products and services by doing keyword searches on Google and other search engines, by reading blogs and forums for reviews of products and services, and by jumping on social networking sites to ask their peers about their experiences with certain products and services. By the time buyers are ready to talk to a seller, they are already equipped with information about the company and its products or services.

Only you can judge if you or your organization is ready to get involved in social media. Should your organization get started on social media now, knowing that it will take a complete mindset shift? What kind of mindset shift you ask? It is a mind that is open to all kinds of possibilities, and below are samples of questions you must ask yourself to check if you or your organization has the right mindset to use social media. If you answer yes to most of them, it's time to take the social plunge.

- Are you willing to learn and educate yourself and/or any employees in your organization?

- Are you ready to make changes to your organization's culture and reinvent the use of office time?

- Are you willing to be open about two-way dialogue instead of the one-way communication that we are all used to?

- Are you prepared to listen and understand what your audience is seeking from you online?

- Are you willing to do the research and take the time to strategize?

- Are you willing to experiment and be patient when results don't happen overnight?

- Are you able to put in true time dedication and commitment?

- Are you committed to keeping your site, blog, and profiles updated with fresh content?

- Are you willing to be authentic about the good and bad in your organization?

- Are you ready to relate to people no matter how receptive or antagonistic they are to your message?

- Are you ready to make your online marketing about your audience and not about yourself all the time?

- Are you willing to mix a little of your personal life with your business to humanize your brand?

- Do you have the "relationships first, business second" mentality?

If you did not answer yes to most of these questions, then your organization either may not be ready or you are still not convinced that social media can build recognition, trust, and revenue for your business. In that case, we hope that the best practice success stories in this book will transform the way you think about the online world forever.

I can tell you that without the social web, my business and many other businesses would not exist today. I was able to go from a local entrepreneur in Southern California to a world-known speaker and author with practically zero marketing dollars. I have built a strong online community of amazing supporters, developed relationships with people all over the world, and have clients who reside in different countries. And, I was able to do it all by sitting in my home office working on my online visibility by sharing my knowledge and expertise, and building genuine relationships. All it took is passion, an open-mind, focus, commitment, and consistency.

Remember, being mute and avoiding participation in the online world may tarnish years of brand equity and give the upper hand to your competition. If you're not taking advantage of this opportunity, know that your competition *is*. Participation on the social web will no longer be an option as more and more people spend increased amounts of time communicating online. Thus, online transparency may still be a choice now, but will soon be an unavoidable requirement if we want to stay in business tomorrow.

I trust you will enjoy all the incredible success stories in this book, and hope you join us in this exciting online journey by opening your mind, thinking outside the box, and coming up with some creative and innovative approaches to engaging the community.

Named as one of the "smartest people in social media," Mirna Bard is a business and social web strategy consultant who inspires organizations and entrepreneurs to leverage the Internet, so they can attract bigger and better opportunities for their business. She has helped many businesses create a sustainable strategy so they can consistently attract new prospects, build stronger bonds with customers, empower employees, boost leads, and increase sales. Mirna is also an author and world-known speaker as well as an instructor of social media at the University of California, Irvine, CA. She has a bachelor's degree in advertising and a master's in business.

Mirna Bard
mirnabard@gmail.com
@MirnaBard
http://facebook.com/SocialWebStrategyConsultant
http://www.linkedin.com/in/mirnabard
http://www.MirnaBard.com
http://www.MirnaBard.com/blog

My Personal Learning Network

by

Eric Andersen

If I were to think back just five years ago to how I consumed information and interacted with the world around me, it would be a radically different picture than my experience today. As I recall, what is now known today as "social media" was at that time a combination of two things: blogging and a Web site called MySpace. What is now known as "Web 2.0" was at that time just a conference. And what is now known as the iPhone did not yet exist. Wow, how things have changed in just a few years.

My response to the early social media platforms of blogging and MySpace could not have been more different. As an IBM employee, I knew people who were blogging on technical topics both internally and externally, and while I did not have the time to blog myself, I did find time throughout my week to follow a number of blogs and forums and occasionally post comments or contact the blogger directly. This soon became a standard element of my learning routine, something that has always been important for my role at IBM.

MySpace, on the other hand, represented something that had no value to me whatsoever, an online network intended purely for social interactions (as opposed to professional interactions), and I didn't need some Web site to help me make or keep in touch with friends. Besides, these Web sites were time-consuming, mundane, and, like text messaging, primarily for teenagers, right?

So, I stuck with reading blogs. This became yet another component of an already fragmented part of my professional life, learning. At IBM, and especially in an organization like Global Business Services (GBS), focusing on learning and keeping your skills and knowledge base up-to-date is critical for working with customers on a daily basis. As an IT architect in the custom development space, my primary roles are to understand technologies available in the marketplace, communicate them to clients, select the right components based on customer requirements, and design and implement architectures to support large, complex systems. Therefore, I not only had to keep my existing web development and J2EE technical skills current, but I also had to keep abreast of new technologies, new software products, open source projects, frameworks, advances in hardware, and even industry trends (at the time primarily in retail and the travel/transportation).

To put it bluntly, learning poses a major challenge in a billable, client-facing environment. Finding dedicated time to spend away from a customer project for training purposes was extremely difficult, and even online and virtual training still required periods of dedicated time, which was often out of the question.

Everyone I knew in Services had a different approach to keeping their skills current. Some specialized in certain areas (i.e. product or technology focus), and thus focused their learning only in that particular area, often using technical literature such as O'Reilly books or IBM Redbooks. Others attended the occasional conference or technical event as a way to learn about the latest technologies and trends. And others looked to online resources such as blogs and technology news sites. At the time, I was mentoring a number of junior IT architects, and one of the most frequent questions I was asked was how IT architects could best keep their skills and technical knowledge current and relevant for customers.

I looked to my own strategy for the answer; I had always considered my ability to keep up with technology and the latest trends a core strength, so I hoped I could mentor others in this area. While my personal learning at times included some of the previously mentioned areas, my weekly thirst for technology information came primarily from a combination of:

- Technology blogs
- Technology and business magazines (Computerworld, Information Week, etc.)
- Web sites such as Slashdot and IBM's Developerworks
- Technical books (O'Reilly, IBM, etc.)

For a while this approach worked, though it was time-consuming, erratic, and often prone to missing important trends. I also had no way to easily catalog what I was reading, search and reference previously read material, or share this material with others. Some of these were minimally possible using Google searches, but clearly this was not an ideal solution.

Now on a completely unrelated note, I joined Twitter in May of 2008. I believe my initial experience matched that of nearly everyone else upon joining: utter confusion as to its purpose. Laura Fitton has a well known signature line: "Twitter's the stupidest app you've ever seen"—and it's never more evident than when you first sign up. I did have a handful of friends using Twitter at that time, and my first step was to follow them. Most of them tweeted about three or four times a week, and I should note, still do. I did not have a smartphone at the time, and I set up my account to both send and receive tweets via text message. My usage, in terms of both reading and posting, was minimal for nearly a year; little did I know what impact it would eventually have.

Fast forward to April of 2009, when I begin hearing more about Twitter from colleagues at IBM, primarily bloggers and others in the social computing space.

Most were just trying it out as well, so I decided it was time to find out more. I wasn't disappointed.

After a few simple web searches, I found a number of articles and blog posts on how to get started on Twitter. Although I don't remember the specific articles, they provided some simple steps to take and recommended people to follow in the technology domain, and this was the real beginning of my use of Twitter. In addition, I remember watching a video, which is a Google Tech Talk that Laura Fitton gave at Google in May, 2009. Much of my early understanding of Twitter came from this video[1].

At this point, I began seeking out people to follow in a few key areas: technology, social media, Boston, and IBM. For the most part it was not difficult to find people with these interests, but once I did and I began truly consuming Twitter, everything changed. My Twitter usage increased significantly, from almost nothing to close to thirty to forty tweets per day. I wish I had access to these early tweets, and although Twitter certainly has them stored somewhere, I had not set up a third-party Twitter backup/archive service that early on.

Those first few months of real Twitter usage were mostly a combination of learning about the platform itself, learning how other people were already using Twitter, and tweeting things about my life and of interest to me. I would guess that most of my Twitter usage during this time was engaging with others (@replies) rather than fully public tweets. This pattern has stuck with me, even to this day. Despite heavy tweeting of links, I still hover around 60-65% @replies.

It wasn't long, however, before I started to realize the potential for learning and connecting with others. I was suddenly now connected to a "stream of consciousness" thinking from major tech bloggers, industry experts, news sources, and more. Not surprisingly, all of my existing learning sources (blogs, Slashdot, tech news, etc.) were on Twitter. But, not only did I get the pure news stories, people were providing their own spin, and so Twitter became a human source of information. I could not only learn about news and technology, but receive expert opinions and thoughts on these topics as well, while sharing my own opinion, for what it was worth. For the first time, the learning process became clear, and I was able to consolidate and simplify a number of different areas of learning and keep up-to-date on news. It was at this point that the light bulb went off for me. Twitter was a true game changer.

And yet, even this was still a beginning. In mid-2009 I began attending various "tweetup" events in the Boston area, and I began meeting folks who I had only known online via Twitter. It was incredible to suddenly connect face to face with folks I had never met before, and yet whose interests and everyday lives I already had a connection to. It was at this point that I realized that I was also using Twitter as a way to interact socially with others, not just for learning and news,

---

[1] http://j.mp/LFGoogleTalk

but to begin and develop new friendships and relationships, some of which could be further extended in person. Suddenly my initial thinking about the usefulness of MySpace had changed. Here I had found a tool which could simultaneously provide vast, customized, targeted learning, along with more traditional "social network" experiences of friendships and everyday conversations.

Thanks to Tweetstats and other Twitter analytics tools, these various stages and overall progression can be visualized quite clearly. Below is a graph which simply counts my tweets, by month, throughout all of 2009 and so far in 2010:

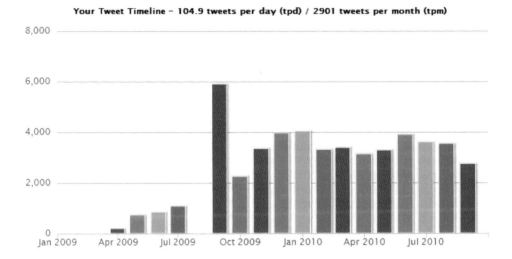

Your Tweet Timeline - 104.9 tweets per day (tpd) / 2901 tweets per month (tpm)

As you can see, once I began following others in my areas of interest in April and May of 2009, my posts to Twitter increased from close to zero to a significant monthly number. I'm actually not sure what happened in September 2009—I suspect this might be a bug in the analysis.

Today, I tweet about 100-120 times a day on weekdays, though much of these are still @reply conversations. I actively use a number of tools to access Twitter via the web, desktop, and iPhone, and I interact with hundreds of different people on Twitter a week. This intersection between personal and professional, learning and social utility, has had a major impact on my day to day life and how I interface with the world around me.

And yet, I sense that this is still just the beginning.

Eric Andersen is a Senior IT Architect with the Emerging Technology and Architecture Service Area in IBM's Global Business Services division. Eric has played a lead role in defining architectures and overall technology solutions for a variety of IBM customers across multiple industries. He is currently the lead architect for IBM's Professional Marketplace, a global workforce management solution for matching employees to projects and clients. His areas of expertise include enterprise search, integration architecture, social computing, workforce optimization, and GIS. You can find Eric on Twitter at @eric_andersen.

Business and Social Media

Garrett Popcorn: Social Media from Zero to Sixty

by

Alecia C. Dantico

Garrett Popcorn Shops: History and Tradition in Chicago

Garrett Popcorn Shops has been a part of a Chicago tradition since 1949 when it opened its first shop at 10 West Madison Street. For the past sixty plus years, Garrett has, in its own words, "focused on fresh, delicious comfort food," creating an unparalleled brand experience that now stretches into New York City and two international locations. Almost everyone in Chicago has a Garrett Popcorn story, whether it's a story of waiting in line as a child or smelling their amazing, fresh CaramelCrisp and CheeseCorn right out of the hot kettle. People who travel through Chicago tell stories of getting Garrett Popcorn at the airport, and most transplants to Chicago will be able to tell you the story of the first time they tasted this delicious, gourmet treat. For many who grew up in Chicago, Garrett Popcorn is one of the famous food experiences that is always associated with the Windy City.

The classic shop on Michigan Avenue (at the original at 670 North Michigan location and now the newly re-opened flagship at 625 North Michigan) has historically had lines around the block, with people of all ages impatiently waiting for their bag of "The Chicago Mix," a sweet-and-salty combination of CaramelCrisp and CheeseCorn that Garrett has called "wildly pleasing" for the past twenty years. The Garrett brand is inherently social, allowing people to bond over a classic blue-striped tin of popcorn goodness. In fact, in 2002 and again in 2005, Chicago's own Oprah Winfrey named "The Chicago Mix" as one of her "Favorite Things," explaining: "It is so good! I love when you mix the cheese with the caramel!" In Chicago for the weekend? Be sure to plan enough time to wait in lines of "historic proportions," typically wrapped halfway around the block and back!

Rev Your Engines...Starting a Social Media Program

Garrett Popcorn is a unique brand that fits squarely into the history of Chicago. So, how did they translate that distinctive experience into a social, online experience?

In some senses, a brand like Garrett Popcorn Shops is a perfect fit for a social marketing and promotional program. Their six decades of storefront presence in Chicago, coupled with a "secret recipe" passed across three generations, provides ample fodder for storytelling.[1] It is rare to find someone from Chicago who lacks a Garrett Popcorn story—no matter their current global location. Social media platforms provide a means to connect those stories across time zones, locations, and generations. And, of course, the act of sharing a tin of popcorn with family and friends is an inherently social activity. Since the stories have been told and retold for generations, starting a social media program for this brand was as straightforward as listening to the conversations already in progress and joining those conversations when and where appropriate. In some ways, talking about Garrett Popcorn Shops online became the equivalent of friends gathered around a tin of popcorn, talking about topics of interest to them: weekend and holiday plans, favorite movies and books, and of course, the goodness of Garrett Popcorn. This brand was almost made for socialized interactions in online media. What's more fun than sitting around with your friends, noshing on fantastic popcorn, and chatting? The community member's deep, pre-existing engagement with the brand (and its stories) provided a comfortable setting to foster genuine conversation and authentic relationships.

Once the Garrett Popcorn Shops' senior management team fully committed to the philosophy of a social media program, the program launched in June of 2009. The program had been created from scratch, starting with the hiring of the initial program director who crafted the job description, the initial strategy, and roadmap. The position was initially described as follows:

> The Social Media Strategy & Distribution position is responsible for managing all aspects of social media as it relates to the Garrett interactive presence, including both web and mobile platforms. The position will act as the Garrett Popcorn Brand Evangelist with respect to social media activities, ensuring that the Garrett brand is represented consistently and appropriately across all interactive distribution channels. The position will also work to establish an integrated customer and user experience across both the offline and the online distribution channels. The position will design and implement the Garrett social media strategy and roadmap, a strategy designed to increase Garrett brand awareness and drive traffic to www.garrettpopcorn.com in order to monetize that traffic.

At the onset, the Garrett Popcorn Social strategy was to leverage platforms where the Garrett Brand advocates were already engaged in order to develop a conversational channel to surprise, delight, and serve customers—no matter their physical location. The strategy was designed to tap into and harness the passion and energy that the brand enthusiasts were already demonstrating on an almost daily basis, telling the stories of their love for Garrett Popcorn.

---

[1] http://www.garrettpopcorn.com/about/

First Steps: Listen, Learn, Join

The initial Garrett Popcorn Social Media roadmap emphasized three key principles: listen, learn, and join. Listen to the existing conversations. Learn who's saying what and where they are talking. Join the conversations.

The initial steps of the program called for an audit to determine where passionate brand advocates were already talking about Garrett. Following the initial audit or gap analysis, learning the types of conversations popular among advocates was the next step in the process. In other words, while talking about the source of the popcorn kernels may have been top of mind for the brand team, it was not likely that this would be a topic of conversation. The steps of the program included the following:

- Conduct an audit and gap analysis of the existing Garrett brand presence in the social media sphere, listening to what consumers are saying and how they are talking about the brand in this space.

- Humanize the voice of the Garrett brand by developing employee profiles and deploying those identities in the interactive space. Speak the voice of the brand in interactive media and social networking sites to engage in authentic, honest dialogue with consumers.

- Develop and implement a social media engagement strategy, including tools, policies, and plans, integrating the strategy with existing marketing campaigns and company strategic initiatives.

- Develop a long-term social media engagement roadmap in order to foster dynamic, bi-directional conversations with both the core Garrett customer base and the expanding customer base (younger demographics).

- Seize control of the Garrett brand within various social media tools and activities by disabling unauthorized accounts and building bona fide branded accounts in the following tools sets:

  - Facebook
  - MySpace
  - Twitter

- Recommend and deploy an appropriate mix of additional communications strategies and tactics for the Garrett brand, with the goal of driving additional traffic to the Garrett's web site, including:

  - Blogs
  - Social Bookmarking and Tagging
  - Communities and Discussion Groups
  - Video

- Develop a set of best practices and recommended rules of engagement for the use of social media and the Garrett brand; develop a corresponding internal training program for all brand and product managers in order to ensure unity and integration of social networking activity/approach across the organization.

Next Steps: Leverage

After the initial listen, learn, join phase of the program, the next phase called on the brand team to leverage—leverage the social conversations and turn them into genuine relationships with the brand. Tactically, the next phase of the strategy was accomplished by following a few key principles and best practices common in the social media space:

- Respond to every direct comment and message about the brand, whether positive or negative, reaching out to provide customer support and service in a number of different platforms, including:

  - Twitter (including DM responses)
  - Blogs
  - Facebook
  - Flickr
  - Customer Service (e-mail and telephone)
  - E-mail

- Use free tool sets for other casual mentions of Garrett Popcorn Shops, including common misspellings and slang[2]

- Follow (almost) all who mention Garrett Popcorn Shops on Twitter (except known spammers and pornography)

- Engage in genuine, authentic conversations with people in order to build long-term relationships

- Refrain from excessive push-marketing or sales

- Monitor and maintain social presence as close to 24/7 as possible (social media never sleeps)

- Respond to customer complaints or inquiries seriously and as quickly as possible

- Tell stories together with the community; be willing to tell personal stories and make a personal investment in the community

---

[2] A good free tool set used to aid this process was www.search.twitter.com.

- Allow the community to set the tone and direction of the conversation, drawing lines at inappropriate or otherwise offensive content

- Measure the success of the program, tracing traffic to the Garrett Popcorn Shops Web site[3]

- Have fun with the community and experiment

Garrett Popcorn Shops: "Blue Tin" Social Media Personality

The signature Garrett Popcorn Shops tin is a blue-striped tin, easily and instantly recognizable by many who pass through Chicago. Accordingly, the avatar chosen to represent the brand was the classic blue-striped tin on both Facebook and Twitter. Post by post, every time that Garrett Popcorn "spoke" in social media channels, the classic blue tin would appear in the community member's news feed or stream. So then, how does a popcorn tin learn to speak? In order to maintain the spirit and energy of the brand, what kind of language does a tin use? How will it connect to the members of the community?

The first step towards creating a viable social media personality is to create a "socialized" voice of the brand—a voice that while maintaining the core brand elements and essence, remains loyal to the conventions and colloquialisms of social media platforms, primarily Twitter and Facebook. In the case of Garrett Popcorn, the personality of the blue tin was fun, outgoing, and sassy. Again, eating popcorn is an inherently social activity, one typically shared with family and friends. To mimic that positive energy, the tin adopted a personality that could have the freedom to talk about fun activities, especially those pertaining to Chicago. To the extent possible, the blue tin tried to adopt a gender-neutral position, responding equally to male and female centered dialogue in the various social media channels.[4] The blue tin was also very chatty, joining in almost any and all conversations about Garrett—**seven days a week**. The tin was also integrally connected to the Chicago community, supporting Chicago history, traditions, teams, and brands—especially other iconic brands in the food space. And, the blue tin was definitely a foodie, talking recipes and restaurants with almost anyone who wanted to discuss those topics—whether they were centered around a specific Garrett experience or not.

While the voice and persona of the blue tin were definitely fun and outgoing, the tin also had a more serious side. For example, when a community member asked a question about a store location or product availability, the tin would switch to a less ludic voice in order answer questions and solve challenges as quickly as possible. The tin was also able to provide information regarding product ingredients and nutritional information, often pointing community

---

[3] Other tools used to measure and monitor the program success included: Twitter / Facebook Grader, Tweetstats.com, Tweetlytics.com, TweetReach.com, TopFollowFriday.com, and Facebook Insights.

[4] In fact, many who finally met the person behind the blue tin, social voice of Garrett Popcorn Shops, had not been able to discern whether this individual was male or female.

members back to the informational portions of the Garrett Popcorn Web site.[5] So, for as much fun as the blue tin was able to have, playing in the community and bonding with its members and advocates, it was also able to answer serious questions and provide timely customer service assistance. The socialized voice of the brand was flexible and multi-dimensional enough to serve both ends.

Constellation of Forces

Any good social media strategy should fit within a comprehensive, marketing and promotional strategy, one that marries the online and offline experience in a holistic, integrated program. The Garrett program was no exception. The social media team made a conscious effort to connect with the marketing and store operations teams in order to make sure that all programs and messages were as coordinated as possible. For example, during the Valentine's Day period, the creative treatments on the Web site were changed to emphasize the pink-striped tin, as were the treatments on the e-mail marketing messages. The in-store displays and window treatments were also dressed in pink to celebrate the holiday. From a social media perspective, the Facebook and Twitter avatars were both changed to the pink-striped tin, and the Twitter background was dressed in a similar manner. By the end of the initial phase of the program (June 2009 through March 2010), Garrett Popcorn Shops had 3,600 Twitter followers and an additional 3,600 Facebook community members, all of whom had been acquired without the support of any dedicated ad buys or coordinated print media campaigns.

Part of the reason that the Garrett Popcorn Shops social media program was able to go from zero to sixty so quickly was due, in part, to what the brand and management teams liked to call a "constellation" of factors. In fact, 2009-2010 was a very big year for Garrett Popcorn Shops. In early 2009, Garrett opened new Chicago shops on Navy Pier and in the Merchandise Mart, and it also participated as a vendor at the Taste of Chicago for the first time. Press and media relations programs for those events (and the corresponding "grand opening" celebrations) were part of the "buzz" that was already being generated about Garrett in the Chicago media; the social media program functioned to amplify that buzz. October 2009 was also a banner month for the Garrett family of brands. That month marked the sixtieth anniversary of the Chicago tradition, and it also saw the return of the Garrett Popcorn Shops to a new flagship location on Michigan Avenue.[6] Being an integral part of Chicago history and tradition, the grand re-opening of this shop created a virtual media frenzy in Chicago, again heightened and accentuated by a strong social media presence.

The internal and external Garrett teams—advertising, e-mail, store display, marketing, finance, sales—worked very hard to coordinate promotional efforts across the different platforms, using social media to emphasize coverage in print

---

[5] http://www.garrettpopcorn.com/service/nutritional.aspx.
[6] Construction had forced Garrett Popcorn Shops to close its original Michigan Avenue location at 670 North Michigan in May of 2008. The shop reopened on the Magnificent Mile at 525 North Michigan Avenue in October of 2010.

outlets and to generate excitement around the various store openings and celebrations that took place in 2009 and into 2010. Celebrations, both "in real life" and in the virtual realm were cross-promoted in all message distribution channels, using the power of tweetups to enhance excitement around the various shop openings. The virtual aspect of Twitter and Facebook connections were further leveraged to connect the New York location of Garrett Popcorn Shops (Penn Plaza) to the festivities back home in Chicago.

Going Global: History and Tradition Beyond Chicago

During the course of the initial social media ramp up during this time period, Garrett Popcorn Shops expanded into two international locations, Dubai and Singapore. The coalition of brand evangelists that had bonded with Garrett on the Twitter and Facebook platforms became a critical piece of the launch and promotion strategy for the international shops. Initially, the senior management team had not wanted to draw undue attention to these external locations outside of the United States. However, given the reach and the power of social media, it was not long after the openings that folks from abroad posted pictures and told their stories about finding a taste of Chicago in such unexpected locations. In particular, the Garrett Popcorn Facebook community members posted snapshots of the shop within Candylicious in Dubai, the largest candy store in the world.[7] Fans posted great stories of taking their children to visit an iconic Chicago tradition, an experience that helped them to recapture their own childhood memories. Also, in a manner that's not atypical for social media enthusiasts, when the Dubai Mall's Aquarium leaked due to a crack in the glass, the Garrett Popcorn Shops Facebook community members immediately posted their own accounts of the story on the Garrett page, and most expressed concern for both the shop and its employees. The Facebook platform allowed the management and brand teams in Chicago to connect with on-the-ground resources and community members in Dubai, bridging time zones and crossing continents to make sure that all was well at Garrett Popcorn Shops, despite the flooding in the mall.

Twitter was also an integral part of the promotional campaign for the shop opening in Dubai.[8] Via a contact made on Twitter, the social media team was also able to secure a promotional spot for Garrett Popcorn Shops in one of the gift suites at the Dubai International Film Festival in December 2009. Following on the heels of the buzz and excitement generated from the Michigan Avenue re-opening and the anniversary celebration the previous October, Twitter activity for the brand reached an all-time high, averaging close to 120 tweets per day.[9] During this heightened activity and through the course of casual, relationship-building conversation on Twitter, the team connected with public relations representatives from DPA who were able to secure a spot for the Garrett team in the gift suites at the film festival. A press release was issued to announce the

---

[7] http://bob.vg/garrettpopcorn.
[8] http://bob.vg/dubaifilmfestival.
[9] Source: www.tweetstats.com.

event, and Twitter/Facebook activity back in Chicago helped to amplify and accentuate the conversation.

Social Media...It Takes a Village

Social media, when it works as designed, should be a collective, collaborative effort between the brand and its constituents. In this medium, the quality of the conversations and the depths of the relationships built and fostered will underwrite the success of any given program. No matter how precise a strategy, unless a brand (and its senior management team) supports the collaborative, collective philosophy at the heart of social media, success across these platforms will be elusive and nearly impossible to attain. Garrett Popcorn Shops approached social media as varied and distributed channels to engage in bi-directional conversation with people who had already expressed an affinity for and an interest in the brand. In a sense, Garrett used social media to manage customer relationships on a micro level, building friendships and bonds tweet by tweet, post by post, photo by photo. Garrett took the time to build and invest in the quality of those relationships, conversing with people about topics of interest to them; Garrett was not afraid to participate in the conversation, even if the topics of discussion did not always center around the brand. Approaching the space as more than a promotional avenue, Garrett was able to solidify bonds with its customers—genuine relationships that it will be able to carry forward into future campaigns and celebrations. Garrett gave as much to its community as it allowed its community to give back. It is in the center of this reciprocity that the success of social media lies. At the end of the day, it was the whole village, the international community, sharing stories and connecting over a tin of Garrett Popcorn that allowed this social media program to flourish.

Alecia Dantico serves as Vice President, Digital, at Weber Shandwick, where she works to develop social media strategy and build integrated digital, marketing, and communications programs. She has over fifteen years of experience with cross-platform interactive strategy, digital marketing/communications, and technical web development. Her experience includes both B2B/B2C and C2C in start-up, agency, and in-house environments, with a special emphasis on new media and word-of-mouth marketing. She has advanced knowledge of online consumer behavior, social networking, and interactive communities. She recently completed a second MA in English with a concentration in Gender & Women's Studies. She tweets at @danticoa.

Alecia C. Dantico
danticoa@yahoo.com
@danticoa
http://facebook.com/aleciadantico
http://linkedin.com/aleciadantico
http://www.danticoa.com

The Little Cupcake That Could

By

Robert Fine and Lev Ekster

CupcakeStop had not been in business for more than two months when I came across it in August 2009. I was looking for interesting Twitter speakers for a New York City event, and I was floored at the number of followers this new truck in Manhattan had for simple cupcakes. Okay, they're not just simple cupcakes, they're amazing cupcakes, some of the best on the East Coast. There aren't too many places where you can find Margarita, Mexican Chocolate, Egg Nog, and Green Apple Martini cupcakes[1].

Lev Ekster was born in L'vov, Ukraine, in 1983. He lived in Austria and Italy before moving to Brooklyn in 1990. Later Lev attended Ithaca College and New York Law School, graduating with honors in May 2009. While attending law school, he was on his way to securing a position at a major international law firm, but the change in the economy took that off the table. During late nights studying, Lev would take breaks to trek to a popular bakery to wait in line for a sweet treat, but was disappointed with what was supposed to be the "best of the best" the city had to offer. Lev decided he could do better. Thus, the concept for CupcakeStop was born. And New York City's first mobile cupcake truck offering high-end, delicious, fresh-baked cupcakes of every variety was launched on June 3, 2009.

He went through daunting start-up procedures, but obtained and wrapped the enormous new truck he procured with the company's signature logo that he designed. He created and launched the company's Web site, www.cupcakestop.com, and then personally taste tested nearly 1,000 cupcakes until he found the perfect fit.

Now, here's the interesting part of the social media story. Two weeks before the launch of the first truck, social media was not even a part of Lev's marketing plan. But he decided at the last minute to setup a Twitter account and use that as one way to get the word out about when and where the truck would be in

---

[1] Christine Lagorio, "Building a Cupcake Empire," Inc.com Online Magazine, May 24, 2010.

Manhattan. Practically overnight, the Twitter account had followers in the thousands, and within two months, it was quickly approaching the 10,000 mark.

Today, what was once the little cupcake that could is now the little cupcake that can. Less than eighteen months after launching the new truck, Lev now has two full-time trucks, two storefronts (one in Manhattan and one in Montclair, New Jersey), twelve employees, and a growing mail order business with overnight shipping of cupcakes pretty much anywhere you can imagine.

But it isn't all whipped cream and cherries. It's a small startup business that has the same stresses as others. Eighty-hour work weeks, sales that are very dependent on the weather, and growing competition.

Lev manages the Twitter account, personally responding to individual tweets, sending pictures of happy customers and newly unveiled cupcakes, and staying engaged with his clientel. Last October, as the Yankees and the Phillies were duking it out for the World Series, I tweeted Lev a friendly bet: if the Phillies won, he had to provide two dozen cupcakes that say "Phillies Win." And if the Yankees win, well, of course I have to pay for two dozen that say "Yankees Win." As hard as that loss was, in the end, I still had two dozen amazing cupcakes to eat. It was better than eating crow.

Today Lev utilizes both Facebook and Twitter so customers can find information about all his baked goods in real time. Currently, CupcakeStop has a reach of close to 20,000 people through social media.

Lev donates leftover cupcakes from the day to City Harvest, a New York-based nonprofit organization dedicated to feeding the homeless. In addition, he has organized events for the Jewish Law Students Association, with proceeds going to JNF Blueprint and Amit Children. He has participated in three Cystic Fibrosis fundraisers, and is also involved with a community service program with Dorot, delivering holiday care packages to the elderly. Other organizations Lev has worked with include the Glad to Give Charity and Cupcakes for a Cause, benefiting pediatric cancer patients.

@CupcakeStop
http://www.cupcakestop.com

Creating the Ultimate Multimedia Blend with Olympus

by

Michael Bourne

In April, 2009, Olympus came to Mullen, the agency where I've worked for a decade, with a challenging assignment: launch a new camera standard, the PEN E-P1, one of the smallest interchangeable lens cameras in the world that shoots brilliant stills and HD video and offers an array of creative controls – a true multimedia device. In the competitive consumer electronics market, Olympus was looking for a marketing campaign that would be as innovative, nimble, and smart as the E-P1.

The story we told about the PEN E-P1 had to be as original and entertaining as the camera and get the core tech aficionado target salivating about shooting with the ultimate gadget. Given that the E-P1 was an enabler of a better online social experience, producing videos that look amazing on YouTube, and still images that dramatically enhance your Facebook profile picture, we leveraged social media channels to secure broad awareness for the camera. After all, images and video are all about sharing and self-expression. What better place to do it than in social media?

Over the course of several months, our Olympus client had come to see the value of using social media because Mullen had set up the brand's outposts in Facebook, Twitter, YouTube, and Flickr. To drive camera sales, it was necessary to develop buzz for the product prior to the launch on June 16, 2009 and beyond through both traditional and social media efforts. Olympus measured online buzz by tracking clicks to videos about the E-P1, hits to its company site at http://getolympus.com/pen, mainstream media and blogosphere coverage. Olympus also measured sales of the E-P1 that resulted from the widespread good news about the camera.

To identify the ideal E-P1 consumer, Mullen implemented its proprietary "Modes of the Mind" brand planning methodology in order to determine which of the seven modes of the minds would best describe the target E-P1 consumer mindset. To identify the target, Mullen conducted online research to identify their primary modes as "informed" and "entertained." To connect with what we called the "Visual Generation," we decided to reach them via their over-indexing behaviors: participation in social networks, viewing of online videos, and their propensity to surf the Internet. We also determined that the primary target for the camera skewed older, which focused us toward Facebook and Twitter that have an older, more tech-savvy user base.

Based on our research, Mullen and Olympus crafted the line "What Will You Create?" that reflected the new multimedia convergence of the technologies in the PEN, and served as the centerpiece for all communication about the E-P1. From the seed of this positioning, a memorable campaign was born.

"Will it blend? That is the question."

Prior to the announcement of the E-P1, a curious short video was released on the net. In it, a geeky-looking middle-aged man in a white lab coat, who himself aligned well to the camera's retro-chic aesthetic and appealed to the target tech early adopters, says the inimitable phrase "Will it blend? That is the question" and then proceeds to put a large Olympus Digital SLR camera into a blender. Then, after the blades pulverize it, he throws in an Olympus point-and-shoot camera, resulting in an explosion.

Of course, I am talking about Blendtec and its nutty CEO Tom Dickson, famous for the viral video series sensation "Will It Blend?" Working with Olympus and Blendtec, we produced a teaser video released a couple weeks before the announcement date, fueling enormous speculation as to what would happen if a compact camera and a DSLR were combined.

Then, to give the camera a memorable birthday kickoff, Mullen coordinated a media event in New York City that brought together key influencers from both social media and traditional media circles. The stage was set in the penthouse of the Hotel on Rivington, with floor-to-ceiling windows looking out on the vista of lower Manhattan, filled with fifty top tier media, bloggers, and VIPs. Participants watched the premier of the launch video "Will It Blend?—Take Two: The Full Olympus Multimedia Blend," during which Tom stuffed a wider variety of Olympus equipment into his blender—DSLR, point-and-shoot, lens, camcorder, audio recorder, shredded art—to see what would happen, resulting in the Olympus E-P1 pouring out of the blender. The crowd and everyone viewing the video at home or in the office were wowed by this "launch by video" approach and clever humor.

We then boarded a water taxi to use the camera on Coney Island where the camera's full capabilities could be demonstrated. All the while, Mullen was tweeting live from the event, posting to Facebook and Flickr, and directing everyone to the video.

These videos were the focal point of an all-out integrated campaign that took advantage of Olympus' growing social media network, connecting its presence on Twitter, Facebook, and YouTube, and using a little PR magic to help generate attention and stimulate consumer participation. The total social network was linked up to the company channel for the brand to further drive traffic to http://getolympus.com/pen

We secured incredible awareness for the E-P1, and the resulting blog chatter on tech sites like Gizmodo and Engadget, mainstream media coverage from the *New York Times, Popular Science, PC World, Washington Post*, and the tweets in the twitterverse were astounding, with millions upon millions of positive impressions. In addition to giving the camera a wonderful review, *WIRED* magazine wrote:

"This is how you make an ad. What you are about to see starts off like any other 'Will it Blend' episode, but this special edition is a collaboration between Olympus and Blendtec. Once the second camera goes in, you'll easily guess the ending, but I won't spoil it here. We'll just say that this is the kind of smart, innovative advertising that Olympus was famous for right back to its Olympus Trip/David Bailey TV spots."

For a time, the videos earned YouTube top honors: Number Six Most Discussed in the world, and Number Eight Top Rated in Entertainment Category in the world. Demand was so high the camera immediately went on backorder. The two Blendtec videos were viewed close to a million times. Between sales of the camera and the value of the media coverage, it's fair to say that Olympus more than recouped the costs of the campaign.

As the incredibly prescient Marshall McLuhan once said, "the medium is the message." This was never truer than for the launch of the E-P1 that utilized the various social media channels used by consumers to spread the word. It was a unique launch in that the release of the video was timed to the release of the camera. Instead of providing just a static news release and product shot, we creatively demonstrated the E-P1's value and provided bloggers with the content (a hilarious video) that they could use to spread the news. In the realm of social media, valuable online content is synonymous with your actual product.

Unlike traditional PR campaigns that rely on targeting just media, the campaign by Olympus and Mullen collectively established relationships with key influencers via Twitter for several months prior to the announcement of the camera. Together, both client and agency operate the @getolympus handle for the Olympus brand, uncovering and engaging with the most influential people on Twitter who are interested in photography, Olympus, and the Micro Four Thirds format employed by the E-P1. We interacted with these influencers prior to launching the E-P1 so that when we did formally launch the camera, we would have an existing base of followers to spread the word about it to their communities. Collectively, we established the Twitter site as the de facto site online for information about the E-P1, and continue to operate it as of this writing along with www.facebook.com/getolympus, www.flickr.com/groups/getolympus, and www.youtube.com/getolympus. This last social site would become increasingly central to the camera company's next effort: the launch of the mass consumer Olympus PEN E-PL1.

The PEN Is Now Mightier

After launching the first-generation Olympus PEN cameras using only social media in 2009, Olympus tasked us with another challenge in 2010. The mass-market PEN, the E-PL1, was on its way, but now the target was general consumers. That meant the PEN would compete against mega-brands like Canon, Nikon, and Sony that were fast developing their own compact interchangeable lens digital cameras.

In the face of such Goliath-like competition, the silver lining was that our David was a powerful new camera designed for anyone looking to step up from their point-and-shoots to something significantly better. Like its predecessor, the Olympus PEN E-PL1 was a hybrid of professional digital SLR image quality, HD video, and point-and-shoot simplicity. Now anyone could easily capture incredible pictures and videos at the push of a button.

Working with the Olympus PEN team, Mullen's Media, Creative, and PR/Social Influence departments joined forces to conceptualize a highly integrated and unique approach. We started with a great asset—the new PEN's large following of knowledgeable advocates. The plan was to engage them in a series of media activations that encourage conversation and social advocacy and result in more word of mouth than media spend alone could afford. We concepted a big brand platform that revolved around a simple and provocative premise: "Look What You Can Do."

The "Look What You Can Do" platform showed how easy it was for anyone to unleash their inner pro photographer at the push of a button. Our big idea had a crucial and unusual twist: we would shoot all the elements of the campaign with the actual camera itself. Let's not tell people "Look What You Can Do," let's show them what they can do was our mantra.

Every touch-point sought to be a real world proof of the big idea. And the entire industry was taking notice. It's amazing what happens when creatives and media and PR get together.

As with all product launches, Olympus had the goal to meet or exceed sales expectations and increase brand awareness and preference in an extremely crowded and competitive category by making its media spend work harder. The company also wanted to benefit from the halo effect of leveraging emerging technologies that would present Olympus as a technological leader.

Mullen embarked on a two-pronged planning approach to develop our solution. Prong one was conducting research to gain insights into the consumer's mindset. Mullen brand planning and research capabilities were employed. The second prong consisted of reaching our consumer in places and ways that competitors were not, so we could have a significant media presence.

We launched with our strategy to activate social advocates via Facebook, blogs, Twitter, YouTube, forums, and Flickr. The campaign debuted with a branded YouTube channel featuring a crowdsourced contest—the "PEN Your Story Challenge." We asked consumers what they'd do with five thousand dollars and a free PEN E-PL1. Submissions came pouring in, thanks to advertising as well as six "shout out" videos from notable YouTube directors like Erik Beck (Indy Mogul) and Threadbanger with large subscriber bases. Like Blendtec with the first PEN, leveraging the power of Internet celebrities was essential to engaging consumers.

We teased the upcoming creative and connected fans and hand-raisers to the camera's potential with Facebook engagement ads and Spongecell ads, encouraging prospects to endorse the camera in their social feed. This provided Olympus with a base from which to grow longer-term advocacy and additional conversation in the future.

As the cameras became available, we integrated media placements that built on the "Look What You Can Do" themes, including:

- An ad in the launch issue of *WIRED* magazine's iPad edition.

- The world's first robust camera demo using augmented reality (www.getolympus.com/PEN3D), which used print in a non-traditional way—by debuting an insert in *WIRED* and *Popular Photography* as a tip-in card that, when activated on users' computers, took the shape of the actual Olympus PEN in 3D. Augmented reality has been used before in other ways, but more as a gimmick than as an actual, working, in-depth product demo. This was as close to having the camera in your hands as you can get without actually having it in your hands. Furthering the viral nature of the experience, it could also be shared socially.

- Fifteen, thirty, and sixty-second brand television spots actually shot with the PEN, to prove the high-quality video capability of a point-and-shoot camera that shoots broadcast-quality television. And, to demonstrate the camera's HD screen, we developed customized animated billboards that began playing clips from the program in which the ad was airing.

- Singles and spreads also shot with the PEN in major consumer magazines.

The end result is a campaign that showed consumers what they could do, and they responded. We used cutting-edge technology to bring the camera and our strategy to life for consumers, enabling them to directly experience and participate in ways Olympus competitors didn't offer. We also melded the power of traditional media (TV, online, print) to drive participation in new social and digital media, to orchestrate a comprehensive campaign that supported the "Look What You Can Do" brand platform.

Looking back on how social media has shaped Olympus over the past two years, it's evident that the company has embraced consumer-centric marketing by becoming more generous with its brand. Instead of blasting messages and slogans out, it is inviting consumers to participate directly with its products, to share a laugh, to share an experience, and to show what Olympus cameras can do when they use them. When the grand prize winner of the "PEN Your Story Challenge" won a trip, from Atlanta to New York, to see his video play on the large video board at the USTA Center during the Olympus-sponsored U.S. Open Tennis Championships, it was a seminal moment and a harbinger of even greater things to come.

Michael Bourne began a career in public relations just as the bloom was starting to fade from the dot-com rose, but at a time when consumer electronics were expanding in the digital age. Having served as managing editor of *Tokyo Journal Magazine* in Japan before going into agency land, he has an affinity for technology from the East and a reporter's eye for what makes a story work. He's been bringing innovative and complex technologies down to the human level ever since.

A diverse mélange of acronyms, the tech he's promoted has ranged widely—from the world's first quantum cryptography network, to a hydrogen-powered Hummer, anti-sniper sensors, podcast transcribers, social media apps, and digital music players. While promoting all of these innovations and more, his modus operandi has been to make all of the benefits easily understandable to garner maximum exposure for clients that have included Olympus, General Motors, BBN Technologies, Springpad, and The Monitor Group among others. He blogs and tweets as Bournesocial.

Michael Bourne
bournesocial@gmail.com
@bournesocial
http://bournesocial.com

FuegoMundo South American Wood-Fire Grill

by

Todd Schnick

The whole idea started when the future owners traveled to Latin America on vacation. They stopped in a small joint to have dinner, and discovered wood-fire grilled food, with a healthy kick. "We must bring this concept to Atlanta," they decided.

Thus was launched the idea that became FuegoMundo South American Wood-Fire Grill. The purpose? To create a restaurant with a fusion of food styles from around Latin American, but in addition, food that was both affordable, delicious AND healthy.

My name is Todd Schnick, and I run a small marketing shop in Metro Atlanta. I first met Masha, now the owner, in summer 2008. She told me she had an idea for a new type of restaurant in metro Atlanta, and asked if I was interested in joining them on the journey. It was a thrill to work with people who were willing to try some new things, and let me experiment with some marketing strategies that were bold, yet mindful of limited budgets. The restaurant opened in June, 2009.

I wish I had an easy formula for you to follow. Some sort of magic pill to take to replicate what was done at FuegoMundo South American Wood-Fire Grill. But I don't. In the end, it was about connecting. And talking to people. And building relationships.

Months before the restaurant actually opened, we got active on Twitter. And started blogging. In fact, the early blog posts showed people the progress of our construction. This was a lot of fun, in that a lot of folks enjoyed seeing the place come together. They felt like they were a part of the experience, that they were coming along for the ride. This built a sense of community, and we could tell that people were wishing us to succeed...

But the concept that really got us launched on the social web was when we invited our new Twitter friends to participate in a test run of the as yet unopened restaurant. We scheduled four large private parties, all friends from Twitter.

We packed four parties from engaging with our audience on Twitter. Folks came in, and we had them experience FuegoMundo, ordering whatever they wanted, and gave our full staff a legitimate hands on experience, testing the ordering process, food prep, service staff...the whole nine yards.

This provided us a fun way to interact with our new audience, and talk about what worked, what needed improvement, and the changes we were making from the experience. And the beauty was, although we did NOT ask them to, most of our guests got on Twitter and talked about the new restaurant. Many blogged about the experience. Shared pics of the new joint. Told their friends about it.

In the end, we had an enthused network of connections already buzzin' about the place long before the doors officially opened. And the best part? It was free. Well, apart from the effort and commitment to making it happen. Creating an opportunity to engage with an audience, built around a shared experience, was so much more powerful than trying to broadcast - one way - details about a grand opening. Many of these original Twitter followers are still our best customers 18 months later...

Another part of what aided our success utilizing the social web was our efforts to solicit feedback and opinion from our online audience. This is in large part how we, for instance, used both Twitter and Facebook. When we wanted to test new ideas for the menu, we would ask our community to vote on it. This usually followed a video featuring our owner describing the potential new options, and/or a detailed blog post demonstrating potential recipes. We would then literally ask people to vote on their favorite option. People loved the chance to participate and be a decision-maker on the menu.

Made them a part of the family!

We've recently launched a new program with Foursquare, running several tests to see what helps us best reward our loyal customers. Although we haven't been running this program long enough to fully see how it impacts business long term, we have seen enough evidence of one thing... And that is the impact of the social web on geolocation.

When we launched our Foursquare program, we promoted it heavily on Twitter and Facebook. We blogged about our promotions, and released videos (that featured our current Foursquare Mayor) on YouTube. As a result, the check-in rate saw a dramatic increase. A few weeks later, we stopped promoting our Foursquare program on social media as a test, and as a result, observed the check-in rate dramatically decrease.

From this, we understood that engaging your online audience does significantly impact the success of other marketing programs...particularly if you have been engaged with your online network for a while, over a year in our case. Blasting our community with specials, discounts, and one-way messaging wasn't nearly as effective and making them a part of the FuegoMundo family...and actually caring about them.

Todd Schnick is a marketer, blogger, radio show host, speaker, trainer, political strategist, and distance runner. Since 2003 Todd has started six companies including The Intrepid Group LLC, The High Velocity Organization, and Dreamland Interactive; marketing firms serving various markets and sectors. Messaging, strategy, and social media integration fall squarely within his key areas of expertise. Todd launched his career in politics serving as aide to a U.S. congressman. He later served as political director of the Florida GOP during the 2000 recount and has run two state political parties (Nevada and Georgia).

todd@intrepid-llc.com
@toddschnick
http://Facebook.com/todd.schnick
http://www.linkedin.com/in/toddschnick
http://intrepid-llc.com
+1-404-931-0969

Leveraging Social Media to Reach Customers and the Community:
A Case Study of Network Solutions

by

Shashi Bellamkonda

As leaders in Web-based services, Network Solutions' constant goal has been to help small businesses succeed online. Network Solutions (NetSol) once was the sole provider of domain names on the Internet; however, it now competes in a crowded marketplace, leading as a focused provider of small business online tools. While Network Solutions still manages more than 7 million domain names, it also manages over 1.5 million e-mailboxes, and more than 350,000 Web sites—in addition to providing a wide variety of additional services for small businesses. Many are not aware of the many new online small business tools and services available.

In 2008, any online conversations about Network Solutions were based on outdated information. An initial benchmark in July 2008 conducted by Livingston Communications (now CRT/tanaka) put negative conversations about Network Solutions in the social media at 64%, when in fact, the company has excellent customer service. For three consecutive years, our Hazleton, Pennsylvania, customer support center has been named a J.D. Power and Associates Certified Call Center, providing "An Outstanding Customer Service Experience." (For J.D. Power and Associates 2008 Certified Call Center ProgramSM information, visit www.jdpower.com.) Building a bridge with this net-savvy audience is an important goal and formed the foundation for the social media strategy for Network Solutions.

A Four Point Strategy:

Brand/Reputation Management

- Negative mentions were mitigated by Network Solutions' proactive commenting and reaching out to customers through social media channels. Commenting has paid off as a good tactic to reach out to customers and let them know their feedback is valued. The increase in comments from Network Solutions has a direct correlation to a decrease in negative blog comments.

Connecting With Customers

- Listening and monitoring helped Network Solutions connect with customers in social media channels

- Network Solutions has a Twitter presence—@Network Solutionscares (http://www.twitter.com/netsolcares)—performing about two thousand engagements per month on Twitter

- The engagements on Twitter have been a successful retention strategy for customers

Community Outreach

- Network Solutions' community engagement and social activities generated organic positive mentions

- Speaking engagements, creating and analyzing small business needs, and the GrowSmartBusiness conference increased positive mentions

Get New Business

- Network Solutions offers coupons on Twitter through the account @NSoffers (http://www.twitter.com/nsoffers) and through Network Solutions' Facebook page (http://facebook.com/networksolutions)

- Traffic from links to Network Solutions from conferences and posts about the Network Solutions community outreach generates incremental revenue

- Events organized by the social media team also leads to added revenue, as attendees use the coupons provided or think of Network Solutions first when they make a decision to purchase online tools for their business

- Under certain circumstances, the social team received requests for coupons and offers from customers of other registrars to transfer and become a Network Solutions customer

Tactics

<u>Listening</u>

Using monitoring tools to find brand mentions.

- Monitoring tools: Radian 6, Google Alerts, back type alerts, team approach to response
- Twitter Customer Support 3rd Party Tool: http://hy.ly—classify as crisis, general issue, or technical customer service problem (network issues, volume, etc.)
- Engage in a variety of places: blog posts, Twitter via @Network SolutionsCares Technical Forums

<u>Participating</u>

- Attending small business, Web design, and developer conferences and events
- Influencer and blogger outreach
- Crisis management support
- Training of internal advocates

<u>Contributing</u>

Creating content for users through blogs.

- Network Solutions Conversations: http://blog.networksolutions.com
- Small Business Success Index: http://growsmartbusiness.com
- Women Entrepreneurs: http://www.womengrowbusiness.com
- Start-up Entrepreneurs: http://www.unintentionalentrepreneurs.com
- Millennial Mentoring: http://www.WhatsNextGenY.com

<u>Holding events</u>

- Annual GrowSmartBiz conference
- Meetups for entrepreneurs and small business
- Tweetchats

<u>Speaking at conferences</u>

- SXSW, IABC, PRSA Digital, Small Biz technology conference, local chamber of business events, Twitterville book launch, Affiliate Summit

The Team

The Network Solutions social media team is led by Shashi Bellamkonda, Director of Social Media (a.k.a. the Social Media Swami). He reports to the VP of

Marketing at Network Solutions, and manages a team of four bloggers to assist with the social media properties and the brand's online presence. There is also an executive support team of three to respond to consumers. Additionally, the team relies on social media agency, CRT/tanaka, as an extension of the team.

Top Accomplishments

- Enjoying a positive sentiment online compared to the negative mentions in 2008

- Shift in perception of Network Solutions as not just a domain registrar but also a thought leader in small business growth

- Network Solutions is often referred to as a company that has effectively leveraged social media to maximize customer satisfaction

- Won the 2008 SNCR Award for Excellence in Corporate Reputation Management using social media

- Won the 2009 Golden Quill Award for Excellence in Social Media

Conclusion

In the real time world of communications, it is important for all businesses to invest in a conversation strategy to listen and participate in dialogue with customers and community, and doing it wisely gives them a great audience development resource.

Something Old, Something New

by

Cordelia Mendoza

The possibilities of social media are endless in how it can take a business to another level. It's basically a gift to business people. All we have to do is be open to the outreach possibilities. To me, it's the most exciting thing available to businesses today. But in the antiques business, it's another story. Antique dealers all over the country have been crying the blues for the last few years about the decline in collectors and the lack of young people that are interested in antiques. My response is that there will always be collectors on every level, from low-end to extremely high-end fine antiques. Antique business owners can learn to adapt to the Web and its tools and the way today's buyers seek information and make buying decisions. If they don't learn to adapt, they won't make it.

Social media is a part of my workday routine. But I've discovered that I'm a minority as a user of digital marketing and social media for my antiques business. For some reason, this field of retail has far less percentages of business owners involved than other industries. Because I willingly do anything that involves social media, it's difficult to understand how business owners can't see the potential and don't jump on board. To me, it's a no-brainer. I immediately got excited about new media, particularly Twitter, when first introduced to it. I jumped in with both feet and learned by watching and doing. I soon found that it was a fun form of work. I started adding a variety of tools, including LinkedIn, Digg, Twitter, Facebook, Yelp, Blogger, Reddit, Ning, e-mail blasts, and YouTube. Twitter and Facebook appear to be the best for my business purposes, along with my blog. Previously, when I held a promotional event in my store or needed to make an announcement to my customers and the public, I'd take out a paid ad in the local newspaper and trade papers, send out a press release, and mail postcards using the U.S. Postal Service to more than three thousand customers—all at a hefty cost. Reaching people by direct mail was always, hands down, our best marketing tool. Now, I collect e-mail addresses from customers and send out flyers or special event invites through a mailing list provider ("Your Mailing List Provider"—www.ymlp.com—is what works for me and the best value for the money). I also blitz events on Twitter, Facebook, CraigsList, my blog, Kijiji, the events page on my store's Web site, and Eventful.com. That's all I do, and my results have been excellent. From a first-hand experience, I believe sending e-mails through a mailing list provider is an absolute necessity for any small business.

Tourists from the East Coast, the Midwest, the Southwest, and the Pacific Northwest have come into the store and said they learned about our shop on Twitter. A woman, on vacation from Ohio, came into the store and said she saw me on Twitter. Another, from Texas, recently came in because she'd read my blog. It's not unusual when people see our store's Web site or blog, but I am still surprised (and delighted) to hear them say they found us through Twitter. It shows that a simple 140-character post not only connects you with people online, but it facilitates connections offline as well, and is proof positive when people actually show up at your door.

We regularly redisplay our store. Whenever we decorate or create new window displays, I take photos, write a blog post, and then tweet about it. Blogging is useful when new merchandise arrives, particularly unusual items. I again shoot photos, quickly load them up, and write a blurb about them. Customers love it! I do the same when we create new displays and vignettes of merchandise. If our store windows are changed out, they get photographed and a blog entry is posted about them too. It builds a customer following, and it's in real time. An antiques magazine recently contacted me and asked if they could publish posts they'd read on my blog in their print magazine as well as in their online magazine. How cool is that? They published a blog I wrote about the history of iron beds. And another blog I wrote, about English Staffordshire white ironstone china, was picked up by another online magazine. There is no paid advertising that could get me that kind of industry-targeted visibility.

As for Twitter, one thing I don't do that I see many others do is post merchandise. A lot of Etsy and eBay sellers post their auction and store items on Twitter. That's like making a cold call, which can come across as too forceful and an in-your-face sales tactic. At the store, if we create a fabulous display with fresh merchandise, I'll photograph it and write a tweet that goes something like this:

> @CottageAntiques Had a blast changing out our display windows in r store today; spent the whole day decorating: http://(then post the twitpic photo).

To draw more people to the Web site, I'll write something interesting about the store, like when Rachel Ashwell, a well-known designer who made shabby and worn furnishings trendy, came into our store to shop recently. It's tweetable material. Later, a piece of furniture she purchased from us was on her company's blog in a photo tour of her London apartment. Tweetable again, including the photo. My goal is to broaden the market for antiques through social engagement.

Since my Web site and blog are listed on my Twitter page, people can easily find us. It only takes a few minutes out of my day to tweet. Another thing that has worked for me—but I'm careful how often I do it for fear of losing followers—is to post a photo of an unusual or unique item. I obtained a 1901 White House cookbook, which is not that common. It was a wonderful find, so I photographed it and posted it on Twitter with a remark about how lucky I was to locate such a great piece of American political memorabilia. Within a couple of hours, a woman saw it on Twitter and contacted me to ask if it was for sale. She had once been a First Lady's speechwriter and worked at the White House. I happily packaged the book and shipped it off to her. That was my first sale because of a tweet, and I had only been using Twitter a short time, so it was a real motivator to continue using that technique. The truth is I get very excited about terrific finds and love to share.

Our store's Web site hits have increased since I first started using social media. I get a lot of news about the antiques business via Twitter. It's a great tool to use for listening. News is breaking every second, so it's important to stay tuned and pay attention. Old school doesn't work any longer when it comes to antiques. And sharing information with customers is a large part of our web strategy for attracting business. It can work for other purposes too. For example, one Sunday night, my sister copied someone's tweet and e-mailed it to me. It read, "@LifesAPet: Very Small Spayed Female Chihuahua Needs Rescue/Adoption."

I had not been looking to adopt another dog, but when I clicked onto the link and saw that dog's little face, that was all it took. On Monday, I was on the phone with the shelter. The next morning, I was on the road driving to the Los Angeles area to retrieve the five-pound Chihuahua, who was found on the street, taken by animal control to a shelter, and then put on their euthanasia list. There is no question that Twitter and other forms of social media are having a huge impact on adoptions and save rates at shelters.

A big bonus with social media is that it makes it possible, like never before, for small businesses to compete with large corporations. Web marketing is an even ground and an open field. The audience is there for anyone who goes after it.

Another thing that works for me is staying up to date with what's happening in the social media world, not just what's going on with antiques. I read voraciously about social media, follow people who are leaders in the field, and generally keep my ear to the ground. This alone helps my business and the nonprofits I work with. In my case, it encourages me to do even more and not be left behind.

In addition to doing social media for my store, I'm a volunteer coordinator of an annual garden walk to raise funds for Rady Children's Hospital. The most recent event, after more than a year of a bad economy, was the most successful in nine years with record-breaking ticket sales and sponsorship/donor funds. And it was all done online, launching a very simple social media campaign, putting it out there anywhere and everywhere possible. For the first time ever, we had sponsorships come through the Web site without previous personal contact. The ticket sales through the Web site were also the highest ever. It opened the eyes of many people in our hospital auxiliary, enough that I was asked to join the hospital's main auxiliary board to help with its social media and membership drive countywide. Our auxiliary has been held up as the model for what can be done through social media for the other twenty-two hospital auxiliaries in San Diego County.

It's an exciting time for any nonprofit, small business, large corporation, or—last but not least—the antiques world. It's never too late to get involved and begin making things happen in a different way than ever before. I look forward to moving ahead with whatever changes occur. Sign me up!

Cordelia Mendoza is an antiques expert, estate consultant, and shop owner in a coastal community of San Diego, and is a volunteer social media coordinator for a nationally known nonprofit organization.

Cordelia Mendoza
@CordeliaMendoza
@CottageAntiques
@BestFriendsDog
http://www.cottageantiques.biz
http://AntiqueCottage.blogspot.com

More Twitter, More Rentals

By

Eric Brown and Becky Carroll

Customer Experience is a Relative of Customer Service

Customer experience many times gets lumped into the customer service bucket. Our mind equates enhanced customer experience with improved customer service. As business owners, and consumers alike, we all strive for better customer relationships. Excellent customer service is the starting point, but many times our quest to increase customer service is a race to eroding profits. Assuming your business already has great customer service, perhaps you could gain better leverage by *enhancing the customer experience.* Let's start by looking at the offline experience, and then we'll take a look at how we can weave it together with social media to create an excellent customer experience.

Customer Experience and Social Media Have a Common Bond

The paradigm shift for a business to focus on enhancing the customer experience is also a gateway to the two "E's" of social media marketing, Emotion and Engagement.

We have all heard about the Four P's of Marketing (Product, Price, Place, and Promotion), but what about the new "Two E's," Emotion and Engagement—are you fully utilizing them? Companies that offer a great customer experience have strategically planned those two areas, both online and offline. For an example of how it is used at Urbane Apartments in Royal Oak, Michigan, think about how much people love their pets. In our boutique property management business, we decided to go after the pet people market and accept pets. Many places accept pets, but they usually have weight and breed restrictions, as well as a hefty pet deposit. We decided to keep it simple, and we implemented the "Urbane Loves Pets" program—no fees and no breed restrictions. The theory is this: if we have a good resident, they will likely have a good pet. In conjunction with this program, we worked very hard on an enhanced resident-screening system, resulting in attracting great residents, which has improved collections. A nice side benefit to accepting pets.

Note that the triumph of this program isn't about accepting pets. It's about "Urbane Loves Pets," which has successfully evoked positive emotions in prospects and residents alike. Consequently, we own the local people pet market. If you are going after sliver markets, go after them with a vengeance and own them.

Make It a Playful and Engaging Experience

We can't all have an exciting brand such as Apple or Nike, and many business verticals are actually a little boring. Apartment management falls into the really boring category. Apartment hunting falls right in there with going to the dentist—not much fun.

Given that, Urbane wanted to lighten up the entire leasing process. If you're apartment hunting at Urbane, you will pay a visit to our Centralized Leasing Center, known as Urbane Underground, which is anything but typical. There are farm-watering troughs with tropical plants. A forty-five foot long bamboo planter. Crazy music playing. A tropical bird hanging out. A conference table that hangs from the ceiling with no legs. Anything but typical. In fact, it is very whimsical, fun, and *engaging*. And to really engage a prospect, **we do shots** with them before they leave (energy shots that is). This creates an offline experience that carries into the online, social media conversation. Why? Because we have touched their emotions, we have created an experience that engages, and we have created an environment where they can envision themselves and their friends. Remember, no one cares about your product; they care about themselves and their lifestyle.

Bring the Experience Online – Event Marketing with Social Media

At Urbane Apartments, we love a great party, and we often partner with other brands to really make these events rock. We find that when complementary brands pool together resources, the sum of all the parts equals much more than can be leveraged alone. Additionally, when you partner up with local and national brands, they may well have a much broader social media reach and following, which can be very helpful in drawing a much larger crowd than going it alone.

For example, Urbane Apartments partnered with BlackFinn Saloon, a local watering hole, the good folks at Vitamin Water, who have hydration for every situation, and Pink Pump, the hottest little shoe boutique in Royal Oak, Michigan, to create a fun community event. We only used Facebook to market the event; however, it wasn't just our Facebook fan base that brought in the guests. The reach for the invite also included the fans of each participating partner, so our overall social media reach expanded exponentially.

Girls, Guys, and Foursquare Draw in the Crowd

Although the weather didn't cooperate, the event drew a great crowd. A steady parade of dressed-up gals brought about a load of boys, and everyone seemed to have a great time, including our photographer. We tied Foursquare into this event to bring the engagement online. Guests first came to "check in" at the Urbane Underground (remember, this is our Centralized Leasing Center) and be photographed. While there, they received a bracelet for free appetizers at the BlackFinn Saloon and admittance to our fashion show. This helped spread the word about the event to those who couldn't make it to the party, as well as create more buzz among the participants.

It Is About Your Larger Community

If you have ever heard of a #tweetup, we switched that up a bit at Urbane and decided to have a #laughup. We were chatting over coffee as we were going over some last minute details about the event, and we were musing over how many of the anticipated guests were actually Urbane Residents. My reply of, "Who Cares!" sort of put everyone off, so let me explain. First, of course I care about our residents, and while I do care if they come or not, I have a greater interest in providing an event that is remarkable. Something different than the average Joe. Something that breaks away from the pack of event marketing commodities. I want our larger community to attend, and the people out there who talk about us and will talk to their friends about us. Based on the turnout, I think we accomplished that. We had about seventy-five people attend, enough to accomplish a Foursquare Swarm Badge from all of the check ins.

Results - When the Community Tweets About You

We have experimented and indulged in several different types of social media marketing and customer experience enhancements at the Urbane Lab. The projects ranged widely, but the best-leveraged campaign we have done was from a co-sponsored trip to SxSW (South by Southwest), one of the top social media conferences. What has unfolded from all of these social media marketing initiatives is this: the collective local community has tweeted about the Urbane Life *extensively.*

More Twitter, More Rentals

Although I have found significant benefit to our social media marketing here at The Urbane Way, from the effective use and practice of Twitter, I never really believed that Twitter would ever help us rent more apartments.

In the beginning, Urbane Apartments, like many other apartment operators starting out with Twitter, tweeted about our "rent specials" to no avail. We quickly ceased taking that direction (because no one cares about your specials). We even changed our Twitter handle, from @UrbaneApts to @UrbaneLife. We now have over three thousand relevant, local followers, and we monitor for events via TweetDeck in the cities where we have apartment communities. Not only do we have followers, but our Web site traffic has spiked significantly, and we recently experienced our highest physical traffic month in April (the same month as the co-sponsored SxSW trip mentioned earlier). In the eight years we have been in business, our occupancy rate is nearly 100% (in a challenging Michigan economy).

Tweeting is the New Leasing Requirement

While many of my apartment-marketing peers may find this inappropriate, we are requiring our leasing agents at Urbane to start to focus on increasing their Twitter following, and on posting a minimum number of tweets and Facebook updates. We are not suggesting that Twitter and Facebook should take precedence over leasing apartments and resident retention, but I am convinced that a steady and consistent outreach to the community through tools such as Twitter and Facebook will further build and solidify our digital footprint, and our customer relationships.

Let's Connect

The backbone of the above social media interactions is connection. People want to connect with other friends and acquaintances with similar interests. Customers are much more socially connected in this day and age, and many of a company's "marketing" activities are now taking place *between* customers (ratings, reviews, blog posts, tweets, etc.). As marketers rush to the social media space like a herd of cattle, some may miss the point. The directional flow of marketing has forever changed. No longer does buying a larger block of advertising mean there will be increasing sales.

That does not mean that each customer does not want to be treated as an individual by the company. Customer-focused marketing has less to do with sending separate direct mail pieces to each person as it does with treating different customers differently. Customer-focused marketing is mostly about managing the entire customer experience. In order to do this properly, one needs to understand the needs of the customer. Now that many customers are interacting online, it is easier to listen and hear what they want. Companies need to make sure they act on what they are learning, before their competitor does. And if you go beyond listening to social media marketing, it can have an extraordinary reach for your product or business.

Potential prospects pick and choose to be part of your social media community, and they can leave at any time. Unlike traditional advertising where you are shouting to the masses, this type of marketing requires your business to create something of genuine interest to your prospects. A brand's blog or online magazine can provide an excellent platform for your customers and prospects to share and connect, as well as a great way to augment your customer's experience and bring the community together.

Eric Brown's background is rooted in the rental and real estate industries. He founded metro Detroit's Urbane Apartments in 2003, after serving as Senior Vice President for a major Midwest apartment developer. He established a proven track record of effectively repositioning existing rental properties in a way that added value for investors while enhancing the resident experience. He also established The Urbane Way, a social media marketing and PR laboratory, where innovative marketing ideas are tested.

Eric Brown
eric@theurbaneway.com
@eric_urbane
http://www.facebook.com/TheUrbaneWay
http://www.linkedin.com/in/apartmentveteran/
http://www.theurbaneway.com/
http://www.theurbanelife.com/
+1-248-767-4460

Becky Carroll is the founder of Petra Consulting Group, a strategic consultancy focused on WOW customer experiences. In her main role, she is the Community Program Manager for Verizon. She is responsible for developing the strategy for the community forums as well working with her team to integrate the community with other Verizon social media. Becky's business blog, Customers Rock! (http://customersrock.net), is listed in the Top 5 of the Top 50 Customer Service Blogs. She teaches the "Marketing via New Media" class at UC San Diego Extension. Previously, Becky was a Senior Consultant for Peppers & Rogers Group and worked at HP for 14 years, including as the Director of Marketing for the UK and Ireland.

Becky Carroll
becky@petraconsultinggroup.com
@bcarroll7
http://facebook.com/rebeccacarroll
http://linkedin.com/in/beckycarroll
http://customersrock.net

Technical

Social Media Analytics

by

Pek Pongpaet

Social media analytics is where the rubber meets the road. You can spend all day on a social media site, promoting your brand and spreading links around. You can even get more than a few people to engage in conversation around your brand. The concept of social media analytics isn't what's new here—it's the technology that's important to look at.

Google Trends notes the weakening use of Web 2.0 and new media, as the terms are overthrown by social media. This is just one reflection of a larger movement that shifts social media beyond early adopters, teens, or any narrowly rendered consumer demographic.

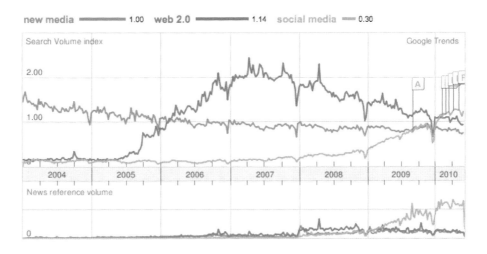

For years, social media outlets have been hyped as a place for marketers to push brands and gain eyeballs. But that social media activity became more fragmented with the opening up of networks creating more places for users to leave their bread crumbs of conversation. From one corporate blog entry, you could get comments on your site, Twitter, another blog, or Facebook. How do you capture, aggregate, and analyze all that data to see how successful your social media campaign really was? How far is your reach actually going?

In the past, pure Web analytics fell short. They were unable to follow through on the promise of targeted marketing measures because they were unable to capture every aspect of a given social media trek. To truly analyze your social media activity, you need to be able to follow your brand correlation with a user, wherever it goes. This involves a multi-faceted approach to maintaining correspondence and tracking measures for social media users, which we'll parse out later.

In the mean time, you'll need to focus on picking up that trail of social media activity in order to determine your success, return on investment, and next steps toward growth. This requires new technology—which we're seeing around the use of APIs and data analysis networks that have better ways of looking at your social media activity—that is finally able to measure your reach. This means more validation around the act of social media marketing, and more benefits from the resources poured into social media analysis.

Fortunately, a fleet of new concepts, services, and businesses has emerged in the past year to provide the means for calculating results around your social media activity.

Converting The Intangible

The importance of such technology lies in its ability to make your social media activity tangible. Take the raw data of your users and convert it into something that can be measured against itself, other data sets, and additional standards set for various distribution methods (i.e. display advertising). Not only does this standardize your own social media activity, but it builds out a framework to follow with future campaigns, budgets, and other planning measures.

One way in which new technology is being applied to the conversion of social media activity is through real-time analytics. This is a trend that has gained a significant amount of traction in recent months, in part due to the success of public-sharing platforms like Twitter and Facebook. These networks have raised consumer comfort levels around sharing their personal preferences, while prompting direct conversations to take place between brands and consumers.

These platforms leveled the playing field in yet another way—the raw data being collected from these public conversation mines is also being offered up by the platforms themselves. Twitter and Facebook, among others, have APIs for developers to tap, generating pools of real-time interactions that can be re-grouped around any given demographic.

Real-time capabilities introduce another layer for contextualizing the new, readily available data. Instead of determining the relevance of a blog entry by the number of links that are directed its way, you can see how recently it was published. This adds another perspective for filtering through data, enabling publishers, developers, and advertisers to connect with consumers in a more immediate fashion. Real-time social media has converted the Web into a giant conversation, instead of a series of static pages that are updated at various points in time. The type of information exchange that can be achieved through direct conversation is much more effective than a board of sequentially updated posts.

Another technology innovation contributing towards improved social media analytics is location-based tagging. Smartphones' GPS capacity, coupled with a booming mobile app marketplace, has led to an array of applications that can geo-tag nearly anything. Photos, credit card activity, social meetings, jogging routes, and shopping patterns—all of these are possible through the collective capabilities of mobile technology. These countless parameters drive more opportunities for publishers, brands, and developers to reach consumers in a direct manner, with each interaction becoming an opportunity for social media analysis.

Social Media Metrics

For a better idea on what social media metrics to measure, look at your objectives and your path to reach that goal. Do you want more Twitter followers, more sales, or more ad clicks? What actions do your users and followers need to take in order to help you achieve your objective?

Pure Web analytics can give you basic insight to your user behavior. What links do they click on, from where are incoming links originating? This can give you some ideas on the best placement for your ads, buttons, graphics, sign-up links, and other calls to action.

Beyond pure Web analytics, however, you'd also like to know how many users find you on Twitter versus Facebook, and how they're influencing their friends on those networks, so some of that traffic and activity can come back to you. Are they already talking about your brand, and if so, how do they feel about it?

For this, you'll need more social media-specific metrics. How often are your tweets being retweeted, and by whom? How does your brand rank amongst others involved in social media campaigns? What actions are user-initiated, and which need a little prodding?

Some examples of social media metrics to monitor:

Embeds/installs: How many users have placed your embeddable video or widget on their site or social networking profile?

Searches: How many users have searched for you within a social network setting?

Rankings: How do users view you as a brand, and how visible are you within a given social network?

Registrations by channel: How many users sign up for your site through a Facebook app versus an iPhone app? What social networking integration do you have for single sign-in options?

Influence: Not just page views, clicks, and impressions or time on site, etc. Things like retweets, influencer score, sentiment, number of mentions, comments, velocity, reach, and followers.

Sentiment: How do users feel about your brand, and what language is being used in association with your brand?

Some of these metrics are relatively simple to assess. Others, like sentiment, involve more calculations. You'll have to look at the language used in individual tweets, along with the context of how those tweets are shared. One problem social media analytics had early on was a shortage of tools that could automate this analysis process. Those that were able to gain metrics like this were paying a pretty penny for such services, which were still limited to the type and amount of social networking information that was available for processing.

Open standards have increased the amount of raw data that is accessible to you, even when it's data that pertains specifically to your brand or social network. New ways of appropriating raw data have emerged to help you extract what you need from social media activity.

Perhaps you'd like to know what the conversion rate is for various steps a user must take when registering for your social network. Mashable outlines the Funnel Analysis method for measuring conversion rates, using Twitter's sign up process as an example.

Funnel Analysis

One critical kind of analysis that social apps require is called Funnel Analysis. This is a way of measuring conversion rates, which is the lifeblood of all applications. The term "conversion rate" refers to the total number of visitors who came to a site, compared to the number of visitors who did a desired action (such as creating an account or purchasing an item).

The Marketing Funnel

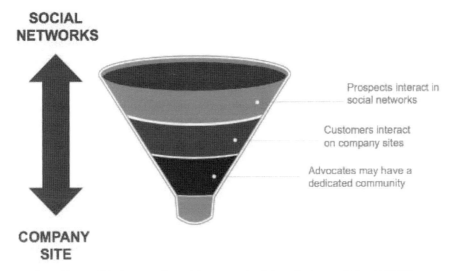

http://www.slideshare.net/jeremiah_owyang/social-marketing-analytics-4464428

What Funnel Analysis gives you is a more granular way of analyzing conversion rates. Instead of simply looking at sign ups divided by total visitors, you figure out the steps that have to be taken to get a user to sign up and measure the individual conversion rates between steps. As you can see from the image above, there's often a pretty steep dropoff between each step, giving you the namesake funnel shape. (Note: the image uses made up stats and is for illustration purposes only.)

This more granular look at conversion rates can have surprising results. Let's take a look at Twitter's signup funnel:

1. Hit homepage
2. Go to signup page, fill out registration form
3. Browse suggested topics
4. Add e-mail friends
5. Search for someone

As you can see, the signup process is pretty complicated, and will benefit from detailed analysis. We might find, for example, that there's a huge dropoff rate (a "dropoff" occurs when many of the people who made it to one step don't make it to the next) at the "add e-mail friends" step. Once we've discovered a dropoff rate like this, we have to figure out the root cause. The dropoff rate at the "add e-mail friends" step could mean that users are unsure how to continue, causing them to leave, or they might not want to add their e-mail information. We would have to test to make sure.

Ultimately, Funnel Analysis is about finding and improving trouble spots in a Web site. With continual analysis, changes can be measured and ideas can be tested over time.

We've gone over some metrics that are useful to consider, but let's dive a little deeper and compare other measurements that you'll see throughout the industry. It's important to look at multiple sides of your measurable data, as it can offer guidance lending to the survival of your business. There are some pitfalls to watch out for, and other areas that are beneficial. Let's take a look.

Vanity Metrics Versus ROI

Vanity metrics are the ego-boosters, often lauded by press releases and internal reports. The fluff stats that don't get at the heart of user activity could swirl around millions of page views, hundreds of clicks-per-minutes, or thousands of sign ups on the first day. But the relevance missing from these vanity metrics is sustainability.

You can brag about a million page views, but that doesn't offer any insight to the origin of those page views, how engaged users were once they reached your page, and if they thought highly enough of the content to share it across the social Web. Where vanity metrics fall short is in their ability to measure a return on investment (ROI), as there's no measurable follow through on such fluff stats.

In order for a business to move forward with testing, improvements, marketing, and growth, a close analysis of user behavior is in order. Otherwise, resources allocated to a particular social media campaign are lost in translation. A business cannot operate without a constructive amount of self-assessment.

Quantitative Versus Qualitative Metrics

Along the same lines of vanity metrics versus ROI, quantitative versus qualitative metrics look at two types of data sets. A quantitative set of data is objective, offering raw information with no analysis. Qualitative metrics are more subjective, offering insight to the correlation between any two points of data in one or more sets.

Both quantitative and qualitative metrics have their purposes—they offer multiple perspectives on a larger system. What's important to note for social media, however, is the ongoing evolution of data set analysis in these fields. For most, quantitative metrics are akin to page views and other flat data that doesn't peer into sentiment.

Qualitative metrics extract user feelings, giving more dimensions toward determining the relationship between your brand, a user's retweet, and their reasoning behind sharing your brand with a friend. The more levels you can acquaint yourself with your users, the better you can approach and serve their needs.

Ways To Measure Meaning

As social media metrics take their next big leap, it's necessary to understand a few ways in which the meaning behind your actions can be analyzed. As you dig down into the reasons behind user action, you'll also better understand your business, marketing, and growth needs. Studying how consumers interact with your brand can, in fact, tell you a lot about yourself (the brand).

Sentiment

Sentiment is one way in which your users' actions can be measured. As previously noted, sentiment is a qualitative metric that can be far more insightful than a quantitative metric. Studying the natural language and grammar used in shared social media content can provide some clues as to the sentiment around your brand.

Natural language consists of the vocabulary used, and with what frequency. How many times was your brand name mentioned in a series of tweets, and what other words were mentioned in the same sentence?

The grammar of those sentences adds another layer of analysis for sentiment metrics, as it looks at the relationship amongst words used. This reveals the context around which those words were used, showing you a peek of the process behind your users' actions.

Are people responding positively or negatively to your brand name, or social media marketing campaign? How far is that sentiment spreading, and where can it convert, in a helping or hindering manner, into action taken around your brand?

The use of sentiment analysis is still in its infancy; it's one of the major steps forward in social media metrics, but we've only tapped the tip of the iceberg. At its most basic level, sentiment metrics are still keyword driven. Algorithms and bots can only dissect so much of human intent. Even with another human going over your users' tweets, the context can be misunderstood.

In order to get the most accurate results, you'd need that human follow-up system. This can get costly as your business tries to scale social media metrics. Remember your objectives around the ROI of your campaign, and strike a balance between resources and results.

As more data sets become available for cross-network and cross-app analysis, more correlations will be made. This will be a result of standards currently being established. We'll discuss this standardization process in more detail later in the chapter.

Social Customer Relationship Management (CRM)

Dealing with social media metrics ultimately means dealing with individuals. Your activity is comprised of individual actions, all of which need to be assessed, monitored, and addressed. You'll find that there are typically a handful of active users that drive the social movement of your app or product. Measure the reach of your influencers, and seek ways to appeal to them.

There are plenty of ways to learn from your influencers. Look at their past interaction with your brand, and how they've spread their message to their own friends and colleagues. What types of recommendations are they making, and are they positive or negative about your brand?

Once you've determined who your primary influencers are, you can begin communications with them. Perhaps they can test your upcoming features and offer feedback. Maybe they'd like to help spread the word about a new product you're unveiling, which could lead to a widespread social endorsement for your brand.

There are a number of tools that aid you in CRM, such as Radian6 or StatusNet. These tools provide central consoles for organizing bug fixes, customer comments and questions, and help desks. They provide a back-end for your team to handle such communications from an organizational viewpoint, as well as client-facing tools to make it easier for your users to submit their concerns and suggestions. These tools can often be fully incorporated into your existing Web site for a seamless user experience.

What We Have Learned

"Social media is like teen sex. Everybody wants to do it. Nobody knows how. When it's finally done there is surprise it's not better." - AvinashKaushik

So far we've looked at the importance of social media metrics, and how it's evolved with new trends and analysis tools. We've looked at the ways in which social media analytics can be measured, and the important metrics around this analysis. Now let's see how all that data can be applied for your purposes.

It's important to remember that analytics are part of a larger plan for growing your business. Social media metrics give you insight to your previous and current effects, all while creating a roadmap for determining your future course of action. What you learn from social media metrics can help you achieve several of your business goals.

Start by looking over your former campaigns—where did it succeed and where did it fall short? Which users interacted with your social campaigns, and at what points were they doing so? What can you do next to improve on your last campaigns?

We've mentioned several tools and services that your business can benefit from when analyzing all of this data. But here are some specific things to remember during your analysis:

Key Performance Indicators (KPIs)

These are the points you've determined before rolling out a new campaign, so you have set metrics to focus on when doing your social media analysis. To do so, you're going to be studying your qualitative and quantitative data sets closely, providing clear-cut points of comparison for before-and-after analysis of your social media activity. This is critical towards your business development, as it acts as a self-assessment tool in relation to your social media campaigns.

KPIs need to be actionable and quantifiable, and provide comparative analysis. These are directly tied to your social media objectives, as they outline what actions you'll take. Would you like more repeat sales? What metrics can you look at to determine previous visitor actions around sales in order to achieve an increase in the future?

Dialog KPIs In Action

Share of Voice:

$$\frac{\text{Brand Mentions}}{\text{Total Mentions (Brand + Competitor A, B, C...n)}} = \text{Share of Voice}$$

Audience Engagement:

$$\frac{\text{Comments + Shares + Trackbacks}}{\text{Total Views}} = \text{Audience Engagement}$$

Conversation Reach:

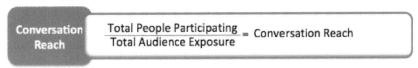

$$\frac{\text{Total People Participating}}{\text{Total Audience Exposure}} = \text{Conversation Reach}$$

http://www.slideshare.net/jeremiah_owyang/social-marketing-analytics-4464428

Standardization

Standardizing your metrics as much as possible will help you in your analysis, particularly when it comes to determining and analyzing your KPIs. Whether you're looking at Web site engagement or ads that convert into sales, leveling the grounds of data comparison will help you reach important conclusions more efficiently.

Support KPIs In Action

Social Media Issue Resolution Rate:

Issue Resolution Rate

$$\frac{\text{Total \# Issues Resolved Satisfactorily}}{\text{Total \# Service Issues}} = \text{Issue Resolution Rate}$$

Resolution Time:

Resolution Time

$$\frac{\text{Total Inquiry Response Time}}{\text{Total \# Service Inquiries}} = \text{Resolution Time}$$

Customer Satisfaction Score:

Satisfaction Score

$$\frac{\text{Customer Feedback (input A, B, C...n)}}{\text{All Customer Feedback}} = \text{Satisfaction Score}$$

http://www.slideshare.net/jeremiah_owyang/social-marketing-analytics-4464428

This is something you can do with your own data, but it's a movement that's taking place across the industry. Social media advertising in particular is seeing the effects of standardization, determining industry-wide metrics that you can apply to your own data sets. How do you compare to your competitors, and what new standards can be reached to help you better analyze your data? Sentiment as a metric, for example, is currently being standardized around natural language and grammar.

In all, it's important that you choose metrics that can actually translate into the context of your business. For your own purposes, you'll need to define metrics beyond "attention metrics" in order to sieve out the points that are reflective of your business goals. Metrics are key to the development of your social media campaigns, as they will help you streamline your efforts and make the most of the tools that are available to you.

Pek Pongpaet
pek@firesnakelabs.com
@pekpongpaet
http://www.facebook.com/PeksPage
http://www.linkedin.com/in/pekpongpaet
http://blog.pekpongpaet.com
http://firesnakelabs.com

Anatomy of a Social Media App: A Case Study of Tap Hunter

by

Melani Gordon

TapHunter.com is an online service providing the quickest and easiest path for beer aficionados to find their favorite craft beers. Not only are we a craft beer search engine and iPhone app, but we are also focused on building a community, inspiring beer enthusiasts, and supporting craft brewers.[1]

The Beginning

The idea for Tap Hunter came to founder Jeff Gordon, a longtime craft beer fan, as he tried to stay on top of what beer was on tap at local bars and breweries. Keeping up meant checking a variety of Web sites and newsletters every day. That became such a hassle that Gordon, who used to build Web sites at his day job, had a better idea.

The next month, he and I launched the Tap Hunter Web site to a flurry of local buzz. Since then, Tap Hunter has caught the attention of a big beer company and allowed the Gordons to travel to New York City and Vancouver to cover beer events as experts. Our momentum has been so exciting, as this is the most successful idea that Jeff and I have collaborated on together. (We are serial entrepreneurs.)

A friend of ours even made the Tap Hunter iPhone app for us for free because he was so excited about it. It is imperative for the craft beer revolution that more consumers get introduced to it, and that will happen through sites like TapHunter.com.

A Big Break

---

[1] Learn more at TapHunter.com.

Shortly after launching the site, our names became synonymous with colleagues and friends: "The Gordons are the beer gurus." That's when we received a phone call from Anheuser-Busch InBev to cover an event in New York City for their premium brand: Stella Artois.

We accepted and had a trip of a lifetime. Tap Hunter covered the Stella Artois World Draught Master title in NYC via blogging, Twitter, and Ustream. This was the first time the Stella Artois World Draught Master Competition would be held in the U.S., after being hosted in Leuven, Belgium, for the past twelve years. The timed competition took place in front of an esteemed panel of judges, including Food & Wine magazine's Ray Isle, Bon Appétit magazine's Andrew Knowlton, Stella Artois Draught Master, Cian Hickey, and 2008 U.S. Draught Master Winner, Anthony Alba.

What Is It All About?

TapHunter.com is an online service that lets you search for your favorite craft beer on tap at San Diego and Seattle area breweries, brew pubs, local hideouts, and more.

- Find your favorite craft beers: Tap Hunter scours the Web and pulls beer lists from local bars to keep you posted on the hottest craft beers on tap. Once you belly up to your local hideout, you can even notify us that your favorite beer on tap is empty.

- Tired of arriving at a local hideout to find a line around the block for the "cask" special of the night and then learn it's been empty for hours? With TapHunter.com, you'll stay up-to-date on the latest taps.

- Quickly find what you're looking for: Search by bar, beer or location...even from your iPhone or Blackberry. And yes, we're social media savvy; you can also track your favorite beer through RSS or Twitter. We'll notify you when it's on tap in your area.

Social Demographic Breakdown

- Age: 25–45
- Gender: 70% male
- Marital Status: 55% single, 39% married
- Combined Household Income: 23% $100K+
- Educational Level: Majority some college and undergraduate degree
- Purchase craft beer 5+ times per month
- Visit local brewery or pub 1–5 times per month
- Home brewer
- Enjoys climbing, biking, dining out, camping, snowboarding, sporting events, video games and travel

Making It Social

We focus the Web site on being social and local. By integrating with social networks (Twitter and Facebook), users can stay updated through many different channels. Users can contribute to the site by helping keep the location tap lists updated. Each action they take on the site is rewarded on a point system to incorporate a "gaming" element to the user experience. The iPhone app is designed to be used "on-the-go" and has location based searching built in.

Twitter: There are city specific Twitter accounts so we can cater to their specific audience and culture. We often find ourselves making recommendations on what craft beer to pair with this weekend's BBQ.

Facebook: We post geo-targeted posts. A review on a Philly festival most likely doesn't interest our San Diego fans. And we're careful not to create too much noise. They have to be targeted posts.

Flickr: We take pictures at every event, whether it's a festival or at a friends house home brewing party. People love to see and feel the vibe of gatherings and tag themselves in photos.

Our Motivation

The fanatics keep us going with our mission. This is a perfect example of the craft beer consumers who just plain get it.

Here's one of our favorite fan blog posts to date:

"I have personally been using the Tap Hunter iPhone app for about 8 months now. Personally, this app chooses where I go to enjoy a great craft beer. I know what I'm going to drink BEFORE I get to the bar/brewery, and I know approximately how long I will be there before I pack up and head to another location for another great craft brew that I found on Tap Hunter.

What I don't understand is how some breweries haven't jumped all over this yet. THIS APP WILL INCREASE YOUR CUSTOMER BASE! Even after 8 short months, I would not be able to function as a craft beer "guy" without my Tap Hunter app. The user-friendly interface allows me to easily pick my city by sharing my location, and then calculates the distance to my nearest craft beer watering hole. I then choose the spot, peruse the list of beers that are accompanied by their respective brewery name, and the Abv of the beer listed. If there was anything lacking, it would be a "style" designation so we know if Corona is a Stout, Lager or a Poison.

Head on over to Tap Hunter.com and check out what they have to offer. You can thank me with a beer the next time you see me." — Stonepurist

In addition to co-founding TapHunter.com & TapHunter.tv, Melani Gordon is the principal of gWave Consulting. Melani leads a team that helps clients enhance their Internet presence to build brand awareness through the use of search engine optimization, strategic marketing, and online marketing communications. Melani has more than eleven years of technology and Internet marketing experience. Prior to forming gWave, she served as marketing manager at an Internet technology company, where she led the marketing, branding, and communication efforts for more than 20,000 real estate agents and brokers. Melani also has been a key player for several San Diego interactive agencies and Internet technology startups.

Melani Gordon
@melgordon
http://www.linkedin.com/in/gwave
http://www.facebook.com/gwaveconsulting
+1-619-894-0384

Verticals

ConnectedCOPS

By

Lauri Stevens

Law enforcement agencies, especially at the local level, are implementing social media tools into their operations. But like many businesses, government groups, and other organizations, it's a slow adoption rate. Few of those agencies using the tools are leveraging them to their full capability, and fewer still *really* understand how to incorporate the tools strategically into their agencies. But that's changing. That isn't to say that law enforcement is all that far behind other types of organizations. This chapter will provide an overview of the current state of law enforcement's use of social media, provide a critique, and explore some of the ways that it might look like in the future.

Police at all levels of government, state, local, and federal, use social media to engage citizens, recruit, enhance their reputations, and provide information. They also use it to prevent and solve crime. For hiring purpose, many agencies are leveraging the tools to perform very thorough background checks on potential new recruits.

Current Social Media Use by Law Enforcement

I'm asked frequently how many police departments use social media. Getting an accurate count is pretty hard to do. I will say that when Twitter first came out with lists around October of 2009[1], I spent that entire weekend listing every law enforcement department with a Twitter presence that I could find, and it numbered just under 400. As I write this, eleven months later, the @LAwSComm law enforcement agency lists approximate 1,200 agencies worldwide on Twitter. That's not including the numerous individual cops on Twitter. While I make every attempt to keep track of them, and have listed agencies in Singapore, India, Spain, Mexico, the Netherlands, and many other countries, I'm sure I've missed a few if not many.

But just because 1,200 agencies are on Twitter doesn't mean 1,200 agencies *use* it. Some set up accounts and haven't tweeted for several months or at all. Certainly Twitter isn't the definitive measuring tool. I refer to it because it's "countable." The important takeaway is that law enforcement globally is realizing that social media is here to stay, and that despite the risks, the benefits are far

---

[1] MG Siegler, "Twitter Expands Lists Beta Testing. A Great New Feature." TechCrunch, Oct 15, 2009,. http://techcrunch.com/2009/10/15/breaking-twitter-begins-lists-rollout/.

greater. My casual observance of an increase from 400 to 1,200 would indicate— albeit unscientifically—a 200% increase in just eleven months on just one platform.

What we can also observe is that whether using Twitter or other social media tools, law enforcement is increasingly realizing the power they have in their own hands to increase communication with citizens and involve them in law enforcement activities. Police are sharing information about crimes, wanted persons, traffic or upcoming events, and general education. They're realizing that they can dissolve the media filter[2], increase the speed at which information gets out to the public, and share more information because they are no longer dependent upon news editors to determine the newsworthiness of the information.

For community engagement purposes, police departments are also adopting Facebook in large numbers. Paralleling some of the same themes with Twitter, not all of them allow postings by others. But the departments with Facebook walls open for posting by and large receive more comments from citizens, and the huge majority of the comments are expressing appreciation for the work they do or are quality discussions of the topic at hand. When the comments are critical of police, chances are many people step forward to balance the criticism with positive observations or clarifications.

Law enforcement agencies are becoming more aware of how to increase and manage their own reputations. They're learning how to monitor Twitter or use social media monitoring tools or watch blogs to see what people are saying about them, thereby gaining insight into how to alter their messages to the public.

They're also increasingly realizing the business parallels for policing. In my workshops with law officers I point out that big business is losing control over their brands because of the increase in communication on social media by customers talking about them. But while the IBM's and Coca-Cola's of the world are grasping to maintain some control over their images, law enforcement stands to gain control. For any police department, their brand is their reputation. Since they previously had little if any control over what reporters said and had no vehicles with which to respond, they now are in the envious position to increase control by paying attention to what's happening online and acting on it strategically. Some agencies are recording their own press conferences, or even creating their own video news programs and have YouTube or Vimeo channels. Most aren't taking it that far, but are enjoying the public relations benefits of distributing information directly to citizens through Twitter and Facebook.

When the Vancouver Police Department (VPD) was preparing for the Olympic Games in 2010, they needed more cops—about two hundred more cops. So back in 2007 they tried an innovative new method to recruit. They hopped onto

---

[2] Dan Alexander, Spin. ConnectedCOPS.net, September 10, 2009. http://connectedcops.net/?p=316].

Second Life[3]. At the end of May of that year they held a virtual recruitment seminar in their virtual police department. Only thirty plus people showed up, but it was still a huge success. According to VPD Director of Communications Paul Patterson, nobody who attended the online seminar actually signed up to become a police officer, but the PD received so much media attention for their innovative approach that the "earned PR" was substantial. So much so that they were able to recruit all the new officers needed[4].

Police departments are realizing that in order to recruit the tech-savvy young people that they desire, they need to be where they reside. What the Vancouver experiment proved is that smart and savvy use of the tools can communicate that the department isn't stuck in the dark ages, and to a potential new recruit it's a strong sign that the department is forward-thinking and therefore an appealing place to consider for a career.

Effective internal communications has always been a goal for many departments. For continuity in investigations or other case work, progress is sometimes stymied when an officer is off-duty for a couple of days and takes important information with him because it exists only in his head. With the proliferation of third-party collaborative tools, progressive agencies are facilitating the sharing of information among its members.

Even more exciting than the internal communications area is the degree to which law enforcement is increasing communications within the law enforcement community across jurisdictions, up and down from local agencies to federal and back again.

Other sites internal to the police profession have been formed to bring law officers together. Communities have been built on Ning, Yammer, and many other community-building platforms. Police are a tight group. With such technical tools available they are enjoying the opportunity to connect with fellow officers globally.

Another significant area worth mentioning is the career-enhancing opportunities being realized by individual officers. Even with LinkedIn alone, cops are discovering golden opportunities to promote themselves, to learn from their colleagues by joining LinkedIn groups, or to enhance their current work by making new connections. Upwardly mobile officers especially like LinkedIn because of its professional atmosphere and the ability to retain privacy. Even officers who scoff at the suggestion of being on Twitter are finding the benefits of LinkedIn. Public safety related groups number in the dozens focusing on high-tech crimes, police training, Internet safety, executive communications, and even one dedicated solely to discuss the use of social media within law enforcement.

---

[3] VPD: Virtual Police Department. The Vancouver Sun. May 29, 2007. http://bob.vg/vpd.
[4] Paul Patterson, Interview, June, 2010.

With Crime, Social Media Is A Double-edged Sword

Social networking tools are making it easier for police to investigate and prevent crime. The same tools are also making it easier for criminals to plan and carry out crimes, and thus challenge law enforcement in new ways. The challenge faced by law enforcement is to keep up with the criminal element while simultaneously using the tools to their advantage.

With greater ability to disseminate information, it's easier for citizens to make themselves aware of the types of information police are looking for, and it's also much easier for people to report crimes they wouldn't have before, either because they didn't want to have their names connected or because they felt the crime wasn't serious enough to warrant calling 911.

Crime Stoppers programs are reporting that anonymous tips are increasing and many programs credit social media. In Toronto, for example, the officer who ran the Crime Stoppers program is also Toronto's top social media "know-it-all." Constable Mills credits social media for how he raised anonymous tips nearly 200% from 2007 to 2009[5]. Crime Stoppers programs are nearly all volunteer run and many have little or no funding. So creatively incorporating free social media tools into their process has been successful in many ways. Some Crime Stoppers programs have figured out to put a "leave-a-tip" tab on their Facebook pages. It takes a tipster to the same Web reporting form used elsewhere, and with 500 million people using Facebook, the hope is that more people will become aware and take the easy step of clicking and reporting what they know[6].

Sometimes, it's just too easy for cops to get their guy. Like when the 19-year-old robber in Pennsylvania checked his Facebook account during a robbery and forgot to log out[7]. In a separate case, another 19-year-old in Brooklyn had his robbery charges dropped when he was able to prove that he made a post on his Facebook page from his father's apartment at the time of the robbery[8].

---

[5] Scott Mills, "Toronto Crime Stoppers Gets 10,300 Anonymous Tips for 25th Birthday." ConnetedCOPS.net, August 17, 2010.
http://connectedcops.net/?p=2723.
[6] Lauri Stevens, "New tab on Police Facebook Pages for anonymous tip/crime reporting." ConnectedCOPS.net, August 9, 2010.
http://connectedcops.net/?p=2626.
[7] David M. Williams, "Robber leaves Facebook logged in at scene of crime." ITWire.com, September 23, 2010. http://www.itwire.com/opinion-and-analysis/the-linux-distillery/27940-robber-leaves-facebook-logged-in-at-scene-of-crime.
[8] Jacqui Cheng, "Teen's Facebook update gets robbery charges dropped." Arstechnica.com, November 12, 2009. http://arstechnica.com/tech-policy/news/2009/11/teens-facebook-update-gets-robbery-charges-dropped.ars.

When investigating the rape of a young girl, Los Angeles area investigators were stumped until they turned to social media. One of the key pieces of the case was a photo of one of the two attackers. Knowing the general vicinity of where the subject lived, they were able to compare the photo to Google map images and eventually identified the exact house in which he was standing in front of. Further advances in geolocation technology allow investigators to often see the location a photo was taken or even the exact location a tweet was sent.

In all cases investigated online, there's a digital trail of evidence, and more and more law officers are receiving training in how to collect and preserve it. So as pedophile rings develop, law enforcement in a few recent cases were able to follow the 1s and 0s and crack international operations. In Poland, 102 men were arrested after a two-year investigation that started with the photo of a naked girl being circulated on a social networking site[9]. In a separate incident, law enforcement agencies in Australia, Canada, and the UK, along with Child Exploitation and Online Protection (CEOP), cracked an operation distributing photos of children "suffering horrific abuse" over Facebook[10].

Inventive police organizations are creatively trying other measures to make our world safer. To combat driving under the influence (DUI), cops in at least three jurisdictions tried posting names of people arrested for driving under the influence. The Honolulu PD posted arrests on their Web site each week and took it down after two days. Evesham Police in New Jersey were posting names and other details of DUI arrests on their Facebook page, and the Montgomery County (Texas) District Attorney's office was tweeting DUI arrestees' names during "high-drinking" holidays. But in each of these three examples, law enforcement has pulled back after receiving criticism largely over privacy issues and that none of the people had been convicted.

Facebook pages have been known to be both a great source for intelligence gathering and a place that can interfere with an investigation and cause a great deal of stress to cops on a personal level. After the G20 in Toronto in June of 2010, police came under fire for alleged acts of police brutality. The Facebook pages that sprung up calling for investigation into the alleged wrong-doing garnered tens of thousands of fans in some cases. Toronto Police even let their accusers post on its own Facebook page. While the posts caused the controversy to grow, and negatively affected officer morale, the cops were also literally handed immense amounts of intelligence in the photos and videos posted by their critics.

---

[9] Gemma Fox, "Police in Poland smash pedophile ring with over 100 arrests." Digital Journal, September 10, 2010.
http://www.digitaljournal.com/article/297331.
[10] UK Parents Lounge, "Pedophile ring busted hiding on Facebook." Expose Report News Magazine, August 29, 2010.
http://www.exposereport.com/enews/index.php/sex-offender-news/128-pedophile-ring-busted-hiding-on-facebook.

In Multnomah County, Oregon, in the case of missing 7-year-old Kyron Horman, sheriffs' investigators were distracted at least in part from working the case because they had to address erroneous information being spread through public speculation over whether the step-mother was involved in the child's disappearance[11].

The opportunity to commit crimes in the digital world is abundant. But law officers know that opportunity to solve crime is also theirs to determine. Digital trails don't run dry.

The Need For Strategy, Policy, and Training

It's not the wild, wild west—shoot now and ask questions later. Early law enforcement adopters of social media are full of examples of one cop who followed the "it's easier to ask for forgiveness than permission" theory of life and created a Twitter and Facebook account for their agency because they were progressive thinkers, and to them the benefits of these tools was beyond obvious. These people are pioneers and innovators. We're passed that phase of adoption. In his book *Crossing the Chasm*, Geoffrey Moore describes five types of technology adopters: Innovators, Early Adopters, Early Majority, Late Majority, and Laggards[12].

I would put the law enforcement profession in the second phase of adoption, still described as early adopters. The closer we move towards adoption by the masses, the more police leaders are realizing the need for sound policy. Indeed, policy is imperative and relatively few agencies have created one to guide their staff. I've written on the topic, invariably pointing out that social media policy for law enforcement is very similar to policy for other industries (such as honoring copyright, privacy, and intellectual property) but special considerations are necessary for law officers. Among the special considerations are deciphering between off-duty and on-duty use, use of department logos, command-staff authority, special conduct issues and the implications a mistake could have on one's career or a court case[13]. Additionally, policies are needed to guide the process of using social media to cyber-vet potential new recruits as well as using the tools to conduct investigations.

And there's another special consideration that I tend to harp upon, which is competence. Many of the problems that have come up could have been alleviated by increased knowledge on the part of officers using the tools. Too often cops say they thought only a few friends could see what they posted on Facebook. Or they

---

[11] Kate Mather, "Rumor mill in Kyron Horman disappearance reaches fever pitch." The Oregonian, June 17, 2010.

[12] Geoffrey Moore, Crossing the Chasm. Harper Business Essentials, 1991. ISBN: 0-06-051712-3.

[13] Lauri Stevens, "The Ingredient of a Solid Social Media Policy for Law Enforcement Agencies." ConnectedCOPS.net, August 17, 2009. http://connectedcops.net/?p=42 and http://connectedcops.net/?p=2483.

lack appreciation for technological advances. A police officer wouldn't allow regular folks to claim ignorance of the law as an excuse for breaking it. Similarly, police officers need to make a better effort to know what they're doing with the technology before they use it, and they need to be held accountable in that regard. Herein lies the argument for professional training.

Cops train and train and train. It is staggering the amount of training they undergo just to remain current in firearms qualifications and other duties germane to the job, let alone special training required to accept the responsibilities of a K9 officer, a school resource officer, a collision deconstructionist, a motorcycle cop, a SWAT officer, etc. The law enforcement profession is realizing that even something as seemingly simple as Twitter has a lot to it and they should be thoroughly trained before representing their department. In fact, at training sessions when I make the statement to the group that if you give a cop a gun and a taser, you can give them Twitter, invariably someone jokes that cops could do a lot more damage with Twitter than with a taser.

Ideally, law enforcement agencies will evaluate their goals thoroughly before policy and training even come into play. For most departments, having a presence on Twitter, Facebook, and YouTube is quite an accomplishment and they're proud of it. Few, if any, realize the types of benefits achievable with true and deep engagement with constituents. Fewer still realize the advanced benefits that can be achieved with a thorough strategy applying the technologies to all areas of the operation.

The C.O.P.P.S. social media method helps law enforcement social media practitioners grasp such goals. I developed the method to help police evaluate the who, what, when, where, why, and how. The C.O.P.P.S. method provides a framework to step through the five-step process of evaluating Citizens, Objectives, Plan, Policy, and Schedule[14].

By carefully identifying the various demographics they want to reach, either because there's a perceived problem or need for more information within it, and then determining an agency's objectives/goals with each and every identified demographic, large agencies in particular can develop a strategy that potentially implements a social media program into several areas of operation, each one a separate program as part of the whole. The result is a comprehensive strategy that incorporates consideration for needed resources and training, the adoption of a solid policy, and a rollout schedule for implementation.

---

[14] Lauri Stevens, "The C.O.P.P.S. Social Media Method™ for Cops." ConnectedCOPS.net, March 3, 2010. http://connectedcops.net/?p=1634.

Stupid Cop Tricks

Cops seem to have a knack for getting themselves into trouble. And when they do, the traditional media loves the story. Cops could probably figure out how to get into hot water anywhere, but problems abound on Facebook.

When a bus carrying tourists from Hong Kong was hijacked in Manila, the Philippine National Police (PNP) received criticism for its handling of the situation. The PNP admitted they handled it badly, citing lack of training[15]. It didn't help that officers' involved then posted photos of themselves smiling in front of the bus, taken at the scene. Eight hostages and the gunman died in the incident. Police posting of photos of themselves was not well received[16].

In East Palo Alto, a police detective posted a comment about "open carry," which refers to the carrying of unconcealed and unloaded guns in public. Open carry is legal in California. The detective, allegedly joking, posted on Facebook to another officer that people who practice open carry in his town "should be shot." The department faced protests by open-carry advocates and an abundance of negative press coverage. An internal investigation found that the detective had violated department policy.

In Sandy Springs, Georgia, an officer posted on his private Facebook page that he would "be working with plain clothes tonight," referring to a drug case being investigated by the FBI. One of his Facebook friends saw the comment and reported him. He's been fired but is pursuing the case in court[17].

An officer in Bozeman, Montana, resigned under pressure after posting that there should "be a law saying police can take people to jail for being stupid." It didn't help that it came right on the heels of a national media spotlight on Bozeman for requiring anyone applying for a government position in the city to cough up usernames and passwords to their social media profiles[18].

In the UK, eighteen officers were disciplined for comments made about police car collisions on a site called "Look I've had a polcol." Polcol is short for *police collision*. In several of the postings, officers bragged about their having wrecked their police vehicle. One post included a photo of an officer showing a "thumbs-

---

[15] Manny Mogato and James Pomfret, "Philippine police admit to botching hostage crisis." Reuters, August 24, 2010.
http://in.reuters.com/article/idINIndia-51027020100824.
[16] "Facebook photos of Philippine police stir more anger." Yahoo! News, August 30, 2010. http://bob.vg/pnppolice.
[17] Alexis Stevens,, "Officer: Facebook postings didn't warrant fire." The Atlanta Journal-Constitution, December 9, 2009. http://www.ajc.com/news/north-fulton/officer-facebook-postings-didnt-235017.html.
[18] Scott McAndrew, "Bozeman fired up over officer's Facebook posts." Online Marketing Performance, September 15, 2009.
http://www.onlinemarketingperformance.com/bozeman-mt-facebook-police/.

up" standing in front of the cruiser that was pinned under a tree. The site has since been shut down[19].

Stories about cops getting themselves in trouble on Facebook could probably fill this book, but it surely doesn't end there. Some cases have made their way to the Supreme Court of the United States. One recent case was CITY OF ONTARIO, CALIFORNIA v. QUON involving a SWAT officer who used his pager to send sexually explicit messages on his work pager. The high court ruled in favor of the Police Chief, who had the messages evaluated to see if the officer was going over his monthly usage allowance because of work-related or personal messaging. The officer had been paying overage charges out of pocket in exchange via verbal agreement with his supervisor for the right to use the pager for personal use, despite the fact that written policy prohibits it. The justices decided that his Fourth Amendment right to privacy had not been violated[20].

A second example is the case of CITY OF SAN DIEGO, CALIFORNIA v. JOHN ROE. The Supreme Court reversed a lower court finding that Officer Roe's First and Fourteenth Amendment rights of free speech had not been violated. While off-duty the officer had produced videotapes of himself masturbating. He was in a non-official police uniform (when clothed) and sold the tapes on eBay[21]. Officer Roe was fired when his commanders learned of the officer's extra-curricular activities, which he sold under the name "Code3stud" on eBay. His activities were discovered by a sergeant who found other items offered for sale by Roe and then discovered a link to an adults-only section[22].

These examples are raised because they reinforce previously made arguments about the need for policy and training, and a requisite maturing of the social media industry, both in terms of acceptance as the norm by law enforcement and acknowledgement by users that social media isn't about playtime. It's about putting smart social into media and leveraging the energy in the technology to potentially change policing in profound ways.

---

[19] Matthew Moore, "Police disciplined for Facebook crash boasts." Telegraph.co.uk, June 23, 2008. http://www.telegraph.co.uk/news/uknews/2180276/Police-disciplined-for-Facebook-crash-boasts.html.

[20] Supreme Court Of The United States. CITY OF ONTARIO, CALIFORNIA, ET AL. v. QUON ET AL. Decided June 17, 2010. http://www.supremecourt.gov/opinions/09pdf/08-1332.pdf.

[21] J. Scott Tiedemann. City of San Diego v. Roe: Its Impact on the Discipline of Officers for Off-Duty Speech. Liebert Cassidy Whitmore. http://www.lcwlegal.com/newspublications/Articles/PastArticles/IMLA_01_02-05_Tiedemann.htm.

[22] Supreme Court Of The United States. CITY OF SAN DIEGO, CALIFORNIA ET AL. v. JOHN ROE. Decided December 6, 2004. http://www.supremecourt.gov/opinions/04pdf/03-1669.pdf.

Why Are Police Hesitant To Use Social Media?

Quite regularly, the phone rings and a police commander on the other end wants me to tell him or her how s/he can convince the chief to adopt social media. When moderating a panel of chiefs at the California Peace Officers' Training Symposium, I posed that question to the panelists. Of course, those three chiefs were already believers. But the first chief to answer the question, Sacramento Chief Rick Braziel said in jest, "Get a new chief."[23]

Some chiefs can be hard-headed for sure. But as more departments use the tools and more opportunities and benefits are being realized, more and more of them are coming around and beginning to explore the networked world. The primary reasons for the hesitation include fear of the unknown, lack of understanding, lack of resources (including personnel and time), as well as inherent legal challenges, especially because they've all heard about the "stupid cop tricks" mentioned above. But professional law enforcement organizations are beginning to address the topic in their annual conferences. Police command colleges are adding social media content to their curricula, in some cases hosting several days of social media content at a time[24]. The SMILE Conference is an event dedicated solely to bringing information about social media and the Internet to policing[25]. As the delivery of professional education proliferates, and understanding of social media spreads, their reluctance to jump on board will shrink.

As one commander said at a training event, "we don't want to be the test case that ends up in court." Law enforcement is a conservative profession by tradition. That should surprise no one. If they make a mistake, criticism flies at them fast. It's imperative that any social media initiatives they undertake be measured and strategic with sound governance in place.

SMILE

In the summer of 2009, as I was brainstorming ideas on how to bring this information to law enforcement, one of the ways that occurred to me was to create a conference that was dedicated solely to law enforcement and social media. But I had never put on a conference and didn't even know where to begin, so I tucked it in the back of my head for later. Then, early in September, a friend who also was producing social media conferences suggested I work with

---

[23] California Peace Officers Annual Training Symposium, April, 2010.

[24] Leadership in a Cyberworld. Institute for Law Enforcement Administration. March 24–26, 2010. Plano, TX / Annual Training Symposium. California Peace Officers' Association. May 25–27. Los Angeles, CA. / PERF Annual Meeting. Police Executive Research Forum. April 15, 2010. Phildadelphia, PA. / Leadership training. POST Command College. June 14 and July 15, 2010. Folsom, CA. / Pearls of Policing. Canadian Police College. Nov 1–5, 2010. Toronto, Canada.

[25] The SMILE Conference. http://www.thesmileconference.com.

him. I wouldn't have to worry about the logistics, only the content. It was a match made in heaven!

So we came up with the name SMILE to mean "Social Media in Law Enforcement." The SMILE Conference was scheduled for April in Washington, DC. Three months prior, I found myself without my planning partner. As we already had put it out there, I felt obligated to carry through. All of a sudden, I was an accidental conference producer.

The conference was a tremendous hit within the law enforcement community. So much so that we were able to attract high level speakers from all over the country, as well as Canada, the UK, and The Netherlands. We also garnered extraordinary attention from the press with stories in the Huffington Post, Mashable.com, and many law enforcement publications. We had eight hours of hands-on training, a full day of community engagement and communication topics, and a full day of investigations and crime prevention. A true testament to the success is that we've seen instances of people using the acronym SMILE to refer to the *concept* of using social media within law enforcement, without intending to refer to the conference at all.

More SMILE conferences are to come, possibly two or three a year. But we have tweaked the acronym to "Social Media, the Internet, and Law Enforcement." The change reflects a need to incorporate other topics such as information sharing, data mining, geolocation, and other important related Internet topics.

Final Thoughts On What's To Come

There are too many variables to attempt to accurately predict the future of law enforcement's use of social media and Internet technologies very far into the future. But looking out short term, we can articulate a few observations with some certainty.

Law enforcement is becoming more comfortable with engagement online and law enforcement agencies are placing greater emphasis on the recruitment of new officers with college degrees. As technologies improve and law officers become better educated, new and innovative ways of leveraging social networking and other Internet tools for enhancing community policing through increased engagement, solving crimes with powerful new intelligence, and gathering techniques will develop as well.

Two particularly exciting areas to a communications professional like myself are information sharing and predictive policing. The speed with which information is gathered and analyzed, in addition to the exponential growth in the amount of information available will provide law enforcement with the challenge of how to gather it all and then what to do with it when they do. New Web-based computer programs already exist that will help law enforcement visualize potential crime in real time. The programs work by pulling data from all known data sets, social networking platforms to include local blogs, newspapers, and every other form of publicly accessible data. They then recognize patterns in the cultivated data that will allow law enforcement to predict, with great accuracy, future risk of criminal activity.

New technologies will facilitate information sharing among law enforcement agencies. Traditionally, law enforcement has had a culture of competitive one-upmanship from one agency to another, both vertically and horizontally. New technologies will make it possible to remove the human element from that process and facilitate the sharing and analysis of all information available.

The world is getting smaller; law enforcement is getting smarter and more efficient. Additionally, citizens who are also armed with more information are growing more aware and taking greater responsibility for partnering with law enforcement to keep their communities safe. There is no doubt that technology related to the Internet and the real-time Web is becoming more integral to policing. There is also zero doubt that law officers at all levels and on every continent will continue to find ways to leverage new technology tools to decrease crime and improve safety and quality of life in profoundly exciting ways. The potential is exciting and significant to policing, and could possibly mean a paradigm-shift to a true community-oriented policing approach involving citizens in the solutions and cops who are approachable and engaging. It's called the #bluewaveofchange.

Lauri Stevens is a social media strategist for law enforcement. Lauri has over twenty-five years of experience in media: social media, interactive media, Web, television, radio, and high-tech market research. Lauri is the founder and principal of LAwS Communications, a media consultancy for law enforcement. LAwS specializes in media management, with an emphasis on social media. LAwS provides consultation in social media strategy, policy, implementation, and training. She is the Producer and Creator of The SMILE (Social Media the Internet and Law Enforcement) Conference and the C.O.P.P.S. Social Media Method.

Lauri Stevens
Lauri@lawscomm.net
@lawscomm
@smileconference
http://www.facebook.com/LawsComm
http://www.facebook.com/TheSMILEConference
http://www.linkin.com/in/LauriStevens
http://www.LawsCommunications.com
http://www.TheSMILEConference.com
http://www.ConnectedCOPS.net
+1-978-764-9887

The Quantified Tweet — Healthcare and Social Media

By

Phil Baumann

In recent years, people have taken a deeper interest in the data around their lives. People are increasingly gaining interest in tracking this data. There's even a name for this movement—the Quantified Self.

In healthcare, tracking relevant data is key. But it can also be cumbersome, and so developing methods and tools that enable the easiest and most convenient means of collection are critical to widespread adoption.

The emerging technologies of our time are creating novel opportunities for all kinds of connection. Social media is enabling and inspiring new ways for people to share their stories with others.

But what we call social media is not in fact strictly social media—it is repurposed technology that provides more than just social connection. They enable connection not only among people, but things—machines to machines, people to machines, and virtually any other kind of item to another.

Currently we are undergoing an inflection in communications evolution. People and industries from all over the world are catching on to social media and folding them into their daily lives and operations to share stories, update their friends, and their network.

In light of these kinds of connections, we may need to expand our definition of social from the kinds of relationships between people, like the relationships and connections between the cells in our bodies, to connections computers have on the ground to satellites in orbit above out planet.

But it's the non-social uses of digital technologies, including social media, which will reveal to us worlds of opportunities perhaps only envisioned in science fiction.

We are only beginning to understand how these social technologies can be used in healthcare.

Of all the emerging media in recent years, the one that may have one of the most interesting—but not so obvious—applications in healthcare is microblogging.

Twitter has come to exemplify this new medium of communication, connection and sharing.

Healthcare Uses of Twitter

A few months before Twitter gained the public's attention, I wrote about how the service could be used in healthcare in "140 Healthcare Uses of Twitter":

1. Tissue recruitment (for kidney and other organs, including blood)
2. Epidemiological survey
3. Disaster alerting and response
4. Emergency response team management
5. Supportive care for patients and family members
6. Diabetes management (blood glucose tracking)
7. Maintaining a personal health diary
8. Adverse event reporting in the clinical setting and other pharmacovigilance functions
9. Emitting critical laboratory values to nurses and physicians
10. Alarming silent codes (psychiatric emergencies, security incidents)
11. Drug safety alerts from the FDA
12. Risk management communication
13. Augmenting telemedicine
14. Issuing Amber alerts
15. Issuing alerts for missing nursing home residents
16. Exercise management and encouragement
17. Weight management and support
18. Biomedical device data capture and reporting
19. Nutritional diary and tracking
20. Coordinating preoperative, perioperative and postoperative care (among pharmacy, nursing and surgical services)
21. Medical service collaboration in the clinical setting
22. Triage management in emergency rooms
23. Census management/monitoring
24. Arranging outpatient care
25. Crowdsourcing for healthcare resources
26. Shift-bidding for nurses and other healthcare professionals
27. Mood tracking (for patients with bipolar and other mood disorders)
28. Patient care reminders in the clinical setting
29. Prescription management, including pharmacy refill reminders
30. Daily health tips from authoritative sources
31. Location awareness during crisis
32. Occupational safety response
33. Hazardous materials communication
34. "Quick and dirty" diagnostic brainstorming between physicians (e.g. "symptom clustering")
35. Clinical case education (residents following attendings)
36. Physician opinion-sharing

37. Promoting domestic violence awareness
38. Raising child abuse awareness
39. USMLE preparation for medical licensing
40. NCLEX preparation for nursing licensing
41. Recruitment of healthcare staff
42. Alcohol and other substance abuse support
43. Issuing and confirming doctor's orders
44. Environmental alerts: pollen counts, pollutions levels, heat waves, severe weather alerts
45. Remote wound care assistance
46. Rural area healthcare communication
47. Micro-sharing of pertinent patient information
48. Micro-sharing of diagnostic results (blood tests, echocardiography, radiological images)
49. Internal facility customer service (a hospital equivalent of @comcastcares—c'mon hospitals!)
50. Publishing health-related news
51. Psychiatric "check-ins" for patients
52. Nursing mentoring and collaboration
53. Publishing disease-specific tips
54. Childcare support
55. Fundraising for hospitals and health-related causes
56. Updating patient family members during procedures
57. Live-tweeting surgical procedures for education
58. Rare diseases tracking and resource connection
59. Reporting hospital staff injuries
60. Tracking patient trends
61. Tracking disease-specific trends
62. Checking hospital ratings with our healthcare consumers
63. Providing around-the-clock disease management
64. Connecting genetic researchers with physicians
65. Publishing the latest advances in biomedical devices
66. Tracking antibiotic resistance
67. Real-time satisfaction surveys with immediate follow-up for problem resolution
68. Issuing asthma alerts
69. Data collection for tracking facility patterns (process performance, supply chain and staffing problems)
70. Live-tweeting medical conferences
71. Keyword tracking of health related topics via search on Twitter
72. Posting quick nursing assessments that feed into electronic medical records (EMRs)
73. Improving medical rounding systems
74. Clinical trial awareness
75. Hospital administration
76. Sharing peer-to-peer reviews of articles of interest
77. Connecting patients with similar disease processes
78. Enhancing health related support groups (e.g. buddy systems for depression)

79. Providing smoking cessation assistance
80. Medical appliance support (e.g. at home: colostomy care, infusion pumps, wound-vacs)
81. Reporting medical device malfunctions
82. Tweeting updates to facility policies and procedures
83. Arranging appointments with healthcare providers
84. Product safety alerts
85. Food safety alerts
86. Information on women's health
87. Pain management
88. Hospital reputation monitoring
89. Publishing hospital-sponsored events in local communities
90. Community health outreach
91. Bioterrorism awareness and preparedness
92. Issuing updates to hospital services to the public
93. Insurance claim management
94. Ethical, permission-based following of patients
95. Micro-sharing consent for surgical and other procedures
96. Patient-sharing of health related experiences
97. Posting "bread crumbs" of facility experiences ("I had a bypass at this hospital and it went well, but the food almost killed me")
98. Patient searches for others confronting similar problems
99. Stress management
100. Mental health awareness
101. Posting homeless shelter needs
102. Food bank resource management
103. Transmitting patient data to patients who are traveling abroad
104. Generating streams of authoritative healthcare content online
105. Exposing medical quackery
106. Mirco-sharing documentation for advanced medical directives
107. Discussing public healthcare policy
108. Developing stronger patient-provider relationships
109. Tracking the safety and efficacy of pharmaceuticals
110. Following health marketing
111. Tracking influenza alerts from the CDC
112. Exchanging/soliciting scientific validation of alternative health claims
113. Following ad-hoc conferences on eHealth (like HealthCampPhila)
114. Tracking toxic diseases
115. Tracking HIV news
116. Issuing/exchanging dietary tips
117. Tweeting what you eat
118. Comparing nursing home performance
119. Coordinating clinical instruction
120. Communicating with nursing supervisors
121. Public safety announcements
122. Tracking FDA guideline updates
123. Tracking the progress of developing pharmaceuticals
124. Broadcasting infant care tips to new parents

125. Publishing vaccination/immunization services locations, hours, and reminders
126. Reporting adverse events to FDA
127. Obtaining information on Medicare and Medicaid
128. Case management functions
129. Clinical education coordination
130. Facilitating patient-transfer processes
131. Patient-information retrieval
132. Reporting breeches of universal precautions in healthcare facilities
133. Posting daily nursing tips
134. Exchanging physician humor (we don't want stressed-out docs)
135. Closing the digital divide with respect to healthcare information
136. Coordinating allied healthcare services during patient admissions
137. Coordinating patient discharges with all services
138. Post-discharge patient consultations
139. Helping device technicians communicate directly with manufacturers
140. Dicussing HIPAA reform in the age of microsharing

Since publication of the list, hospitals and other healthcare organizations have adopted Twitter. For the most part, however, the primary use of Twitter has been for public relations.

Nonetheless, interest in the premise of Twitter's place in clinical operations has been piqued.

Twitter's simplicity of functional design, speed of delivery, and ability to connect two or more people around the world provides a powerful means of communication, idea sharing, and collaboration.

There's potency in the ability to burst out 140 characters, including a shortened URL. Could this power have any use in healthcare? Doctors and nurses share medical information, often as short bursts of data (lab values, conditions, orders, etc.).

But Twitter not only connects people: it has the ability to connect machines. And it's this non-social use of the medium which can be especially interesting in the context of healthcare.

Twitter epitomizes the general direction of twenty-first century communications. It's core feature is a flexible simplicity which enables endless permutations of re-purposed utility.

Twitter is not one thing. It is by itself neither social nor conversational. Rather, it's a pliant and ambient technology that permits several different purposes which can grow around it.

In the healthcare industry, there is often a fine line between caution and fear. It is the fear of change so common in healthcare that I hope we can overcome.

Twitter may be a proving ground of how we overcome our fears, satisfy our cautions, and extend the reach of our health care system with Web-based technologies and communities.

The Data Our Bodies Radiate

Everyday your heart beats a certain number of times. Your lungs inhale and exhale a certain number of times. Your mood shifts, your blood sugar changes, your thoughts stream. But where does the data—the news—of these things go?

The data which our bodies radiate are like streams of thoughts that swiftly vanish from memory. Some of this data is easy to capture: your pulse, your blood pressure, your temperature.

Other data isn't so easy: the size of a neoplastic growth, your potassium level, the number of red blood cells coursing through your veins.

Information, the relevant data needed to make a decision in light of risk, abounds our lives. If you or your healthcare providers don't know about the critical information your body glows forth, you or they might miss the chance to make important decisions about the state of your health.

Glow forth. That would be cool to see, huh? But we don't, we are somewhat blind in that regard. We don't, and never will, have infinite senses omniscient. We are limited and mortal, and yet, it's so human to desire beyond hope to transcend both realities. It's what drives us to live our fullest, to be remarkable and, in some sense, immortal.

But we do create technologies. We can now "see" infrared light. We can view our bones with dangerous radiation, view deep vein thrombi, graph the electric patterns of our brains.

But we too often need huge and expensive machines to do most of these things.

And yet, today's emerging and converging technologies offers the hope of offering powerful and convenient ways to "visualize" and capture the glowing-forth of our bodies' data.

Eventually, augmented reality will be able to further enhance the power of these technologies by illuminating the body with relevant metrics.

The Quantified Tweet Within Your Heart

The tweet is a metaphor for the power of conveying the droplets of data that comprise the larger streams of our lives.

Not only will novel technologies be capable of streaming lone raw data, but they will also enable social connections, expanding the range of fellowship while providing robust arrays of searchable (and researchable) data for science to study.

Furthermore, all this data will have metadata—data about the data. A tweet contains not only the text within the 140 characters, but also the time, location, and any other data that a user selects to tag the tweet.

We are entering a time of tectonic change. In spite of that, our longing for better lives, for health and healing, remains unchanged.

We should use that longing to bring forth novel and convenient technologies that can capture, process, organize and rightfully exploit the precious messages of our health.

Healthcare has often been a demand-side economy. You break your leg, the radiologist and orthosurgeon get paid. You throw a pulmonary embolism, the hospital sends you a cheap survey and an extravagant bill.

It's also supply-side: you have a condition you never knew existed, a company spends billions of dollars on research and advertising and, pop, you have a convenient little pill to take with your bacon and eggs.

The technologies we need to see the data our bodies radiate need an economy.

It may be that smart companies or brave individuals, lone crazy deranged fools, build some of theses technologies. They are on the supply-side.

As we become more aware of these technologies and how we can repurpose them, more of the public will want convenient ways to track their health data.

Meanwhile, entrepreneurs will see the possibilities for new markets to meet the needs of consumers.

What we will need, however, are the processes which enable the right kinds of interpretation of the data which radiates from our skin to the deep core of our invisibly glowing hearts.

Our task is not only to understand these technologies but also to comprehend their influence on the changing ways we see our world. We must strive to understand ourselves with these novel insights so that we may proceed toward a better future.

Phil Baumann is the founder of Health Is Social. He is a registered nurse who blogs and speaks and consults about the role of digital and social media in healthcare.

Religion and Social Media

by

Dave Ingland

In starting Revolution Church Sacramento, one of our key fundamental goals was to connect with people not currently attending church services on a regular basis. Our strategy was simple. Through interpersonal relationships we may have great one-on-one conversations with people, but in order to let the masses know that we welcomed them, social media was extremely important.

At Revolution Church Sacramento, we started with a big dream and an almost invisible budget. It was actually a similar process to how I started a printing corporation from scratch with just a telephone, fax machine, ink jet printer, and a crazy idea to step out on my own in the business world. When I started the printing corporation back in January 2001, social media didn't exist. I relied heavily on telephone and e-mail marketing (instead of conventional print and trade show advertising) to build an international client base, rarely meeting clients in person. Once the business became successful, I still continued to communicate with clients and build trust through telephone and e-mail communication. It helped keep our overhead low and required no marketing budget. This was a great experience to draw from as I made the shift from an atheist in the business world to now becoming the lead pastor of a start-up church eight years later.

In looking at how to make people aware of a new church launching, I saw churches all around us doing conventional marketing such as postcard mailings, door hangers, and Yellow Page advertisements. We didn't want to present ourselves like other churches, because we weren't going to be like them. What better way to present our thoughts, dreams and ideas to those we didn't already know, than to do so in an unobtrusive, inexpensive manner through social media such as Twitter, Facebook, YouTube, and blogging?

For me, Twitter was my go-to tool for connecting with thousands of people. It was free, quick, limited to concise 140 character blurbs, and only those interested in seeing what we were about would subscribe (follow) our tweets. Not only could others follow our tweets, but they could also retweet (rebroadcast) them to their followers and the audience would expand exponentially. It was a very organic, grassroots medium that we as a church were very drawn to.

A core value of the church is centered around building community. I find it to be a core value of Twitter as well. Many look at the church as an institution where a dynamic speaker stands in front of an audience and delivers a speech about God and how to live a life that is pleasing to him. Then the people disburse and reunite again the next Sunday. Some use Twitter in the same way. It is a pulpit in which they can broadcast their viewpoints to those that will follow. However, one can't build community in that manner. Once the message is no longer relevant or they lose interest in the one broadcasting tweets, they disconnect. We used Twitter to help initiate and facilitate conversations. It is through this dialogue that we were able to connect and generate interest with people that would be drawn to what we were doing as a new and different church.

We were very strategic about how we used social media to develop interest since it wasn't about being controversial or grabbing attention; at the core of our social media campaign we were trying to foster a sense of community. Twitter helped us reach the world outside and engage them through our tweets and @replies which then allowed us to make a personal connection once they came out to a gathering or event. When we weren't collectively together in person, we could still continue our connection using Twitter, as well as Facebook and our blog. As a very small, under-resourced Church start-up, one of the things that helped us feel larger and encouraged was the feedback we were getting from around the world via Twitter. I could post something like a prayer request on Twitter and almost instantly receive confirmations from people as far away as Great Britain, Australia, Canada, and Hawaii, responding back that they were in prayer for us. When something amazing happened I would share this with others in our Twitter community and they would respond back with words of encouragement and support. Twitter not only helped us reach others outside of our tiny Church community, but it also made us feel much larger than we were.

Having reached those outside of our initial sphere of influence through social media, we then felt it was equally as important to share what we were doing with others as it was happening. Twitter is a great tool for breaking news in a fast and concise manner, and we as a Church used it to share what we were doing with those that were not in attendance. In a traditional Church service, there is one speaker (preacher) that delivers a message to rows of people all facing him/her. The room is quiet and everyone is asked to give the speaker their undivided attention. We at Revolution Church Sacramento wanted to engage people in dialogue and be conversational in our services. While we didn't always have people in the seats talking back to the speaker, we did pose questions and give moments of pause for them to think and respond internally. We asked people to bring their cellphones and laptops and whenever they felt something should go out to their friends/followers on Twitter, we encouraged them to do so. Whether it be a question, a quote, or their personal thoughts or opinions, we wanted to engage our community in a meaningful way with what we were doing. We wanted to let others know that we didn't exist to be heard, but rather we existed to engage and converse and share our experiences and be open to learning about theirs. Twitter was a great, universal application to allow this interaction because it could be utilized through SMS text messaging on a basic cellphone or through specific apps on smartphones or laptops. We provided a broadband connection, but even that wasn't necessary to allow Twitter to be used. Through this use of Twitter during our services we found that rather than being distracted, people actually followed the conversation more because they were engaged in activity. They didn't have to go to their work or their friends' houses and invite them to a weekend Church service since this was a natural progression through sending out tweets and @replies and discussing what was happening during and after the service. People could also tweet relevant things they heard during the service and go home and reread those tweets and reflect on them afterwards.

There were several times that we had people thousands of miles away asking me more in-depth questions about things that had happened at one of our gatherings that they read about on Twitter. While we may have been together on Sunday as less than twenty people, we were connecting and engaging with dozens more outside of our city. Conversations were developing and relationships were being built with people we may never see in person. We even tied our initial pre-launch services in June 2008 (intended to share our vision with our parent Church's congregation to build initial support) with an international event known as One Prayer (oneprayer.com), which was hosted by LifeChurch.tv in Oklahoma (yes, their name really is a URL!). Revolution Church Sacramento was one of the first fifty churches to sign up for the event, which was initiated to bring churches together around the world to pray together for thirty days. It also allowed individual churches to produce and submit sermon videos that would then be available for download and shared in the churches participating in One Prayer during that month. In a matter of a few weeks, the event grew from our initial fifty churches to well over 1,800 by the time June came around. Many of us involved in the project blogged and tweeted about what was going on. I was overwhelmed at the support and encouragement we received from a global fellowship of churches and individuals during the One Prayer event. There are still people to this day that continue to be friends as a result of connections we made through Twitter back in June 2008.

One of the exciting things we got to do as we worked to utilize social media for building community and bridging the gap between those inside and outside of faith was an opportunity that arose to share our experiences with a group of business executives through a great project known as the Cool Twitter Conferences (recently renamed to Cool Social Conferences), hosted by Cool Blue Company, LLC. It was at this conference that I was able to share our strategy for using social media—particularly Twitter as an engagement and community-building tool—and help those in attendance to think outside of the box with how they thought of social media. Additionally, it brought to the attention of the business and technology sector that they weren't the only ones using social media effectively, and that we in the Church were also reaching our communities with tools such as Twitter, Facebook and YouTube. Even churches in relatively unknown places, such as Granger, Indiana (population 28,284), are making their mark nationally through incorporating social media as a communication tool. It is here that the Granger Community Church employs a full-time Communications Director named Kem Meyer, and their Web site (gccwired.com) is very interactive. They prominently display their latest Tweets in the center of their homepage and have contributions displayed from twenty-four pastors that blog regularly. Granger Community Church has harnessed the power and spontaneity of social media to effectively engage people in community and reach others far beyond the four walls of their Church building. They also use streaming video for those that want to engage even more by participating in Sunday services from their computers anywhere in the world.

Social media has become a marketing and communications game changer! It's free, instantaneous, and its use is already very widespread. People are longing to be in community and to connect with others that they can learn from and engage in dialogue. It has been a remarkable experience to be able to utilize something thought of as commonplace in an uncommon way. It has broken down barriers within the traditional Church and our experience is now becoming something other churches are seeking to build upon as well. Soon, static Web sites and boring blogs will give way to interesting and dynamic content and engaging dialog through social media apps like Twitter and Facebook. People outside of the Church, as well as those within it, will have a voice and their need for community will be realized in ways that aren't limited to Sunday services.

Dave Ingland is a former atheist who left a career as the CEO of a printing corporation to become the lead pastor of a start-up church in Sacramento, which ceased earlier in 2010. Dave has since relocated to the Portland, Oregon, area with his wife Charlotte and is involved in sales and social media marketing for an automotive dealership group. He is the father to Samantha and Megan and stepfather to Matthew and Jaela. In his spare time, you'll find Dave utilizing Facebook and Twitter to stay connected with and to engage the world around him.

Dave Ingland
daveingland@gmail.com
@daveingland
http://facebook.com/daveingland
http://linkedin.com/in/daveingland
http://www.daveingland.com
+1-503-583-4542

Social Media and the Eco-Minded

by

Jennifer Kaplan

Social media is a powerful communication tool for the eco-minded. Green groups on Facebook and LinkedIn allow people to both network and to connect personally. Green blogs and eco-blogger networks provide forums for targeted content to be shared over the Internet. Green Twitter feeds keep time- and attention-pressured users in the loop. Online communities, such as those on Care2.com and Change.org, exist for every eco-topic imaginable, and media sharing sites like Flickr and YouTube are flooded with environmental content. As Maryanne Conlin, founder of The MCMilker Group states: "There are close ties between the green movement and social media. Or maybe it's just that those leaders in the green movement who are on social media have become the mouthpiece for the movement. Or perhaps most likely, leaders in the green movement have figured out how to harness social media to promote their cause."[1] The choice to be green (no matter what the motivation) is most often a personal one, and social media is about personal connections. It is no surprise that green-themed social media is thriving.

Understanding Green Consumers

In order to understand how to best use social media to tap into green audiences, it is essential to understand that not all green consumers are the same. According to research on the green marketplace, only about two-thirds of consumers are interested in buying green products and services for any reason. And when it comes to environmental issues, consumers have different values, different motivations, and different levels of commitment. Some consumers that buy green are motivated by their desire to reward companies that align with their social goals, while some are primarily concerned about personal health and wellness, and yet others are quite practical and looking for convenience and efficiency.[2]

---

[1] Maryanne Conlin, "LOHAS Green Consumers Biggest Users of Social Media- So What?" http://themcmilkergroup.com, April 21, 2009. Posted online at http://bob.vg/mcmilker.
[2] BBMG, "Conscious Consumer Report: Redefining Value in a New Economy," (2009) and "LOHAS Consumers Most Likely to Use Online Social Networks," April 17, 2009. Posted online at http://bob.vg/lohas.

As a result, some marketing messages, and some green practices, tend to be more powerful motivators than others. In a 2006 article in *Environment Magazine*, "Green Marketing Myopia," researchers concluded that consumers value green for health, safety, convenience, efficiency, cost savings, performance, and (at times) status.[3] Regardless of who your customer is, the *nature of the value* you provide to your customers should be at the forefront of your social media messaging. For example, if you operate a home cleaning business that uses safe, organic cleaning solutions, communicating the safety of your service will be a key element of social media activities. Social media is the perfect means to promote the market position of: *We are committed to the health and safety of our employees and customers. We use only safe, organic products during the cleaning process.*

If you're like most business owners, you want to provide value to your customers in a way that gives you an edge over the competition. By being green, you can use your commitment to the environment as a competitive advantage and attract customers who value your environmental offerings. Social media works for this because it leverages the reach of the Internet with the cornerstones of environmental activism: content sharing and direct engagement. By sharing green information with your networks, you are able to converse about the ways in which your green products and services create value for them, or how they don't. Fundamentally, that means being able to seize opportunities to provide offerings that deliver more value to your customers than your competitors deliver.

That said, given the mixed profile of green consumers, you'll want to think carefully about what motivates consumers in your market, and position your social media messaging accordingly. Know which attributes and benefits resonate with your customers and provide thought leadership in that area. If your customers care about health and safety, make sure your social media messaging focuses on health and safety. If efficiency sets your products apart, the focus of your social media efforts can be strategies for increasing efficiencies and reducing waste.

Social Media Tactics

Once you've identified your target audience and determined what motivates them, social media is an excellent tool to craft your messages.

Start to blog. A blog (short for web log) is a diary on the web. As a communication tool, blogging can help you network, make sales, and activate your stakeholders and become a thought leader at a fraction of the cost of traditional media. There are two basic ways to blog about your business. One is to start your own blog and build a reputation as a green industry expert. A good example of this is the blog "Inside Sustainable Packaging"

---

[3]J. Ottman, E. Stafford, and C. Hartman, "Green Marketing Myopia," *Environment*, 48, 5 (2005): 22–36.

(http://blog.salazarpackaging.com), written by Dennis Salazar of Salazar Packaging. Known as a reputable and unbiased source of information, Salazar's blog is effective because it is more than a repository for press releases. It contains valuable information about industry trends in sustainability as well as product information.

The other way to blog is to become a contributor to an existing blog. This can give you a platform from which to communicate your expertise and often requires less time than writing your own blog. Find a blog that reaches your market and ask if they are looking for contributors. Many blogs actively seek writers. Either option provides an excellent way to communicate your green position in a public forum.

The good news about blogging is that you can reach a wide and diverse audience. The downside: it takes time and a genuine interest in engaging the community. It is essential to become an active member of your green online community. In other words, don't use your blog exclusively to promote yourself. Spend time reading posts, comment when you have something to offer, and promote your fellow bloggers. Also, if you want your blog posts to be read, make them personal and insightful. Everyone loves the insider scoop.

Finally, submit your blog posts to popular social bookmarking sites like Stumble.com, Digg.com, Reddit.com, and Tipd.com, as well as to green-themed sites like Care2.com.

Open a Twitter account. Twitter.com, a cross between instant messaging and blogging, is a free Web site where users post text containing up to 140 characters. People receive updates, or "tweets," from people whom they have chosen to follow. You can tweet to announce promotions, specials, coupons, and events; make new blog posts; provide customer service; resend (a.k.a. retweet) links to green content; and convey any other information that can be stated in a few words. There is an active green community on Twitter and a plethora of green Twitter streams. Add hashtags such as #green and #eco to tweets to allow other "Tweeple" to find you.

Post events. If you sponsor and hold events, post them on social event calendars as a way to attract new attendees. Most social networking sites (including Facebook, LinkedIn, etc.) have event listing applications. Greenbiz.com and SustainableIndustries.com offer free, green-targeted event calendars as well.

Jennifer Kaplan has almost two decades of corporate marketing experience with companies including Discovery Communications, Condé Nast Publications, and Lifetime Television. She is the founder of Greenhance LLC, author of Greening Your Small Business (Penguin USA), co-editor of Ecopreneurist.com, and a senior advisor to the Center for Small Business and the Environment (CSBE). She lives and works in Oakland, California.

Big Social Media On Campus

by

Alex Priest

In case you haven't noticed, social media has become a big deal. A really big deal. And on the college campus, it's about as big as it gets.

Social media is so big, that according to the Pew Internet and American Life Project, between April 2009 and May 2010, social networking use among internet users, ages 18 to 29, grew to a whopping 86 percent. That's just one number, but it solidifies a widely held view—social media is changing the way we communicate, especially young people, and it's not going anywhere anytime soon.

But social media on the college campus is even more than just tweeting what you had for breakfast and posting those inappropriate photos from last night's party. It's becoming a way of life and creating a new generation of communicators, whether they like it or not. This, of course, involves a host of complex issues, some good and some bad. It's these issues that I'll explore here.

Are We Addicted?

In February 2004, Facebook was born on the Harvard University campus, the pet project of then undergraduate student Mark Zuckerberg. Today, Facebook practically *is* the campus, with over 500 million users and virtually every college student in America registered on the site. This deep level of penetration by the social network led adults everywhere to question its utility and the wisdom of heavy usage. Today, some question whether students are perhaps *too* dependent on social media for their social lives.

On September 23, 2010, Facebook went through a few hours of technical difficulties. Users were faced with a blank error page, their entire digital social world ripped from their fingertips and lost in the oblivion of the Internet.

It was like ripping a cigarette out of a chain smoker's mouth. Like depriving a coffee aficionado of their morning joe for a year. It indicated to no one's surprise that we as college students and as a society have become pretty well addicted to social media. It's not necessarily a bad thing, but moments like that do show how important these networks have become. There were plenty of jokes while the site was out of commission. Some suggested Zuckerberg was holding Facebook hostage in exchange for promises by users to *not* watch the upcoming Facebook movie, *The Social Network*. There were funny little Farmville quips. And naturally, plenty of people expressed their horror at having to actually be outside, talking to people in real life.

Only the week before the outage, the Harrisburg University of Science and Technology in Harrisburg, Pennsylvania, decided to put their students' social media use to the test, along with faculty, staff, and everyone else at the university. To see just how dependent they all were on these social networks, they decided to just shut them down. They completely blocked access to Facebook and Twitter for one full week on the campus grounds, forcing university Internet users to use more traditional means of communication to facilitate their social interactions, or simply to meet in real life.

It was an interesting experiment, but also one that I think communicated the wrong idea about social media, namely, that using it is bad. It's like deciding one day that telephones are weakening our social skills, and deciding to throw them out. It's as if they looked at this new technology and picked out the select few negative consequences, and then decided to extrapolate those negatives without regard for the myriad of benefits it provides.

If they wanted to see how much we relied on social media, why not do just the opposite of the social media ban? Why not encourage students and faculty to forego using telephones, e-mail, and paper for a week, instead using Facebook and Twitter as the main mode of communication? Perhaps this would show faculty and students the limitations and strengths of social media. Then they could use social media only for the essential benefits they provide, and realize the strengths of the technologies we tend to throw to the wayside in favor of Facebook.

#COMM346

Social media on the college campus can be so much more than just planning events, sharing photos, and "liking" a few witty status updates. In fact, there's a lot of room to innovate, especially *inside* the classroom. In fact, perhaps if there were a little more social media in our education, professors would find it easier to engage with their students and prepare them for the real world beyond the campus borders.

These social media additions don't have to be complex. Let's look at hashtags for example. Simply creating a hashtag for each class like #comm346 or #mktg301 can create a whole new, complementary conversation behind the scenes of the verbal communication taking place during class hours. Having a back channel for communication will enable more students to participate without distracting from a lecture or guest speaker. It allows quiet students to speak up in a less intimidating environment, also allowing the professor to address their questions and gradually pull them into the "real life" conversation. It allows the conversation to twist and turn beyond the boundaries of the syllabus, extending into valuable conversations both before and after class about related topics. Finally, it lets professors see exactly which students are paying attention and actively dedicated to learning compared to those spending their time on social media talking about last night's party.

Obviously this idea isn't one many teachers will embrace, especially those that may be more traditionally minded. But it's also not a hard one to implement, and one that students might embrace strongly if offered the opportunity.

It's time that we stopped looking at social media in the classroom as a distraction and realized that there's no way to keep it out. With smartphones and mobile apps, social media is everywhere, whether the professor likes it or not. The trick is finding a way to make these so-called "distractions" resources for learning that students want to use. It's silly that students are being forced to adapt to old ways of teaching, when it would be far more efficient and effective for teachers to simply adapt to the new ways that students are learning.

The Real World

Perhaps one of the most powerful aspects of social media for college students is that it can provide a valuable connection to the "real world" that many avoid until graduation. At that point, many students are stuck trying to catch up, and may find themselves unemployed until they build the network necessary to fine the job they desire. Social media is every student's chance to get ahead on building a network off their campus so they're well prepared upon graduation.

Students should think of Twitter as the icebreaker. With 140 characters, you can be sitting in the office of your dream company. You can be connected directly to the CEO of a major corporation, or an entrepreneur you admire. And these simple 140-character introductions can lead to significant professional relationships and real-life interactions. By being active on the network and sharing content of value, important professionals on the network are likely to respond and engage with you regardless of age, profession, or education level. And to the students' benefit, young people who excel and differentiate themselves on social media stand out more than older professionals.

That said, students shouldn't expect to just tweet their way to the job of their dreams. It takes persistence, commitment, and an outgoing personality in real life just as much as it does online. Seeking out conferences, speakers, networking events, and even happy hours that allow students to connect with these professionals in the real world is the key to differentiating themselves and making it to the top of the resume pile when opportunities become available. Twitter can open the door, but it's up to old-school networking techniques to help students walk through it.

Privacy is Dead

It's certainly a controversial statement: "Privacy is dead." But hardly a day goes by without a new story of an employee losing their job, a student losing a new opportunity, or someone losing a friend due to an embarrassing or inappropriate photo or status update on Facebook. Privacy, as we've known it for years, has ceased to exist, and this is a lesson students should learn now.

Reputation management is no longer something left only to corporations and public officials. It's a responsibility that extends to everyone active on social networks, and all the more important if they hope to forge a strong career in our networking-based professional society. The careless posting of an unfortunate photo, or failure to "untag" oneself from such a photo, can lead to some disastrous consequences. While Facebook, perhaps unfairly, receives a large portion of the blame for privacy failings, perhaps more of this actually lays on the end user.

College students, naturally, are particularly susceptible to these mistakes, but it's precisely this generation that must avoid them. Every single aspect of one's online life is or likely will be visible by the public, which makes proper presentation of that online persona essential, even in college. If there's one single drawback to social media in college, it's this. And this, of course, only underscores the importance of teaching these lessons quickly and in the classroom—regardless of the student's field of study.

A Bright Future for Students of Social Media

Social media has earned a permanent role on college campuses everywhere. Its role there is different. It serves not only as a news function, but also as an incredibly important social tool. It facilitates friendships, organization, and even intimate relationships. It has the power to create immense popularity and destroy reputations. It can create opportunity...and it can waste it.

Alex Priest is a student at American University in Washington, DC, studying marketing, public communications, and statistics. He has wide-ranging interests, but a particular passion for social media, mobile technology, politics, and marketing. With experience on Capitol Hill and with nonprofits, PR, marketing, and activism, he's seen social media and mobile technology used in a variety of contexts and is constantly looking forward to the future.

Alex Priest
alex.priest@mac.com
@alexpriest
http://facebook.com/alexpriest
http://linkedin.com/in/alexpriest
http://alexpriest.com
+1-270-287-1307

The Media

Social Success In Media & Music - A CBC Radio 3 Case Study

by

Steve Pratt

Media's History of Control

The media has, for most of its existence, exerted a great deal of control over its content and its audience. There are a finite number of broadcasting licenses available, a finite number of frequencies and channels available, and a finite number of competitors that can afford to participate in any given market. And being one of the "chosen few" with the financial and regulatory means to publish or broadcast audio, video, and print content has always meant the ability to choose the best programming for a desired target audience. The media chooses which shows or stories to produce, what day of the week or time to schedule a television show, which songs get played on a radio station, and which stories end up on the front page of the newspaper.

However, with the rapid growth of the internet, file sharing, and especially social media, all of this behavior has been turned on its head. The audience doesn't need to tune in for "appointment" viewing or listening anymore—if they miss the original broadcast, they can record it on their DVR, stream it online, or download the episode and watch it on their own schedule. They don't need to watch advertising anymore because they can skip it or edit it out of their programming. They don't need to wait until the morning edition of the paper or the 6 p.m. newscast to find out what's happening in their community or around the world—the web has created an always-on 24/7 news cycle. Most importantly, the media can't control or restrict the voices of its audiences any longer either. Through the internet and social media, the audience has gained an enormous amount of influence and control over their own content consumption habits.

The question for media of all kinds now becomes: "How do we stay relevant in this new world where we can't call all the shots anymore?" And, as is probably evident to most consumers, most of the media haven't figured it out yet. The impulse to maintain control and restrict user behavior is strong, and yet it almost always fails in a digital environment because audiences will always find ways of getting what they want, when they want it, where they want it, and in the format they want it.

Canada's Public Broadcaster and Its Innovation Lab

The Canadian Broadcasting Corporation (CBC) is Canada's public broadcaster. Funded by a mix of government appropriation and commercial advertising, the English language side of the CBC has a national television network, two national radio networks, and an extensive digital presence.

The CBC ALSO has something called Radio 3. It's a bit of an oddity, though. CBC Radio 3 isn't on AM or FM radio. And it's not really 'radio' in the traditional sense of the word either. I like to describe CBC Radio 3 as a digital music service that includes satellite radio (Sirius 86), web radio, audio and video podcasts, blogs, and the world's largest online collection of independent Canadian music. One of the most unique aspects of the service is that the entire radio station and all the podcasts are programmed with music that has first been uploaded to the Web site by musicians. The closest analogy would be if MySpace used their musician pages to create radio programming. It's been set up in Vancouver, British Columbia, as an innovation lab—a place to experiment and explore the digital realm, attempt to reach new audiences in new ways, and to raise awareness of new and emerging Canadian music.

Social Experimentation

Without the traditional AM or FM broadcasting license, CBC Radio 3 does NOT have a built-in audience. We also don't have a communications budget. And yet we need to continually show audience growth and increased listening to the songs and artists we play. The solution?

Social media.

Not only have we made extensive use of existing tools like Facebook, Twitter, Flickr, and YouTube, but we have designed our entire service around the core values of sharing, audience empowerment, and community. And so far, it's worked better than we could have imagined.

Social Media Questions

Without traditional ratings to measure success, CBC Radio 3 has had to ask and answer some difficult questions around value and growth.

- Why use social media?

- How do you define success?

- What does a social strategy look like?

- How do you measure social media success?

Why Social Media?

There are many valuable reasons for any media outlet to begin extensive use of social media. The top reasons that CBC Radio 3 transformed our service to focus on social music included:

- Develop a passionate community of active online music lovers.

- Create a deeper relationship between hosts and audiences.

- Get clear and honest feedback about what is or isn't working with our programming and our music service.

- Empower our audience to share our content and programming. We believe that if given the right tools and freedom to share, passionate music fans will reach more new people than our own team at CBC Radio 3 can on our own.

- Update audiences about valuable news and information related to Canadian music in a time, place, and format of THEIR choosing. We wanted to be where audiences already were and have our content be unbelievably easy to access and discover.

Defining Success

The web is filled with questions about how to measure social media success. Is it number of followers on Twitter? Number of fans or "likes" on Facebook? Number of retweets? Number of conversations? Balance between positive and negative tone in conversations? The amount of traffic coming to your site? Goal conversions (sales, clicks, views, etc.) from social networks?

Through trial and error, CBC Radio 3 felt that there are no "standard" measures of success that would apply to every person and business on the web. The best way to determine key metrics is to answer a vitally important question: "What are your goals in the digital space?" Also:

- Why does your business exist?

- Why do you have a Web site?

- What are the measurable goals you have for your Web site?

Once you know the answers to these questions, you have one more whopper: "How can social media help you achieve these goals?" Now you should have a much easier time figuring out what to measure and why in the social space.

For CBC Radio 3, our service exists to bring new and younger audiences into the CBC, to raise awareness of new Canadian music, and to experiment with new forms of content creation and distribution. One of the more disturbing statistics with regard to Canadian music is that over 30,000 songs get released by Canadians every year, and yet only 250 of those ever get any airplay on the radio. Our goal is to help increase the volume of Canadian songs played, heard, and appreciated by music fans. So when it comes to determining metrics, the more people who listen to emerging Canadian music, subscribe to our programming, tune into our programming, participate in online conversations about Canadian music, or follow us on a social network, the bigger impact we're having. As a result, we track:

- number of followers on Twitter

- number of fans or "likes" on Facebook

- number of comments and conversations

- referral traffic from social networks to our service

- average time per visit (measure of engagement)

- unique visitors and visits to our site

- frequency of return visits

- podcast downloads

- number of new artists signing up to the site

- number of new songs uploaded to the site

- number of new "fan" accounts created

- number of user playlists created

- number of on-demand songs streamed (active choice in selecting music rather than passively listening to radio)

We also track trends—are we growing in all our key metrics, and if not, why not and what can we do about it?

Next Steps: Tactics For Achieving Social Media Success

Inside the CBC Radio 3, we had a number of long discussions about how to change the nature of our service from being seen primarily as a radio station to becoming a "social music site" or a "music discovery service." Here are the ones we wrestled with the most:

- How would you introduce people to new music and new artists on Facebook? Twitter? Flickr? YouTube? On a blog?

- How can we enlist our audience to help spread the word about Canadian music?

- How can we rethink "radio" in a social context?

A New "Social Music" Focused Strategy

After really stripping our service to the core and examining the reasons why we exist, what our goals are for the future, and what we needed to do in order to grow audiences and relevance, we crafted a new "social" strategy for CBC Radio 3.

One of the key elements, which is highly unusual for a radio station (or any other form of traditional media), was to de-emphasize our radio programming! Not that our radio content doesn't continue to be an enormous part of the value of CBC Radio 3, but defining ourselves purely as a one-way creator and deliverer of content is a very old school way of thinking. We wanted to position ourselves not as the self-appointed leader of a community, but instead as a valuable member of the Canadian music community. We decided that we could not be arrogant and assume that just because we're a broadcaster, we would automatically have audiences delivered to us—instead, we challenged ourselves to "earn" every audience member by focusing relentlessly on creating value. Valuable content, valuable tools, and valuable interaction.

Another essential change to the direction of the service was to focus on audience empowerment. We made a very conscious effort to give up control over some areas of the service in the hopes that participation would increase loyalty, ownership, and passion for CBC Radio 3.

Closely tied to user empowerment is personalization and customization. It is a defining trait in traditional media to program content from one to many, with the "one" assuming that it knows exactly what the best content is for everyone.

In reality, though, everyone is different. Some people want to listen to the radio, some people want to watch TV, some people want to explore a sea of unfiltered music, and some people want to get recommendations from their own trusted network of music influencers. And the only way to accommodate the diversity of ways that people want to discover and enjoy music is to provide tools and functionality that let EACH PERSON choose the ways that work best for them.

The next logical step is that if we allow our audience to customize their own music programming, then the ones who are passionate and talented will become tastemakers in their own right. The ultimate hope is that our service can create an army of tastemakers and influencers, who will share their passion widely with their own networks and reach many more people and feature many more songs and artists than CBC Radio 3 can possibly do on our own with limited staff and a 24-hour a day radio station.

So that's what we set out to do...

Biggest Traditional Media Mistake

If there is one huge mistake that we saw traditional media making over and over again, it was this: they STILL subscribed to the theory of walled gardens. In other words, the majority of digital strategies for media involve fighting the tools that people want to use in the hopes that they can bully audiences into using the broadcaster's own sites to consume content. There are passionate arguments made against the use of YouTube, Facebook, Flickr, and Twitter that generally follow the same logic: "We can't monetize content effectively outside our own site, so let's force everyone to come to us and send cease and desist letters to anyone who posts our content elsewhere."

Bad idea.

At the time of this writing, there are over 500 million people on Facebook, and YouTube is the second most popular search engine on the planet. There are a lot more people on social networks than there are on any digital property owned by traditional media. And every single time an audience member interacts with you or your programming on a social network, their ENTIRE NETWORK gets an update about it. Yet when the strategy is to force them to leave where they already are—a major inconvenience that stops many people from visiting—when people interact with your content, NONE of their social network is notified about it.

Done properly, seeding content freely and widely will encourage users to view and share content quickly and easily, spreading it farther and wider than the reach of your own Web site. And when new people sample your content, they are far more likely to seek out more of it and visit your company's site.

The formula is simple: fish where the fish are and create real value by posting great content and participating in conversations. If you create real value in a social network, the speed and scope of audience growth is significant. Conversely, if you try to twist people's arms into leaving the social network where they already are in order to come to your site, many won't do it and many will resent you for not making it easy to get content they want.

And when content isn't easy enough to access, that leads users to take matters into their own hands and get it the way they want it. And that is how piracy is driven.

It is counterintuitive, but it is very true—in order to grow audiences and reduce piracy, you need to set your content free and post it where people are already choosing to consume their content. And that usually means somewhere other than your own site. Even more counterintuitive for traditional media, make it easy to share your content with whoever they want. Sorry!

If you set up your strategy so that people have to come to your site, sign up or create a login, and THEN get the content, almost no one will do it. So don't do it!

Making Radio Social

One of the biggest changes CBC Radio 3 made was to rethink our traditional radio programming to make it more effective in a social media space. We wanted to take the elements of radio that represented "old-style" media thinking (one-to-many broadcast, control of message, keeping audiences at a distance, keeping the experience passive, relishing the role of tastemaker, etc.) and come up with new ideas of how to make "Radio 2.0" celebrate the values of the social web.

The biggest change was thinking about how to engage audiences while they listened to radio programming. We wanted to turn listening to radio into an interactive experience. So in the majority of all of our daily radio programming, hosts will discuss a question or topic that becomes the theme for that day's show. There's an accompanying blog post, Facebook updates, and Twitter updates, all designed to seed or start a conversation somehow related to new and emerging Canadian music. On-air, the host will then spend a good chunk of the non-music portion of the show showcasing and unifying the conversations that are taking place on our blog, Facebook, and Twitter. If you're listening to the on-air programming, you get a very strong sense that there is a lot of action going on in the social space, that there is an engaged audience participating in conversations in multiple places while they are all listening to the radio show in real time. In the course of a three-hour show, we often get 150–200 comments on our blog, with some shows with great topics reaching as high as 450–500 comments in the same time span. One of our hosts has a weekly program that essentially functions as an open thread in a discussion forum—he simply asks the audience what they want to talk about and lets the radio programming follow their interests and suggestions.

As we've progressed and the hosts have become better and better at not just thinking of the programming as a radio show, but rather a multi-platform conversation, the comment totals have grown significantly, and the passion and engagement of the audience has increased noticeably.

Another interesting initiative designed to give more control to the audience is CBC Radio 3's "Listener Co-Host Initiative." Every week, someone in our audience is invited into the studio to co-host a live radio show with one of our hosts, Craig Norris. They talk about who they are, they help to choose some of the music, and they get to host a real radio show being broadcast around the world.

Finally, from a web design perspective, perhaps the biggest way that we've given control to audiences and music fans is by creating a rich, on-demand personalized music experience, and we are not just relying on a real time passive stream of programming created by CBC Radio 3.

Every single track we play on the radio has a link to a page featuring the artist and links to listen to all their songs on-demand. Any song on the Web site—currently over 100,000 songs—can be played on-demand, shared through e-mail, Facebook, or Twitter, and most importantly, added to a personal CBC Radio 3 playlist. Every music fan on the site gets their own personal CBC Radio 3 page—they can upload a photo, write a little bio, post contact information, list their favorite artists, and create as many on-demand, shareable playlists as they want.

As a broadcaster, we know that our job is to create a popular mix of songs that will appeal to a broad number of people (the "broad" in "broadcaster!"). However, we also know that we will never nail every person's perfect song mix with our choices because everyone is different. The only way for people to get their own perfect music mix is to give them the tools to do it themselves. And if that means that a group of people choose to make their own experience and forgo listening to our traditional radio programming, then GREAT. They are still having an engaging experience with CBC Radio 3. For us, success is not just about getting as many people listening to the radio as possible—it's about getting as many people as possible having a great experience with our music service (not our radio station) and listening to as much new Canadian music as possible.

When people make their own playlists, there are many benefits. First, when a song they don't like comes on the radio, they don't have to leave your service. They can go into on-demand mode and enjoy the music they want, when they want it. Second, they can share their music and introduce their social networks to music that we might not be showcasing on-air. Receiving recommendations about new music from friends is one of the most powerful and trusted ways to get people to click and listen to a song—much more effective than traditional advertising or a message from a broadcaster.

All of this leads to a new role for audiences and music fans—they become tastemakers themselves. If good chunks of our audience create and share playlists of new Canadian music, they will help us achieve our goals of raising awareness of these artists more effectively than we can ourselves. More music will get shared, more artists will get shared, and there will be more personal ownership and passion in sharing that music than anything CBC Radio 3 could do on our own.

Another feature on the Web site is designed to showcase not just audience participation, but audience curation. We have an area on the Web site that shows what users are listening to RIGHT NOW on the Web site—it updates every ten seconds, shows you who is listening (so you can check out their personal page) and gives you artist and song information and a link to play the song. Actual user behavior has turned into a great source of music recommendations for other music fans.

If we can empower our audience to the point where they move from being passive consumers of traditional broadcasting towards becoming active tastemakers, our audience will own a huge part of our mandate as a public broadcaster. They will be helping us achieve the goals of sharing culture, building communities, and supporting Canadian artists. And they will have true ownership in their own public broadcaster—they will be making a difference and they'll know it. And that is where true value and true relevance is achieved in a digital space.

If I can sum it up neatly, my message is this: think more like a public broadcaster. Public broadcasters are owned by the public. The public has a sense of ownership in them, literally. So instead of framing your media programming as "we are the experts and they are the consumers," try instead to think of how your company would work if it were truly owned by its customers, if your company truly became partners with your audience by inviting them in, asking them what they think, and giving them the keys to the factory. Scary for sure. However, the results will amaze you.

One last note around tools and new social media services: don't wait until there is widely accepted belief about best practices or you will be left behind. Social media is ALWAYS changing and you need to get in and get your hands dirty. The only way to learn is by doing. Making mistakes and learning what works for you and your community is much more valuable than sitting on the sidelines watching. If a new service comes along, try it. If your audience asks you to put in a new feature and you can do it, try it. You have to assume that part of your job is learning and experimenting in the digital space—it is constantly shifting and evolving. So get out there, try a lot of ideas, engage your audience, and try to make them real partners and owners in your service. You'll be ahead of 99% of your competition if you can do it.

Steve Pratt is the Director of Digital Music and CBC Radio 3, a multi-platform unit of Canada's public broadcaster that focuses on emerging Canadian music. Radio 3 creates a variety of audio and video podcasts, a Webby-nominated online radio station, a Web site filled with on-demand content, and Sirius satellite channel 86, all of which are powered by user-generated content uploaded by independent Canadian musicians. CBCRadio3.com provides musicians with the tools they need to promote themselves and gives users the tools they need to discover and share the best in new Canadian music around the world. The result has been a public broadcasting success story built on a unique partnership between CBC Radio 3, artists, and audiences. Prior to CBC, Steve has worked with MuchMusic, CityTV, CTV, YTV, and AOL Canada.

Steve Pratt
@steveprattca
http://cbcradio3.com
http://stevepratt.com

Breaking Tweets

by

Craig Kanalley

On September 11th, 2001, the world changed forever. The political, economic, social, and cultural ramifications of that event both in the United States and internationally were substantial. The event was also deeply personal for many, including myself.

It was on that day that I determined I wanted to be a journalist. I watched in awe as reporters covered the story, providing a critical public service at a time of crisis, and how they handled it so well. In the days and weeks ahead, I was glued to the media coverage as journalists pieced together what had happened, why and who was behind it, and the many stories behind recovery efforts and lives lost.

I had always been interested in writing, and at that time, I realized I wanted to go into journalism and pursue public service myself. Not necessarily in front of the camera, as I'm not one for the limelight, but behind the scenes, preferably in print journalism.

In college, I studied print journalism. But an interesting thing happened during that time. I worked at a metro newspaper, the Democrat and Chronicle in Rochester, New York, but at that paper, and around the country, a trend toward online was rapidly developing. And print was seeing mass layoffs.

By the time I was a senior, in 2007, I was Online Editor of the campus newspaper, a position that felt quite natural to me, as I was passionate about computers and technology growing up (my grandfather used to work at IBM and is a mathematics and computer whiz, so it was a bit in my blood). Concerned about job prospects, I realized I wanted to pursue online journalism as a career and do the unthinkable: go to graduate school for journalism.

Many told me that journalism wasn't a field for a Masters degree unless you wanted to teach (I actually was interested in teaching, but I had other motives too). I was told countless times that experience is far more important. But with the cutbacks industry-wide, I knew getting experience was going to be very difficult. I was prepared to make a big move, go to a big city for a master's degree, and do all the networking I could. If nothing else, it would buy me more time, and somewhere along the way, I was sure to find some opportunities for experience.

So, after an intense nationwide search, I decided on Chicago, a city I knew little about, but one that intrigued me as I read about it on Wikipedia. The "Windy City." With a lakefront. And lots of sports teams. Home of a 2008 presidential candidate named Barack Obama. A city preparing an Olympic bid for the 2016 Games. Also the home of Oprah.

There was a lot going on in Chicago when I made the decision, and I was set to begin in September 2008. Little did I know the ride I had ahead of me. It was the ride of a lifetime. And we actually need to back up a little, as the ride really started in August 2008.

On August 24, 2008, I signed up for Twitter. Skeptical at the time, I had heard rumblings about the site for several months at that point, but I didn't quite understand it. I thought, why would anyone care what I was doing?

But CNN anchor Rick Sanchez put me over the edge. I was watching TV one night, and he was talking about Twitter, encouraging people to "tweet" him about the presidential election. I wanted my voice heard, so I did just that. My first tweet was about eating chicken fingers and watching CNN. My second was an @reply to him with my thoughts on his question. He was the first person I followed.

You could tell from the start I was interested in using Twitter for my pursuit of online journalism as a career. Even though I didn't quite get it, I knew it could potentially help me network with others in the business. I had no idea what an integral part of my life Twitter would become and the doors it would open for me.

With the start of graduate school in Chicago on my mind, I followed WindyCitizen.com, an online Web site, interested in a possible internship there. I also followed its founder Brad Flora (@bradflora) and editor Kayla Webley (@kaylawebley). (I should say I did have the opportunity to work with them and blogged for Windy Citizen for several months, the first instance where Twitter helped me do networking and get my foot in the industry door.)

I also followed Colonel Tribune (@coloneltribune), the Chicago Tribune account, in my first week on Twitter. (Little did I know at the time, I would one day tweet on that account when I interned with the Trib in the Summer of 2009.) I found some other journalism tweeters fairly quickly that had pretty good followings: @newmediajim and @jayrosen_nyu. I also followed the Online News Association account @ONA.

Interestingly, of the first ten accounts I followed, only one was someone I knew in real life: Ben Rawdon (@brawdon77), also a journalism student, who I went to undergrad school with at St. John Fisher.

That's how I started using Twitter. Nothing flashy or exciting. But I had a clear goal in mind from the start: networking. Little did I know at the time the true networking potential of Twitter and how I was going to use it to create a global network.

On November 4, 2008, I was at Grant Park for the Barack Obama rally. Win or lose the presidential contest, Obama was going to come onto the stage there and deliver an address. It was an electrifying environment and I was most fortunate to attend. I had seen someone "tweet" about the opportunity to get a ticket to it. Right place, right time, I was one of only several thousand to get a ticket before they quickly sold out.

Amidst that crowd, and throughout the day, I noticed how many people were tweeting their experiences. I realized how Twitter could serve as a place for breaking news, personal feelings, and eyewitness accounts. While I didn't tweet myself from the event, I tweeted after and before it. And I was in awe looking through others' tweets and how they captured the event.

It was then that I first thought of the idea of a single place that collects these thoughts and experiences from Twitter. But the idea wasn't crystalized. My creative juices picked up steam when I found out I was one of four DePaul University students selected to go to Washington, DC, to cover Barack Obama's Inauguration for the student newspaper. I came up with the idea of a Twitter account for our trip, modeled after Colonel Tribune, called "@dannythedemon," a character who would post pictures from the scene and chronicle our experiences. Each of the four of us would post to @dannythedemon while we were there.

Just days before we left for DC, I was DMing with the Chicago Sun-Times about a possible opportunity to freelance for them. Before I knew it, I had a phone call set up with them and they invited me and my three classmates to run a blog on the Sun-Times site. Once again, Twitter provided an amazing networking opportunity.

So in DC, we ran @dannythedemon. Gaining followers on that account and interest as far away as Australia, I started to see the real impact of Twitter. Being there, seeing all the tweets from others, and documenting the event, I thought again about my idea back in November of a single place to find the most interesting tweets.

On January 31, 2009, just eleven days after attending the inauguration in DC, I started such a place on the Web: a very simple personal blog called Breaking Tweets, which I would update with three or four events each day around the world. It would just be a little hobby, something for fun. Personal and nothing more. I grabbed the Twitter name @breakingtweets to accompany the blog and push out updates.

The first event I posted on was the Australian Open. I went to the "scene," narrowing down tweets by geographic location (Australia in this case) for reactions to this event while it was "breaking news." I looked for compelling tweets, people who might actually be there, tweets with emotion, and those with interesting insights. And I treated these tweets as quotes, adding text before them for news context. A week after starting the site, I realized it was going to be something much, much more. People kept following the Twitter account and stats gradually raised on the blog. I thought, hmm...cool...we'll see where this goes.

The first time it *really* hit me that this could be something really big was on February 7, 2009, when I posted a story about a Madagascar protest that had gone violent. Just a few hours after I posted that story, the site was getting a ton of traffic from both Madagascar and a part of France known for Madagascar connections. I thought it was incredible that I was "covering" this tragedy all the way from Chicago, and that so many people were interested in visiting the site.

From there, I was not prepared for how quickly the account and the site continued to grow. In the days ahead, I was getting hits all over the world. Before you knew it, it had hits from fifty countries and the Twitter account had hundreds of followers. It was then I realized I could no longer go about this solo. It had huge potential. I began getting some friends from school to help out in updating the site, as the audience continued to grow. The Twitter account began being followed by editors/producers at CNN, as well as other editors, publishers, and journalists around the country including at the BBC, Associated Press, Fox News, the Los Angeles Times, and the New York Times. I soon saw in Google Analytics traffic from each of these newsrooms and countless others around the U.S. and the world.

I also started to make amazing contacts.

David MacDougall, a foreign correspondent in Baghdad, contacted me after seeing one of his "tweets" on a Breaking Tweets story about the Iraq election. He was so excited about it and asked if he could become a contributor to the site, and I said of course. He helped me through his international journalism experience and I was able to help him learn more about Twitter and social media.

It was MacDougall who helped bring Breaking Tweets to a new level. He began posting several stories a week. We started to e-mail each other frequently and chat on Gmail chat, and he gave me lots of advice and tips from his experiences.

Later, I connected with Guy Kawasaki, an entrepreneur, venture capitalist, and co-founder of Alltop.com, an online magazine rack. Via direct message on Twitter, I pitched "Breaking Tweets" to him as an idea for a new feed on Alltop. Not only did he get back to me about the idea, he gave us a full page and put us under "News." Then, he tweeted about us six or seven times to his 70,000+ followers (he was named by Forbes as the No. 1 most influential Twitterer). Within hours, we were the most popular Alltop page.

Hours after the successful Alltop debut, Kawasaki contacted me privately through Twitter and asked if I and some other Breaking Tweets editors would be interested in meeting him during a brief trip to Chicago. Of course I was ecstatic about the idea and agreed, and had breakfast with him with friends of mine for a whole hour. He gave all sorts of advice, and vowed to continue to support our project by getting the word out, tweeting about it often, and even giving us a free ad on his site. Kawasaki was huge in taking Breaking Tweets to the next level.

I also came across Kent Mensah via Twitter. Mensah is one of Africa's only online journalists, and he lives in Ghana. He contacted me after coming across Breaking Tweets, anxious to contribute. I named him Africa Editor and he began posting several times a week, adding a new dimension to the site with fascinating coverage via African tweets.

Besides these three folks, it was always awe-inspiring to be noticed by major media outlets, such as CNN, the Los Angeles Times, the New York Times, the BBC, and Reuters, let alone to receive private messages from their reporters and editors. That part of the ride blew me away. I've always been a small-town kind of guy, being from Buffalo, New York, and not particularly fond of the limelight. So at times it even got to be overwhelming. But these people were huge in helping the site grow, spreading the word, and keeping my confidence high despite difficulties to monetize the site. Riding the excitement of all these connections I was making, and the tremendous networking opportunities it brought me, within a few months I was posting on Breaking Tweets seven days a week and it quite literally became my life.

I invested every hour into it; it's nearly all I did and all I knew. I made very good contacts and built up a network of reliable sources around the world, and I found ways to search tweets effectively and quickly in situations of breaking news. I was able to break stories myself.

Most notably, on April 30, 2009, there was an attack on the Dutch royal family. I received a tip from Singapore about this at 4:30 in the morning (Chicago time) in the form of a direct message. The Twitter user seemed pretty adamant this was huge news, so I went to my computer and started digging. Not only did I verify what he was saying, but I got the first English-speaking report of the incident up on BreakingTweets.com via tweets and initial local reports. We beat CNN by two hours and the BBC by one hour, and it turned out to be a big story. It ended up being a huge hit on Google, and it spread fast on Twitter as well.

As much attention as that brought the site, it was in June 2009 when it reached its highest point. I knew the Iran election was going to be a significant story, and leading up to it, I posted some stories about it and photos of the rallies from Iranian twitterers. Then I live blogged on election night for six hours. As it became clear the election was going to be a huge controversy and Mahmoud Ahmadinejad was quickly declared the winner by state media, I made a commitment to stay on this story. And that's what I did, posting daily updates for the next two weeks.

As international media was being shutout of Tehran, Breaking Tweets was able to continue its coverage as I built a trusted network of sources in Iran via Twitter. I continued to go to these sources for my reports, as fake accounts and a mess of retweets confused mainstream media. Breaking Tweets became a place to go for reliable information while the media at large was confused. We had the first report of a death at a protest and the first report of communication networks going down. We were recognized for our relentless coverage by the Poynter Institute and saw traffic skyrocket as the BBC, Reuters, the New York Times, and others visited us daily per Google Analytics. At one point, I learned we were even blocked by the Irani Government itself, as our traffic from Iran stopped except from the Iranian Ministry of Foreign Affairs.

It was stories like the Iran election in which Breaking Tweets could thrive. There's a huge, very complicated world with political spin, and it personalized international news, giving it a human touch and raw emotion that can be understood universally. With its emphasis on social media, the site also encouraged discussion and brought people around the world together to talk about such stories. While it wasn't easy to do, aggregating the best of citizen journalist tweets, including pictures and video whenever possible, and verifying information as best possible, the site helped people learn more about the world around them. It was a public service, and that's why I went into journalism in the first place.

As the site was growing, I proposed to DePaul University, where I was attending graduate school, that we make it a class. I knew more content would help it grow, and if there was a group of students contributing frequently, it could help bring it up another notch. DePaul, somewhat to my surprise, agreed.

The class I taught became known as Digital Editing and it was a bit of a novelty: the first journalism class in America focused on Twitter. Students picked regions or topics to focus on as their "beat" and the site started to be updated more than ever before. Like the Iran coverage in June, this was another high point for Breaking Tweets, and this took place in the Fall of 2009.

At this stage though, I had just finished grad school in August, and I only had the class I was teaching and a paid internship at the Chicago Tribune, which also started in June in large part due to Twitter and Breaking Tweets. While Breaking Tweets was my "full-time job" since its inception, I was longing for a real full-time job, and I desperately wanted Breaking Tweets to be it.

But how? It wasn't making any money, despite repeated attempts and different tries of devising a business model. I'm just not a businessman. Frustrated, I met with several entrepreneurs and journalists in the Chicago area to get their input. One talk with Eric Olson, the founder of Tech Cocktail, stood out. He said talk to larger media organizations and try to forge a partnership. Think bigger.

So on September 28, 2009, I wrote to a person I admired more than any other in the new media space: Arianna Huffington. I sent her a ten paragraph e-mail, trying to keep it as brief as possible while at the same time elaborating on my background, Breaking Tweets, and my admiration for The Huffington Post (HuffPost), and asking about the potential for a partnership or some other arrangement, noting I was "open-minded to what that could be."

To my surprise, I received a reply from Arianna in my inbox on October 3rd. She connected me with HuffPost CEO Eric Hippeau, so we could discuss possible opportunities to work together.

After talking with Hippeau, he directed me to HuffPost CTO Paul Berry, and I chatted with him. Berry invited me to come out to New York for an interview for a job called Traffic/Trends Editor; the job description included tracking the real-time Web and breaking news, similar to what I had been doing with Breaking Tweets.

All of this was happening very quickly, but opportunities like this don't come about often. I dropped everything I was doing, and was in New York the next business day. On November 3rd, one month after first hearing from Arianna, I received a phone call from Arianna Huffington herself, bringing the whole thing full circle, and she welcomed me to the team.

Breaking Tweets, or Twitter rather, had helped me get a full-time job. As much as I had hoped Breaking Tweets could be integrated into the Huffington Post, we couldn't quite figure it out, and my job started quickly so I delved into that. Breaking Tweets just kind of stopped, and the contributors had dropped off long before, so it was only me at the time.

Bothered by the fact that the @BreakingTweets Twitter account, with its 15,000 followers, was idle, I approached HuffPost management again. We figured out a way to at least integrate that account into HuffPost, and it now operates as a Huffington Post breaking news feed of alerts around the world. I continue to operate the account, but I now have two fellow editors from the HuffPost who pitch in.

All because of Twitter.

I continue to be an avid user and I use tweets in the stories I file for HuffPost whenever possible, especially in cases of breaking news. The funny thing is, other news outlets are using tweets in stories now too. The concept of using tweets as quotes started on Breaking Tweets at a time when it would be laughable for that to happen on mainstream news sites. It's exciting to have been part of that first wave of Twitter and news integration, and it's amazing how far Twitter has come since.

Of all my experiences, the bottom line is clear: the power of Twitter as a networking tool. It helped me meet amazing people I would have never met otherwise, it opened up doors, and it opened my eyes to a world I didn't know existed. Perspective. Twitter gives perspective. It's never about you, it's about others. And though it's a publishing medium, sometimes all you have to do is listen and tap into the best it has to offer.

Craig Kanalley started working with The Huffington Post as the Traffic/Trends Editor in November 2009. He is a native of Buffalo, New York, has a Bachelor's degree in Communication/Journalism from St. John Fisher College in Rochester, New York, and a Master's degree in Journalism (focus on online/new media) from DePaul University in Chicago.

Craig Kanalley
@ckanal
http://www.craigkanalley.com

Journalism 2010 - Blazing a New Frontier in the Last Frontier

by

Matthew Felling

Twitter is the largest cocktail party in the world, I tell people. There are cliques surrounding you. Clusters off to the side discussing the appetizers at a certain bar, a huddle of sports fans following injuries, an ever-growing throng of political junkies. All great and fun, but a tad self-selecting and narrow, in terms of conversation topics.

To media professionals, the challenge and opportunity of Twitter is to be one of the most interesting people at that cocktail party, with a broad appeal, and a source of information and insight that few at the party can provide.

I work in Anchorage, Alaska, where half the entire state resides. Now, Alaska is an enormous state, but it's a rather small place. The intimacy of having half the state's population in one city, and a relatively small city in the grand scheme of things, is a near-perfect setting for social media connectivity. And the capability of being on top of things a thousand miles away to the north, and five hundred miles to the west, is a fantastic new tool for news dissemination.

How so? The small population of Anchorage means that there is a lot of overlap in terms of demographics, professions, and ages. So while some Twitter news sources (in "The Lower 48," as we call you contiguous souls) can get away successfully with narrowcasting information— for example, what do you want to know about South Dakota grain?—in Anchorage you can truly broadcast a spectrum of information to a large percentage of Alaskans.

As a journalist of an admitted old school bent, the reason I'm in reporting is Edward R. Murrow's claim that journalism is the largest classroom in the world. However, in the 21st century, you're welcome to keep the same tools in your toolbox, but you've got to adapt to the student body.

New Media, New Rules

Obvious statement alert: everything in information dissemination has changed, whether it's your kid's first tooth or a gubernatorial debate. And the first domino to fall in the old technological revolution—possibly going back to the cable-news-'80s, but definitely when the Internet grabbed a foothold in news— was the fact that "film at 11" reportage is dead. You can't go out, work the streets and/or phones, toss your journalistic ingredients together with care into a nicely conceived stew, and lay it out with the presentation of an Edith Wharton novel for your audience when you're ready. This ain't your grandfather's journalism.

You've got to share what you know when you know it. When you are out on the streets working a story, you need to be uploading photos online in whatever format you're choosing. When you're on the phones and you get a snappy quote for a topic, it has to be tweeted immediately, if not sooner. When you're in the process of putting together your story, if a theme or finding is emerging, tweet it, in the strongest yet broadest terms you can.

The previous generation of journalists would consider this suicide, or the equivalent of showing the opposing team your playbook. In all candor, there are still journalists in Alaska who will tweet out, "What did Governor XX say about offshore drilling? Watch my story at five." And that's ninety minutes after I've let the proverbial cat out of the bag. I bet you, though, that the people who heard it from me when I heard it will tune in rather than follow the online bread crumbs from the old school approach.

As a journalist, Twitter is a tool for disseminating information, but it is also an invaluable branding opportunity. It's your printing press **and** your publicist. It's even your telephone, when you're trolling for sources for a story. ("Has your car been broken into this summer?" was a query from a few months back, and that tweet helped me get five victims within minutes.)

Are you showing your playbook to the other guys? Yes. Are you scooping yourself? Yes. But you're also showcasing your reporting and the fact that you've got the key info right now; you've been making the calls, you've been enterprising enough to see something where others didn't. And while "The Others" may end up reporting the story alongside you, you've got two things going for you. Competitively, you've got the head start on them and they're already playing catchup, working from a disadvantage. Crucially, you are branding yourself as "The News Leader," the one that is completely in command of the issues and newsmakers of the day. As a media purist, I never prioritize getting it first over getting it right. But when you stack up being first consistently, day after day, you then attract a following who appreciate what you do.

Speaking, as I was a paragraph ago, of engaging with followers, don't ever underestimate the value of including the audience in the story-writing process. Every week, I host a program called "View from the Hill." Long story short: it's an Alaskan version of "Meet the Press" where I have fifteen minutes of questions and answers with our DC delegation. Every week, I open up the question suggestion basket to all my followers. And while about 80% of their questions are ones I had in the queue already, I am sure to tweet out: "@AKPolitics, I asked Sen. Begich your question," and people have that sense of ownership in a high-profile product. Then there's the 20% of questions that are purely audience-driven: I give them complete credit and cite them on-air. (Which leads to a swell of "Sen. X answered my question" retweets—which is a win-win.)

For followers, it's ownership of the high-quality journalism they're watching. For the journalist, it turns the cocktail party into a brainstorming session.

Variety

Now that we have the journalism perspective addressed, it's time to acknowledge that we are talking about social media after all. And being "Information Man" is a worthwhile goal and cause, but I'll take it further. As I mentioned back in the cocktail party metaphor, there's a lot of conversations going on around you. Lots. So I retweet some of the more interesting stuff I receive.

But I also find headlines from around the world and bring them to Alaska. Yes, I do the occasional Google news search for "Palin," since there's never a shortage of those. But I also do stories about natural resources (oil, gas, coal) since that's our number one meal ticket. Same with climate studies, since we're positioned in a strategic way for global warming and climate change. Then there are the sports headlines: Alaska doesn't have any major league sports teams, but it's full of sports fans and fantasy sports players, so I have a lot of latitude to share just about any sports headline of note. And the goofy stuff, the frivolous things you find, are always worth a tweet.

I learned as a CBSNews.com blogger that variety is the spice of life, and a useful lure for online relevance. As the site's media writer, I would talk about "anonymous sources," shift gears to the latest case of media bias, and then, when people started seeing a pattern, I'd complain about how TBS blew the coverage of the National League Divisional Playoffs. Like a baseball pitcher with a couple of different tools in my repertoire, I would toss in an off-speed pitch to keep readers alert. These days, I never go more than three or four tweets on a single topic, and that's if I'm at a press event or on a story and buried in very specific details. Internally, I have an overkill meter and try to mix things up for people.

You're not going to be very interesting at the Twitter online cocktail party if you're a one-trick pony.

Be Yourself

There was a study early on in Twitter that broke down users into two groups: Informers and Meformers. It's the difference between "President Obama calls on Hamid Karzai to clean up corruption" and "WOOT! Going out for mojitos, dressed to impress!"

Me, I stick with the informers out there, and dabble here and there with the meformers, particularly when there's a conversation to open up. "@LostHater: What's your problem with Locke?" Or if the viewers are tweeting about snow, I try and turn it into an online poll: "When will be get our first measurable inch? Whoever's closest can help with weather, since you know, you're the expert."

But, it's been a transition. For the first six months of my online existence, I focused solely on branding myself as a news source. Like a young elected official just earning his bona fides through hard work, I wanted to gain respect for my professional ability and presentation. Regardless of any new media reality, your credibility is still your most important possession.

Then—and it was not calculated—just by feel, I decided to loosen my metaphorical anchor tie and toss in asides to news stories I tweeted. I allowed myself the wiggle room to provide news and comment. Followers responded en masse:

"It's great to see you're a real guy!"

"Love when you show a little personality!"

"Way to nail that one."

My online identity continues to evolve. Depending on the news agenda of the day, I am sometimes more locked in on breaking news than usual. Then other days, I'll color outside the lines a bit more. And I get the sense that people have a "feel" for it by now; they're onboard for the ride everyday.

So, while I can safely say I've managed an above-average amount of scoops out to my followers in the twitterverse, and built social relationships that are personally and professionally valuable, I'm also the only reporter in Alaska that's been retweeted by TasteeFreez. While that doesn't make me Bob Woodward, it does position me in the 21st century social media reporting game.

Matt Felling serves KTVA and Anchorage as the 6 p.m. and 10 p.m. anchor and general reporter. He also serves as the host of KTVA's "Alaska's View from the Hill." The Washington Post named him one of "Alaska's Best Political Reporters" in 2009, and was the only broadcaster.

He joined CBS 11 after a decade of news reporting, commentary, and analysis inside the Washington, DC, beltway. Before heading north, he was Editor of CBSNews.com's "Public Eye" section, a regular guest host on WAMU's "Kojo Nnamdi Show," and Media Director of the nonprofit, nonpartisan Center for Media and Public Affairs. His writings have been published in the American Journalism Review, Christian Science Monitor, San Francisco Chronicle, Atlanta Journal-Constitution, and the San Diego Union-Tribune.

Government

The Next Generation of Think Tank Communications

by

Rory Cooper

A successful social media strategy is essential for any organization or business in America. As recently as 2009, having a professional Facebook or Twitter account was a luxury and most were simply designed to broadcast a message or advertisement. That is no longer the case. In today's entrepreneurial and connected world, creating a conversation among your stakeholders rises to the top of any communications strategy.

Take Ford Motor Company, for example. When the company unveiled its newly designed 2011 Ford Explorer, its marketing strategy relied heavily on Facebook. And what was the result? According to SocialCarNews.com, it generated a 200% greater return than a typical Super Bowl ad, and at a fraction of the cost. Traffic to Web sites displaying the Ford Explorer saw a jump of as much as 104%.

The Heritage Foundation recognized this trend very early, and has led the Washington policy-shaping apparatus into the next generation of communications.

Of course, embracing entrepreneurial communications is nothing new to Heritage. The think tank was founded more than thirty years ago as an enterprise dedicated to publishing the best policy research and analysis and, importantly, communicating its findings to Congress, stakeholders, and the American public in the most effective and time-sensitive ways.

Embracing the culture of "new media," "social media," or as some call it, "direct media," was simply another evolution in our ability to communicate transformative policy ideas with those who are interested in American governance and civil society.

Platforms and Products

The Heritage Foundation has developed multiple media platforms to showcase our policy research and analysis in a connective way to social media. None of them are revolutionary in their mere existence, but we strive to create revolutionary ways to utilize them.

The Foundry is our blog, run on an open source WordPress platform. The Foundry drives substantial traffic to our policy papers and provides us a significant portal to direct social media traffic. When a research paper or analysis is published by one of our leading experts, we immediately turn the overall message into a blog, preferably less than a thousand words, that give readers the gist of our position. When breaking news occurs, or a story helps underscore a problem we believe we have expertise on, we also use the blog to emphasize a conservative position.

The Morning Bell is our daily e-newsletter and the masthead, if you will, of our daily Foundry content. While we have several other e-newsletters available dealing with specific policy areas or membership updates, The Morning Bell is Heritage's signature communications product, which gives subscribers a look at the major news of the day combined with conservative research and analysis.

With more than 150,000 subscribers and an impressive open rate, it is regarded as one of the most influential e-newsletters in Washington. We build its subscription through aggressive marketing and quality content. We also use it to highlight recent blog posts worth consideration, and to aggregate news content important to conservatives in five easy "Quick Hits" that help give The Morning Bell an extra appeal to the busy reader.

While e-mail delivered content may be replaced at some point by text messages, or network deliverables, it can't be ignored for the time being. Our ability to get thousands of readers to view content at their doorstep (inbox) every day not only increases our reach, but significantly builds our buy in among our audience.

The Heritage Facebook page was at nearly 250,000 fans and growing rapidly in August 2010. The ability for us to reach a quarter of a million people interested in our content is not taken lightly. Heritage has invested in technology, software, and resources that help us optimize how we use this platform. Facebook's integration into our Web site through "like" functionality is critical, as is our ability to strategically schedule content that is interesting to our readers at a particular time, and invites interaction.

Facebook also gives us the ability to stream live events through Ustream.tv, which take place at Heritage. This ability was really underlined one day when we had House Minority Whip Eric Cantor (R-VA) delivering a major address in our auditorium that seats several hundred visitors. While the audience experienced the speech, thousands upon thousands of Facebook fans were interacting with it online. We even made a point to ask questions during the traditional Q&A period from our Facebook audience to legitimize that experience and build that draw.

Facebook helps you develop solutions, find vendors, and integrate your site with the network by providing information on— where else—its Facebook page. How you take advantage of the new Open Graph protocol is important, and Facebook itself helps you understand it, or helps you find who can understand it for you.

In the end, Facebook is about the people who use it daily to stay connected to friends, family, and organizations like Heritage. It is essential you recognize their presence, which is why we integrated a weekly "Featured Fan" campaign that gives fans a closer biographical profile of one of their own. Why does that person follow Heritage? What makes them a conservative? These questions and profiles help draw the community closer together.

On Twitter, we continue that community building by delivering well-timed tweets that strategically drive home our messages of the day, but also encourage interaction and click-through traffic. Our Twitter and Facebook applications are integrated, so we can measure the effectiveness of each separately and how they work with one another. Using specialized software, we're also able to use the Twitter platform for impromptu chats and to build conversations around certain events or videos.

And of course, rounding out the big three with Facebook and Twitter is YouTube. Our YouTube channel allows us to deliver products that synthesize a particular message, or showcase a particular official, thought leader, or even head of state, who often visit Heritage to champion their particular cause. However, the idea of making a video go viral is a good way to get stuck trying to be too slick for your own good. We try to keep it to the basics. Short, simple, and entertaining enough that viewers will be intrigued to find out more—and if they're not, what they take away was worth the few minutes of their time.

Beyond the traditional big three platforms exists much more. Heritage has invested in microsites when necessary, to amplify a specific policy objective or highlight a particular campaign. 33Minutes.com helped promote the original Heritage movie, "33 Minutes," and our missile defense strategy. FixHealthCarePolicy.com was an important hub during the health care reform debate. And NoEnergyTax.com helped us build a social network, using a points-driven system, where users could interact to learn how disastrous more national energy taxes would be on the economy.

But micro-sites have their downside, as they draw visitors away from your home site. So the first priority is to provide your audience with a useful set of tools at home, Heritage.org, and then identify specific and targeted needs and goals for using an external web address.

Beyond the traditional platforms of blogs, micro-sites, networks and video, we are constantly looking at emerging areas we can enter. When Kindle began publishing blogs, we were one of the first to make ours available. It allowed us to build an early following and remain a highly rated blog in our sphere of content. How we use LinkedIn or Foursquare to connect with other networks is also important. If someone checks in using Foursquare, what information are they getting about us, or from us?

And finally, how our content is delivered on smartphones, iPhones, iPads, tablets, and through RSS feeds is scrutinized to keep up with the mobile revolution. The online user experience is moving away from the desktop and onto the handheld. Heritage has to address how those users will interact with us, and guarantee their experience is as comfortable and engaging on the small screen as it is on the big.

Knowing Your Audience

Heritage consists of nearly 700,000 members. Every single one of them invested their hard-earned money in the idea that conservative solutions to our nation's problems exist, that Heritage was the best factory to build these initiatives, and that Heritage could create the output necessary to see them enacted as policy. Who they are, and how they want to be communicated with, is essential before creating a social media strategy.

Beyond the Heritage membership, it is also our mission to put these ideas into the public marketplace. So every audience has to be considered, and their preferred method of listening to, and engaging in, policy debates understood. Whether an 18-year-old college student; a 29-year-old congressional staffer; a 50-year-old researcher; or a 65-year-old retiree—each person's needs have to be measured.

Juggling so many constituencies can be tough. If you try and be too informal and edgy, you may not reach the retiree, and vice-versa; if you send out boring, policy-laden tweets, you will probably have a hard time reaching the college student. Just like with any form of public writing or speaking, you need to capture attention while maintaining the integrity of your brand.

Heritage has spent considerable time testing what does and doesn't work. Analytics are critical to viewing traffic patterns and letting successful practices flourish and unsuccessful attempts at communicating become "lessons learned." Google Analytics is clearly the most widely available way to do this, and Radian 6 is the more advanced tool, but most social media firms now offer plenty of different products to help measure your audience.

But analytics shouldn't just be used to measure internal strength, but also external popularity. Search Engine Optimization (SEO) is the practice of ensuring your work is available to online users searching relevant keywords. So if someone uses Google to search "missile defense", where does our research fall within Google's results? Up until September 2010, this process needed to be nurtured in a specific way to achieve the maximum amount of incoming Google traffic (i.e. analyzing incoming links, urls, etc.). But then, Google threw the SEO world for a loop introducing "Google Instant."

Google Instant now works with the user to create a unique search environment that predicts what you want, as you type it, and gets smarter at knowing what you want. This means that "page 2" of the search results is now less important than knowing how people will instinctively search. This doesn't mean SEO is no longer important, it simply proves that keeping up with these trends and being flexibly smart about your strategy is more important than ever.

Speaking With an Honest Voice

You can know everything about your audience and still be ineffective, if you don't know everything about yourself. One of the reasons social media has become so engaging is that it allows users to hear a voice unvarnished. Through several applications, you can literally become part of an ongoing debate with your audience. On Twitter, you need to communicate with absolute brevity what you want readers to glean, and that doesn't leave room for spin, bloviating, or nonsense.

Considering these factors, it's best to understand that not only must you speak with an honest voice, but know that the social media audience feels it is their responsibility to keep you honest when you don't. Heritage goes to great lengths to ensure its message—whether on Facebook, Twitter, YouTube, or another platform—accurately represents the original policy ideas being formulated.

Former Governor and vice-presidential candidate Sarah Palin has mastered this art. It is abundantly clear to readers that her Facebook posts and Twitter messages are hers and hers alone. They don't give the impression of a communications staff building a personality, as so many other politicians get hamstrung by. And because of this, she has become one of the most influential social media personalities on Earth. When she says something, it invades the mainstream media almost immediately because of the traction her network has, and the honesty that prevails it.

Some other organizations or personas may use a bait and switch approach to lure readers in, and then offer them something different. This is simply bad communications. While they may get that one "hit" today, they would lose a potential supporter. In other words: tease honestly.

This is not a one-dimensional responsibility. Not only must Heritage ensure that its views are correctly represented by its staff, but also that other organizations, blogs, or media outlets are doing the same. Using social networks is the easiest form of research in this capacity.

This also dovetails into having a responsible social media policy. How are employees using Twitter? No organization should discourage the personal use of social networks, but all personnel need to know the potential consequences of a bad tweet, embarrassing Facebook photo, etc. The idea of representing your professional life in all things personal has not only expanded over the decades, but exploded in Washington. The old axiom a young intern might have learned in 1998 was: "If you don't want to see it on the front page of the Post, don't do it." Today, that is: "If you don't want people tweeting it, videoing it, sharing pictures of it, or memorializing it on their network, really don't do it."

Social Media as a Research Tool

It goes without saying that public policy debates are driven by the news—and there are multiple sides to every debate. If you use social media effectively, you can predict how news cycles will develop. Heritage is able to identify what news hooks exist for a particular effort we're showcasing, and what media personalities are interested in covering our point of view.

In the same vein, other organizations with different views are doing the same thing, and monitoring our output. It's critical that we know how we are being represented by competitors and what message they are using to deliver their own ideas into the marketplace. If Heritage sees several liberal organizations using similar arguments in a policy debate, it is only common sense that we develop messages that reflect our answer to that meme.

And finally, it's necessary to know how your members, audience, and listeners are reacting to what you're saying. If someone retweets something from @Heritage, are we seeing what commentary they may have added on their own? Are we reading other tweets mentioning @Heritage? Are we reading comments on Facebook, YouTube, The Foundry blog, and other locations to gage interest, complaints, and feedback and responding appropriately? This is social media 101, but the practice can't be discounted as anything but absolutely essential to the overall mission.

Self Promotion

The myth in social media is that self promotion is a bad thing, when in fact it is a big reason to be engaging online in the first place. Media exist on so many platforms today that you often need to alert one group of action taking place on another.

So Heritage uses Twitter to drive people to Facebook, or YouTube to drive people to The Foundry blog, or The Foundry blog to drive people to The Morning Bell e-newsletter, and so on. But we also use these platforms to drive people to traditional media outlets, like television, radio, and print media. Many products are developed with a particular platform in mind, but you can't limit their exposure to only those explicitly seeking that type of communication.

For example, Heritage analysts spend considerable time in our television studio appearing on national and local broadcast programs, or phoning in to talk radio programs. Whether taped or live, we can encourage our networks to not only view that appearance but react to it.

Driving Membership

While The Heritage Foundation may have nearly 700,000 members, we are constantly looking to grow that number. But constantly hitting an audience with membership drives can have diminishing returns. Heritage earns membership on reputation and quality of content, in addition to the pitches. We need to ensure our content always broadens that connection between listening and joining, as well as makes the explicit pitch when and if appropriate. This cannot be the sole reason for your social content, but it would be foolish to strategically overlook.

Getting Buy In

An "institution" cannot embrace a new way of communicating anymore than you can go outside and have a conversation with a pile of bricks. The "people" who make up that institution have to buy into the benefits, and that requires understanding the needs and wants of your colleagues and the potential, and limits, of social media.

It used to be that an expert might write a compelling paper or article and communicators might help draw out the pitch or create an inviting headline. But today, communicators need to be able to digest the 100 or so character invite to its Twitter audience. The writers need to be able to point out the compelling bullets that could be transformed into a video or blog. There is simply too much information and public policy debate available to rest on your laurels. Heritage examines some issues that almost no other think tank in the world pays close attention to, and in broader areas, delivers critiques, analysis, and solutions untested. But a library of that information is insufficient to move the ball forward, so the experts have to be involved in the process of helping market their ideas.

Nervousness begets nervousness. Media teams have to be able to confidently demonstrate the benefits and measurements of the platforms they're encouraging their colleagues to embrace. Heritage has struck gold in many respects, because the entrepreneurial spirit of the think tank encourages the mindset that accepts new technology. Often, analysts here who may spend their days thinking of national security will go home and bring back innovative ideas on network formation, technology, and metrics. They build their own policy-specific networks to perform all of the functions we have as an institution at the micro-personal level, by letting people know their broadcast schedule, their editorial appearances, and most importantly, their latest research.

Cannibalizing

There is nothing more tempting than to see one Facebook or Twitter network take off and decide to create ten more. But one organization managing several networks can be troublesome at best, counterproductive at worst.

At Heritage, we focus on so many expansive issues that we are constantly considering whether we branch out our feeds to more specialized content. If @Heritage has 65,000+ fans, then maybe we could segment the ones solely focused on health care into a separate stream. In some cases, this might work, but our experience has been that it is a road less traveled for a reason.

Often you see social media managers aggregate the combined total of ten feeds, averaging 2,000 listeners, and tell an audience that they reach 20,000 people. The math doesn't add up. First you have to take out the large number of those who follow every feed because they are superfans of your organization. And then you have to realize the lost potential of each feed, since the management of each takes away from improving the greater strategy. The above example might actually be reaching 10,000 people, but the reach is so much less effective due to dwindling resources. Which takes us to...

Knowing When to Quit or Say No

Sometimes the most innovative way to use social media is to not use it. In other words, metrics can't just be used to see how well you are doing on a particular platform. They also have to be used to determine if the opportunity costs of using that platform are worth it to begin with. Are you spending three hours of labor a day on Twitter but getting minimal traffic back? Is the latest and greatest technology something to spend time and money on, or instead use a wait and see approach?

As Yogi Berra might say, social media is cheap, except when it's not. Yes, you can have a free Facebook page and Twitter account, and you can even cheaply produce quality video content these days. But the time your team spends on these devices might be better spent on traditional communications methods or focusing more specifically on one platform, forsaking the others.

The metrics and measurements we use at Heritage to determine success are analyzed at a deeper level than "good week/bad week" but rather "good idea/bad idea." Many organizations don't spend enough time, or build enough expertise, analyzing readily available metrics. Adjustments are necessary to build traffic and improve content, and usually a roadmap to that end exists, if you merely employ it.

Even at the micro-level. Having a chat or live blog during a major news event might sound sexy, but if the interaction was limited, were the results insufficient to monopolize your team's time, as well as the experts you rely on for other analysis and broadcast reaction?

At some point, some organization will quit utilizing a successful Twitter or Facebook campaign and people will think they are nuts, internally and externally. But a big decision like that might make sense for your organization.

This is not to say you shouldn't use every free and available resource. Not having a basic Facebook page is akin to not listing your business' phone number in the Yellow Pages (remember phone numbers and phone books?). It ignores low-hanging fruit. But some groups or organizations might decide to provide the best possible information to those seeking them out on a platform and then hopefully redirect those seekers to where you have the resources to give them adequate attention. Costs and benefits have to be weighed.

For Heritage, our success is only encouraging more participation, but in today's world, no communications policy or practice is permanent.

Building a Program

If you pay attention to sports, you know that teams build their programs looking several years out. Teams identify what pieces they need to make an immediate impact, but also build towards a long-term goal (unless they're the Detroit Lions I grew up with). This strategy is easily transferred to the online space.

You need to identify where you need an immediate impact, and fill that space. Then think how that growth will help you in the long run. If you only have the resources for one social media focused team member, what strengths are you looking for to lay the groundwork?

Heritage began with a few visionaries delivering a steady stream of content. It grew by adding pieces, using buy-in to diversify content, and building towards a long-term strategy. The more diversified content and diversified platforms we used, the stronger we became in every area. If we saw a "free agent" that could help build an area earlier than planned, we made the strategic decision to move ahead and not miss an opportunity.

It helps when you have high name ID. The fact that the top two radio programs in the nation discuss our work on a daily basis builds our brand recognition, which in turn, drives up our traffic online. This is why social media practices have to also be tied to marketing strategies, so you can cross-promote and take advantage of that recognition.

Change When At the Top

Heritage President Ed Feulner likes to say that you make changes when you are at the top of your game, not at the bottom. It allows you to be more innovative and focus on your long-term success, rather than short-term gain. This methodology has accomplished a great deal for Heritage. We utilize it in social media as well.

For example, what is your benchmark for success on Facebook? 250,000 fans? We did that. But what about a million? We could easily achieve that in the next year. But a million "likes" on Facebook does not automatically translate into success. It is how you interact with those fans, and how you develop tailored content that counts. Activating listeners into participants and members is the end goal. So yes, getting to a quarter of a million fans is worthy of some backslapping and it put Heritage at the top of that particular network in Washington, but taking that engagement to the next level is a more profound achievement.

Right now, we are identifying ways to build our own internal network that connects engaged Heritage audiences together in a unique and profound way, and connects them with the Heritage team like never before. But that is not a step to be taken lightly. We have to identify what users will get out of the experience, what actions we want them to take, what user expectations will be, and how the network will be managed. This is an undertaking that can only be done when you feel your team is already network-savvy.

Who Are New Media?

We can easily get caught up talking about Facebook and Twitter, since those platforms are so new and exciting, and big. But media exist out there that are driving the news in a way that is frustrating. Bloggers, and in some cases, super tweeters, are driving the conversation. What happens if you spend hours and hours wooing a particular journalist of the traditional persuasion, but spend no time interacting with a blogger that has ten times as much influence?

The Heritage Foundation was a pioneer in this outreach. The director of the Center for Media and Public Policy, Robert Bluey, an early adapter for Heritage on multiple platforms, began a weekly roundtable called "The Bloggers Briefing" (#tbb) in 2006. Bloggers of all stripes can come and share information as well as hear presentations on newsworthy issues. The gathering has become something much bigger than just a way to reach out to bloggers. In fact, when Heritage recently released a major product called "Solutions for America," which outlined conservative policy prescriptions for the next decade, we released it to this group and invited traditional media outlets to join them.

Identifying who your influencers are and how they want to be engaged isn't merely a by-product of dealing with new media. It should earn the same level of professionalism and precedence that traditional outreach has received. Beyond working with them on stories, it is important to identify original content that is important to you —and a particular blogger or aggregator—and to get it to them. Incoming links from some blogs might make up 50% of its traffic for a well-placed story.

And then there are the new hybrid media outlets that bridge the divide between bloggers and newspapers. Appearing online only in most cases, but having the investigative infrastructure of a traditional newspaper, these entities can be wonderful places to place commentary, pitch an investigative idea, or deliver a news story. When you consider the traffic The Huffington Post, Politico, The Daily Caller, or others get compared to the circulation and online traffic of most traditional newspapers, it is obvious that they should merit serious attention from a communications team.

Public Policy

And finally, at The Heritage Foundation, we can't simply analyze new trends for personal growth. It would go against our core structure, and ignore the effect the federal government can have in limiting our access to our audience and the first principle of free speech.

Currently, the Federal Trade Commission is considering taxes and subsidies that would prop up certain preferred editorial methods of journalism at the expense of emerging media. Some of the ideas just smack of government arrogance, such as making "facts" proprietary under U.S. copyright laws that would make it costly for bloggers and aggregators to publish investigative information culled from another source (even with proper attribution).

Other ideas being considered blur the lines that separate government from the people who cover it, like tax credits for newsroom hires, or subsidies for "preferred" or responsible media actors, that essentially result in journalists' salaries being propped up by tax dollars rather than free market performance.

And then there are the taxes. The FTC is considering all types of taxes that would help it manipulate the free exchange of information of ideas, including a broadcast spectrum tax that would hurt radio broadcasters, a tax on consumer electronics (dubbed "the iPad tax" by the New York Post), advertising taxes (where upstart Web sites earn the majority of their revenue) and ISP-cell phone taxes. The idea is to soak the new media to prop up the old media. And it's an idea that is costly to all parties interested in these platforms.

And then there is net neutrality, which some would wrongly argue is designed to protect the little guy from corporate dominance online. Unfortunately, as is often the case, the government's manipulation of the market through excessive regulation will not produce any rosy scenarios for the little guy. Broadband prices will go up as network providers are unable to manage traffic effectively, without interference, and your ability to freely use the networks and platforms so freely available today will be obstructed.

But more importantly, we have a free speech impediment. You may think that large corporations will impede content through deliberate broadband manipulation, but that has never happened. And you may think engineers and users can't agree on performance-based solutions and prefer government fiat to solve traffic jams, but engineers have always developed consensus-building solutions. Handing over the keys to Internet content control to the government raises so many red flags that it should give all users of this glorious technological revolution great pause. Having Washington as the traffic cop for all content on the Internet is a risky and dangerous endeavor that could strangle the strategies outlined in this book.

The Next Big Thing

We can all spend hours, days and months considering the next big thing. It is out there. An ambitious entrepreneur is developing something right now that may make these strategies obsolete by 2011. But there are enough "big things" already out there to harness and take advantage of our connectivity right now. Charting your path forward has to be as individualized as your Twitter avatar, and as unique as your Facebook profile. The Internet has redefined what we consider a community. We are excited to be a part of so many communities and we welcome all into ours, @Heritage.

Rory Cooper is the Director of Strategic Communications for The Heritage Foundation, where he coordinates the think tank's external message and internal communications, manages its entire digital communications and social media portfolios, and develops new media partnerships. Cooper also serves as the executive editor for The Foundry, the conservative policy news blog at Heritage, which includes the Morning Bell, one of Washington's most widely read and influential morning e-newsletters. He previously spent seven years in the Bush Administration in a variety of policy and communications roles at The White House and other federal agencies. He began in campaign politics in the 1990s working for several national political organizations and presidential campaigns. He now lives in Hyattsville, Maryland, with his wife Emily, daughter Lillian, and dog Harold.

Rory Cooper
@rorycooper
http://www.facebook.com/heritagefoundation
http://www.heritage.org/
www.foundry.org

Social Advocacy at American Progress

by

Alan Rosenblatt, Ph.D.

The Center for American Progress and The Center for American Progress Action Fund soft launched its social media engagement program in June 2009. As a think tank with a sister advocacy organization, the challenge was to develop a program that reflected our mission of influencing influencers, largely driven by the production of high quality policy research and proposals. American Progress successfully ventured into the blogosphere with its award-winning, research-based blog: ThinkProgress.org (and its subsidiary blogs Yglesias.ThinkProgress.org and WonkRoom.org). Its think tank Web site, AmericanProgress.org, is rich with videos and interactive graphics that make its policy work accessible to a very broad audience. These outlets reach monthly audiences in excess of 2 million and 250,000, respectively.

Wishing to extend its reach into the social web, American Progress developed its social media strategy based on a few key assumptions:

- Experts and individuals are more trusted than institutions (According to the Edelman Trust Barometer[1])

- Institutions are most effective as social media amplifiers of its expert and staff voices

- Social media creates a new class of influencers that include bloggers, online organizers, and ordinary citizens using social media tools to advocate for issues they care about to personal, and often large, audiences

- Social media can be used to reach targeted audiences of influencers, not just the unfiltered masses

- Social media is fundamentally about conversation between and among people

- Social media interactions occur in a public space and cannot be ignored without risk

---

[1] http://www.edelman.com/trust/2010/.

Given these assumptions and American Progress's mission to influence influencers, its social media strategy has prioritized Twitter over Facebook in its early stages, though it has a strong and growing presence in both communities. The organization implemented a decentralized, hourglass-shaped model that focuses on training as many policy experts and project staff as possible to use Twitter and Facebook to promote their own work, comment on the news and events they attend, engage with other experts in their issue area, and occasionally remind their followers that they are human beings. Then the organizations' branded channels are used to amplify their tweets and posts to a larger audience of influencers and others out on the social web.

American Progress pursues a deliberate strategy to build an audience of influencers. As a result, that audience has grown to a combined audience on Twitter of more than 130,000 followers and a Facebook audience exceeding 35,000. As these audiences grow, American Progress is layering increasing levels of organization onto it. This process starts by creating Twitter lists sorted out by issue focus and other affinity groupings on the Action Fund's @CAPAction channel (such as Energy-Climate Influencers and Progressive State Bloggers). Two supporter groups, CAPAction Superactivists and CAPAction Superactivists2, were also created to recognize the efforts of people who help promote American Progress's work and to start organizing them into a more coherent volunteer force. These superactivists get value from American Progress in several ways. In addition to being fed top-quality content, American Progress recommends these superactivists to the broader progressive community on Twitter by retweeting them and recommending that progressives follow them on #FollowFriday (#FF). As a result, many of the people who retweet American Progress channels become followers, that can be reached via private messaging to be asked for specific efforts promoting progressive messages and policy products.

The goal of American Progress's social media program is to create a reciprocal value community where we bring together progressive activists who help promote the think tank's progressive policy ideas and ultimately take part in social advocacy campaigns. These social advocacy campaigns mobilize activists to target messages to policy makers on social media, posting comments on targeted policymaker's Facebook walls and directly tweeting at them.

An essential part of American Progress's strategy includes **comprehensive measurement** of several aspects of its outreach efforts. In addition to tracking the size and composition of our direct audiences on social media, it tracks activity by supporters to promote its work. Using Bit.ly Pro to measure clicks on posted links, even when they are retweeted by others, provides a rough estimate of traffic driven back to the organizations' Web sites. Using the premium social media monitoring service Meltwater Buzz, it is able to measure how often posts are being retweeted and shared via Twitter and Facebook. Using a combination of Meltwater Buzz, Small Act's Thrive, SocialMention.com, and Search.Twitter.com to track what people are saying about the issues and policies, American Progress is able to respond to conversations and further promote its policy work and products. Using BackType.com, along with Bit.ly, it is able to identify what social media sites are generating traffic to specific web products. And, using tools like Twitalyzer.com and Klout.com, it is able to measure the influence of its own Twitter channels and the influence of its key supporter. And lastly, we are using Thrive to measure the reach of our messages through the extended audiences of people retweeting us on Twitter and pushing our messages through their Facebook news feeds.

Some highlights of American Progress's social media successes are presented in the following charts and tables. Figure 1 shows the growth over the past sixteen months of American Progress's organizational and project Twitter channels, while Figure 2 shows the growth of its expert staff Twitter channels.

Figure 1. Twitter Followers for CAP/Action Brand Channels

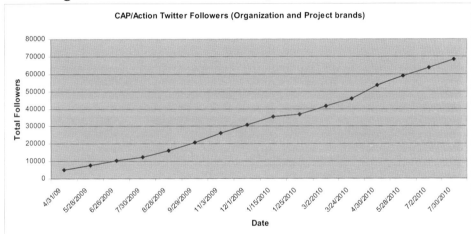

It is important to note that while the branded channels grow their audiences steadily, the staff audiences fluctuate as new staff are hired and other staff leave.

Figure 2. Twitter Followers for CAP/Action Staff Channels

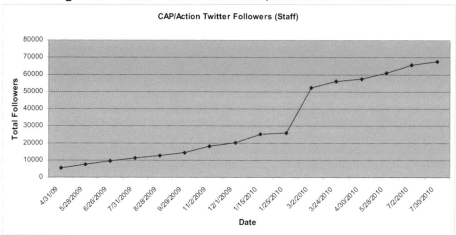

As Figure 3 shows, when combined, the brand and staff channels at American Progress have been growing steadily every month.

Figure 3. Twitter Followers for CAP/Action Brand + Staff Channels

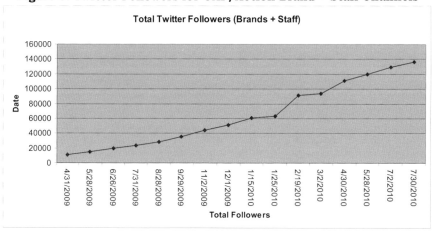

Compared to other think tanks, American Progress's Twitter program is performing very well. As Table 1 shows, not only does it have a larger audience for its branded channels than its major competitors, but it also is far more likely to be recommended (more than 2:1) via Twitter Lists.

Table 1. Twitter Followers and Listings – CAP/Action Brands vs. Other Think Tanks (2010)

Competition	Followers			Lists		
	June	July	Increase	June	July	Increase
Heritage (+ HeritageAction)	53,252	57,856	8.6%	2,922	3,099	6.1%
CatoInstitute	45,070	48,035	6.6%	2,349	2,482	5.7%
AEIOnline	5,098	5,309	4.1%	366	385	5.2%
Brookings (FP, Press, & Blogs)	4,354	4,599	5.6%	526	569	8.2%
All CAP/Action Brands**	**63,658**	**68,154**	**7.1%**	**5,901**	**6,257**	**6.0%**

Overall, the goals for American Progress's social media strategy are to:

- Grow its audience, with particular emphasis on influencers

- Engage its audience in conversation about progressive policies and issues

- Mobilize its audience to promote its policy products and action campaigns

- Create a core community of social media influencers from among its audience

- Deepen its relationship with its audience, generally, and its community, especially

- Leverage its social media network to drive progressive policy ideas into the national debate

Social Advocacy Case Study

One particular campaign that achieved enormous success was an effort by American Progress's anti-genocide program, the ENOUGH Project. This campaign to promote the passage of conflict minerals legislation in Congress has quickly become a best practice example of social advocacy.

As indicated earlier, social advocacy is the current state of the art of online advocacy. It moves advocacy actions to influence policymakers from behind closed doors (e.g. e-mail, faxes, and calls to their offices) to public forums (e.g. their Facebook walls, public messages on Twitter, on their blog comment sections, etc.). By moving these actions to a public forum, policymakers are unable to deny they are getting messages from activists, and if they snub the effort, it is in front of a public audience and is permanently archived. This creates a far more powerful impetus for policymakers to respond to advocacy campaigns.

The ENOUGH Project targeted ten members of the House Foreign Affairs Committee to ask them (nicely) to co-sponsor the conflict minerals bill under consideration by the committee. Within 48 hours, about 500 people posted on the Facebook walls of these members (all told, about 1,200 participated in the campaign). After 48 hours, two of the ten members agreed to co-sponsor. Another three members of the committee who were not targeted "saw the writing on the wall" and also agreed to co-sponsor. Then Chairman Howard Berman (D-CA) took an unanticipated step and not only put the conflict minerals bill up to a vote, but also a second bill identifying the Lord's Resistance Army as an enemy of the U.S., which ENOUGH was pushing up for a vote as well. Both passed unanimously out of committee.

In just a few days, the Lord's Resistance Army bill passed both chambers and was signed into law by the President. The conflict mineral bill was quickly passed by the House, and then amended to the Senate's financial regulation bill, which ultimately passed and was signed into law a few months later.

As a result of ENOUGH's social advocacy campaign, two bills not expected to come up for a vote until next year are now law. And to add frosting to the top of this cake, Chairman Berman contacted ENOUGH and asked if its activists would come back to the committee members' Facebook pages and post "Thank you" messages on the walls.

American Progress's program leverages several channels to implement our campaigns and promotions. It focuses on Twitter because it is the fastest way to reach the most influencers. Even influencers who use other online and offline channels to exert influence are often easily reached via Twitter. It uses Facebook for outreach to grassroots activists, but more importantly, Facebook is where many actions are taken (in addition to actions on Twitter). American Progress also uses e-mail to promote its social advocacy campaigns to our e-mail lists, expanding its ability to mobilize activists.

It is essential that these campaigns leverage several channels in concert. Borrowing from Sir Charles Sherrington's 1904 research on dog reflexes, American Progress recognizes that as in the multiple pressure points on dogs that produce reflexive action when stimulated above a minimal threshold, stimulating several pressure points simultaneously creates a result where the combined effect of the stimuli are greater than the sum of the individual stimuli. In other words, while no one channel of communication may be enough to mobilize activists or policymakers to action, leveraging multiple channels simultaneously will always maximize your impact.

By initially engaging its entire activist e-mail audience and its social media influencer audience, American Progress was able to mobilize a core of diehard supporters, both for the ENOUGH campaign, specifically, and for its ongoing engagement and promotion of its policy work, generally. After casting this broad net, it now knows who among its audience it can depend upon to take action on critical campaigns and promotions.

In addition the specific success of the ENOUGH conflict mineral campaign, American Progress is able to show a rich collection of measurable results. For example, across its most popular social media channels, it is able to generate an average of 20,000 clicks on the URLs it shares with its audience each month. Its tweets are retweeted between 10,000 and 20,000 times each month. Its social media audience exceeds 160,000 direct followers and fans (130,000+ followers on Twitter and 35,000+ fans on Facebook). Its YouTube videos have been viewed more than 5 million times. And it has nearly 50 policy experts and bloggers, as well as about 25 policy project and organizational brand channels promoting its work and engaging its audiences on social media, allowing people to choose what issues they want to hear about and who they want to hear it from.

Beyond these measurable results, American Progress has seen other major think tanks, especially its ideological competitors, emulating its strategy, and dozens of other progressive organizations have asked American Progress to train them on social media strategy. These votes of confidence from competitors and allies alike are a great validation for American Progress's social media strategy.

Alan Rosenblatt is the Associate Director for Online Advocacy at the Center for American Progress and the Center for American Progress Action Fund. He is a frequent speaker and author on digital media, advocacy, and politics, including social networking, blogging, grassroots, and mobile advocacy strategies. He is the founder of the Internet Advocacy Center and the Internet Advocacy Roundtable, as well as an adjunct professor at Georgetown, Johns Hopkins, and American Universities, where he teaches courses on Digital Political Strategies, and Internet Advocacy Communications. He is a blogger at the Huffington Post and TechPresident.com, and a former fellow at George Washington University's Institute for Politics, Democracy, and the Internet. Alan serves on the editorial boards of several scholarly journals dedicated to the study of the Internet, politics, and government, and is a member of the Board of Directors for E-Democracy.org. He taught Political Science at George Mason University for nine years, where, in 1995, he launched the first ever Internet politics course. Alan has a Ph.D. in Political Science from American University, an M.A. in Political Science from Boston College, and a B.A. in Political Science and Philosophy from Tufts University.

Alan J Rosenblatt, Ph.D.
alanrosenblatt@gmail.com
@DrDigipol
http://Facebook.com/DrDigipol
http://www.linkedin.com/in/alanrosenblatt
http://internetadvocacycenter.com
+1-703-282-7157

GovLuv

by

Wayne Moses Burke

Social media is not really about technology. It's about a cultural shift that is enabled by the evolution of technology. I've been working to apply social media to communication between citizens and their elected officials since April 2008 and have learned a thing or two of interest. Some of those lessons relate to social media implementation and some of them relate to how our system of government actually works.

My goals in presenting this case study are to share my knowledge while presenting you with an overview of the trials and tribulations that I've experienced on this fascinating journey.

Who Am I and How Did I Get Into This?

I run a small nonprofit based in Washington, DC, called the Open Forum Foundation. I founded it in April 2008 when I realized the serious disconnect that exists between the citizens of the United States and their elected officials. To my midwestern sensibilities, this conflicted with everything I believed about this country when growing up. Elected leaders make laws that determine how the United States operates, and the people elect those leaders to ensure that their concerns are taken into account during the process. Without any legitimate and reliable means of communication between the two, the entire system is a farce.

To add insult to injury, I knew technology had advanced such that it was possible to video chat with people in India, and yet it was still not possible for every U.S. citizen to reliably send a message to their elected officials that would be understood and responded to in a meaningful way.

Something had to be done.

But first, a little background:

I had come to DC eight months prior to this realization with a freshly minted master's degree in international relations from New York University, effectively no contacts, and a desire to work in foreign policy. Now, my background is both diverse and entrepreneurial, which I thought would be very attractive in the sometimes insular community that is DC politics. I have traveled extensively, both domestically and globally; lived in Michigan, New York, California, and New Mexico; worked in a wide range of industries, including manufacturing, computers, web design and coding, hypnotherapy, and electoral reform; and to top it off, I have a bachelor's degree in engineering from the University of Michigan.

Unfortunately, job hunting is a skill that I have never mastered, and my competition for positions in foreign policy had started their training at the age of 3 and completed internships at the White House, State Department, Capitol Hill, or even foreign embassies. This made my job hunting in DC more difficult than I had anticipated.

The Shifting Nature of Chasing a Big Goal

My realization that citizen engagement was ineffective couldn't have come at a better time. I was intensely frustrated with doing nothing (my take on job hunting) and excited about the prospect of starting an organization and working on something meaningful. And just to be clear: the goal was to enable effective communication between citizens and their elected officials.

Initial Vision

The first night that I came to this conclusion, I barely slept as I began to think about what could be done. I had all the key skills to pull this together. I understood technology and the Internet, I had learned how DC works and begun to build a network of connections, and I had an outsider's perspective. I could see possibilities that someone steeped in the traditions of citizen engagement was blind to. I dreamed of a Web site that would provide everything that citizens, elected officials, and advocacy groups needed to communicate effectively.

So, I started my research. I talked to people that worked on Capitol Hill, such as lobbyists and staffers, to see if my ideas were sound. I spent hours on the Internet trying to determine who was already in the field and what they were doing (there is no need to duplicate good work if it can be supplemented instead). And I began to learn about the complexities of starting and running a nonprofit organization, while simultaneously struggling with whether this could be accomplished as a for-profit.

I was familiar with running small, for-profit companies, and nonprofits are complex in a lot of ways, not the least of which is obtaining and maintaining 501(c)3 tax status. But my vision was grandiose and in the end, I chose nonprofit status for one main reason: I was determined to develop a Web site that would become THE channel of communication between citizens and elected officials. If I was going to build a single channel for communication, it could not be run by a company because monopolies are illegal, and it could not be run by the government because history is filled with dictatorships who maintain their power by controlling the media through which they communicate with their citizens.

I spent the rest of the summer thinking through what I was about to build and clarifying how it would work. I started with social networking functionality that would be immediately accessible to any Internet user, having become popular on sites like MySpace, Facebook, and LinkedIn. I then adapted it so that it would fit the unique constraints that the offices of members of Congress work under. I took into account the needs of advocacy groups, who drive the majority of the messages that reach the Hill today. And I added on educational resources that would be maintained in a fashion similar to the community-based Wikipedia.

I topped this off with a sustainability model that mimicked Wikipedia or NPR. When you provide a system that millions of people use, a small percentage of them making small donations adds up to sufficient capital to maintain and improve the system. I was particularly attracted to this, as it ensured that the survival of the site was based on its ability to meet the needs of its most important constituency: the citizens themselves.

Platform

As I got to know people that worked in citizen engagement and learned more about Internet culture at the time, it soon became apparent to me that a Web site was insufficient to accomplish my goals. My ideas were sound, but I wasn't thinking big enough. Increasingly, people didn't want a destination site for information or services, they wanted immediate availability that fit into their lives with minimal disruption. Twitter was just gaining in popularity and provides the quintessential example. They provided a very simple service[1], but made it easily available for anyone to build on top of through their open Application Programming Interface (API). At the time, there were over 2,000 independently created clients that would enable an individual to access their Twitter account from other Web sites, stand-alone programs installed on a computer, and through applications for the iPhone, Blackberry, and other mobile devices. While related, this is fundamentally different from a Web site.

In my case, this meant creating technology that would be available wherever political discussion was happening, and at the time that it was happening. This should include blogs and online discussion forums, social networking and advocacy group Web sites, and mobile devices via both Internet connectivity and SMS. Of course, none of this relieves the need for a Web site that provides the same functionality and more. This by no means lessened my burden, but rather complicated it, while at the same time showing me what would have to be done if I was to be successful.

Infrastructure

Starting in January 2009[2], a new movement took root in Washington, DC. At the time, it was called Gov2.0, although today it also goes by the moniker OpenGov,

---

1 Exchange of short status messages, http://twitter.com/.
2 And driven in large part by the optimism brought with the change of Presidential Administration from George W. Bush to Barack Obama.

based on the Open Government Memo that President Obama signed on January 21, 2009[3]. This movement was driven by optimism for the value that technology could bring to government, especially in terms of enhancing transparency, participation, and collaboration[4]. This movement found its legs with a series of unrelated barcamps, beginning with TransparencyCamp[5] and followed by Gov2.0Camp[6] and eDemocracyCamp[7]. This was an incredibly exciting time to be in Washington, DC, as government employees, contractors, social media experts, technology gurus, and governmental idealists met to share ideas and figure out what was possible.

It was during this period of knowledge sharing and challenging that I realized I still wasn't dreaming big enough. A single platform could only accomplish so much and it would always allow opportunities for competition. Multiple providers of communication channels would result in a splitting of the data and a consequent reduction in the usefulness of the platform for everyone involved. Given that, I needed to think in terms of developing technological infrastructure. E-mail is a good analogy. There are many providers of e-mail, but they are all interoperable. In this way, the platform that I was developing could be released as open source with a set of standards for exchange of information on the backend that would enable data sharing between multiple instances. This would allow for local customization of the end user interface while still building a fully interoperable system that could link the people and governments of the world in a meaningful and reliable communication system.

With all the organizational paperwork filed, a full understanding of what I needed to create, and a network that included all the necessary connections to build the right technology and get it adopted, I set off to find a developer.

This proved more difficult than I would have imagined.

Luckily, I attended a series of events in New York in late June[8] and reconnected with Jim Gilliam. Jim had gained some notoriety in the Gov2.0 space for WhiteHouse2.com, a site that he built in a week or two with the goal of "imagining how the White House might work if it was run completely democratically by thousands of people over the internet." Everyone I've ever talked to agreed that Jim was the best developer working in the space. He and I had lunch, discussed our goals for the future and found that his skills and my connections in DC were a perfect match. We immediately began planning what

---

3   Some may argue that these names have more specific meanings and deserve to be differentiated in further ways, but that is secondary to this discussion. For all intents and purposes, they can be considered to be synonymous.

4   As laid out in the Open Government Memo, http://www.whitehouse.gov/the_press_office/TransparencyandOpenGovernment/.

5   Put on by the Sunlight Foundation, http://transparencycamp.org/.

6   Initiated by Maxine Teller and led by Peter Corbett, Mark Drapeau, and Jeffrey Levy, http://barcamp.org/Government20Camp.

7   Focused on the participation side of things, http://barcamp.org/eDemocracyCamp2.

8   ParticipationCamp and the Personal Democracy Forum.

we were going to do. I set up meetings with Congressional offices to ensure that we understood their main problems while he cleared his schedule of other projects.

Jim is based in Los Angeles, so we kept in touch via regular Skype video chats. On Friday the week before my first meetings on the Hill, we were scheduled to finalize my presentation, but Jim had other thoughts in mind. He had recently put up a site called Act.ly[9] that utilized Twitter's viral nature to spread petitions. The growth of this site had been phenomenal and had him thinking about the rise of Twitter in the political space and how we could leverage that to our benefit. He proposed that whatever we were about to build should use Twitter for communication. While this was significantly different than what we were planning, and a difficult shift to adjust to, it had several benefits:

1. Part of the complexity of creating a social network is creating the culture of the network. For instance, in some networks it's expected that you will use your real name, in others it's perfectly acceptable to be anonymous. This is just one example of many considerations that need to be made when building a social network. This was particularly true for us since our goal was to build a system that would engender trust and respect between the participants. Twitter had already done this work.

2. Offices were actively adopting Twitter and working to figure it out. If we could support that and become the main interface used by offices, we would be in a good position to add additional functionality and build a site that could accomplish our more grandiose dreams.

3. Political communication was already happening on Twitter. Representatives were tweeting, citizens were tweeting to their representatives, advocacy groups were tweeting and driving political discussion through it. We wouldn't have to attract individuals to have conversations before our platform was interesting, we just had to make sense of the conversations that were already occurring. This was a much easier task.

So off we went, and by early September, we had a beta version running at http://GovLuv.org/[10]. I suggest you have a look at it. It's pretty cool (although I am biased). Our goal was to build a meaningful two-way communication tool that would lessen the inflammatory discussion and enable legitimate engagement between citizens and their representatives. Here are some of the innovations that we built:

1. Identification of constituents. Citizens can put in their address, get a list of their Representatives from local to Federal, and see which ones are on Twitter. Each Representative has their own page. While this constituent

---

9 A Twitter petition site, http://act.ly/.
10 Incidentally, this entire project was volunteer, including the name and design which were contributed by Christiana Aretta, http://storiography.com/.

identification was not verified, it was a first step towards enabling Representatives to distinguish between constituents and the rest of the world.[11]

2. Conversations. We put both tweets sent by the Representative and tweets that mentioned the Representative into the same stream so that the back and forth could begin to be noticeable.

3. Multiple accounts. Each Representative cannot only have multiple accounts, but also distinguish between four different types of accounts: official, staff, personal, and campaign. For the average person, this may not make a difference, but in order to abide by rules in Congress meant that it was very important to ensure that official resources are not used for campaigning[12].

4. Trending Tags. At the top of each Representative's tweet stream, we listed the top ten tags that appeared in their stream. Clicking on any of these would only show the corresponding tweets. This provided a quick overview of what the current topics of conversation were for that specific Representative.

We soft launched GovLuv to make certain we had time to be responsive and solve problems as they came up (they always come up). It was well received on the Hill and by social media experts and the Gov2.0 community, but was lacking in one very important category: adoption by the average user. After considerable deliberation, we came to the conclusion that we were too early in the citizen engagement cycle. We were pioneering new ground, and citizens weren't ready for it yet.

Let me explain. For years, most citizens have been apathetic about what their government is doing (if you doubt this, you didn't grow up in the same America that I did). My personal belief is that one of the main drivers of this is that no one believed they could have any impact on the decisions that were being made, so it was easier to simply ignore the government, or rather focus on the things in life that you do have control over. Fast forward to today: social media has created the promise that citizens can reach out to their Representatives and have an interaction that could actually make a difference. Advocacy groups spread this message and if we can video chat with people in India, this has to be possible, right? Unfortunately, the tools to make this a reality have not yet been created or adopted. It's true that the messages can be delivered, but once an office is flooded with messages that it can't parse, what good has been

---

11 The constituent verification used four methods. For anyone that tweeted to a political Twitter account in the system, these things would happen: 1) their Twitter bio location would be checked, 2) if they used a hashtag zip code, e.g. #20009, to identify themselves, we would pick this up, 3) if they visited GovLuv and logged in, we would pick up the IP address they logged in from and guess their location, and 4) it would be requested that visitors submit their addresses.

12 E.g., Franking rules on the House side and Senate rules on the Senate side.

accomplished? We designed GovLuv to be a huge step in this direction, and in retrospect perhaps it was too huge a step.

Upon further examination of the way social media is being used to communicate to Representatives, we found that it is actually acting more like a relief valve for citizen's frustrations (I refer to it as the cathartic phase of citizen engagement). Instead of having discussions and sending meaningful messages, citizens and advocacy groups are utilizing the available channels to effectively yell at elected officials. The ease with which anyone with a computer or a smart phone may voice exactly how they're feeling at that moment directly to their elected officials has created an emotionally charged deluge of incoming messages. Many of these are not intended to engender discussion, and very few expect a response.

In my eternal optimism, I hope that this emotional discharge will play out and make room for the type of meaningful dialogue that we designed GovLuv to elicit, and not just because I think GovLuv is a great tool (although I do), but because I think it's critical not only to the future of the United States, but the future of good government.

In the meantime, there's other work to be done.

Supporting and Building a Great Community

If I were to pretend that GovLuv's moderate acceptance amongst the public was not disheartening, I would be doing us all a disservice. GovLuv is still live and fully operational: collating tweets, sorting twitter accounts into their districts (over 360,000 Americans identified at this point), and providing a valuable service to certain advocacy groups that see its benefit[13]. Had it become wildly successful, I suppose I would still be working on it full time. But that's not what happened, and I spent December again questioning the direction I was going and whether or not it was the right one.

While I was on the Hill, extolling the virtues of GovLuv and helping offices to understand the value that not only it could bring to them, but also that Twitter and other forms of social media could bring, I noticed something about our interactions. I had the same feeling when discussing GovLuv at conferences and with other social media experts and in the OpenGov community. I was no longer a neutral player in the game of improving citizen engagement. I had a product that I was selling, and it changed the way people interacted with me. Now, this is not to degrade selling a specific product in any form or fashion, except to say that something didn't feel right about it.

While considering my next steps and reviewing the past, I came to another realization at the same time. There will never be a single communication platform that connects citizens to governments. When the Constitution was signed, there were three: personal interaction, letters, and published media, which included newspapers, magazines, and books. Since then, we've only

---

13 Thanks to Alan Rosenblatt.

added more: telegraph, radio, TV, phone, fax, and now Internet-based technologies, and none of the previous ones have gone away (yes, you actually *can* still send a telegram). In retrospect, when I was talking about being the main channel of communication between citizens and elected officials, it almost seems as if I had my eyes closed.

So there I was. Twenty months into something that suddenly seemed as if it was destined to fail from the beginning. After much deliberation, I figured that given the unique knowledge and connections that I had developed, I had two options. 1) Give up the nonprofit and form a company to build what I had originally set out to build (I knew of no one better positioned to do this successfully), or 2) use my nonprofit status to support the community that is building citizen engagement software.

In pondering this, the decision became clear rather quickly. My goal from the beginning was to solve the citizen engagement dilemma that our country finds itself in. As one competitor amongst a growing host, my impact would be limited. But working with the developers and vendors that are building and selling citizen engagement software would offer a unique vantage point from which to make significant contributions to the direction and development of the market. This also fit well with my temperament—I enjoy bringing people together and enabling collaboration even more than I enjoy developing technology. This was a bit of a personal revelation that came as a bonus.

Unfortunately, I had no idea where to start. The concept was there, but the pragmatic implementation plan still lagged.

My next realization was that all the networking I had been doing with the OpenGov, social media, and Congressional communities lacked an entire swath of the citizen engagement market: the established vendors. This includes vendors that sell software to Congressional offices and advocacy groups as well as PR firms that consult on and manage software for advocacy groups. These organizations were not represented in any of the discussions or at any of the events that I had come to think of as determining the future of citizen engagement, not just with Congress but with government more broadly.

So I invited everyone to a workshop called Creating GREAT Citizen Engagement Software[14], where we discussed the realities of the market as it stands today. The result was a realization that the problem with the current system is due to a fundamental mismatch between the expectations of citizens and the capabilities of Representatives to respond. To say it another way, there is a cultural shift occurring in the relationship between citizens and Representatives, and technology alone will not solve this problem. We defined the goal for the two day workshop as to "redefine the relationship between citizens and their elected officials."

---

14 Workshop invite at http://j.mp/GREATces.

Of course, we weren't really able to accomplish this by the end of the workshop, so the attendees agreed to establish an association to continue the work. This association includes developers, vendors of citizen engagement software, and draws from a diversity of organizations, including nonprofits, startups and well established companies whose target audiences are citizens, representatives, and advocacy groups. In short, we started out covering the full range of organizations that are engaged in the market, and are working to expand on that.

It's called the Open Model for Citizen Engagement and is unique in several ways. First of all, it's surrounded by a community that is free for anyone to join. This ensures that citizens, elected officials, and advocacy groups can participate in the discussions along with the developers and vendors. Second, the majority of activities are documented on the Web site[15]. You've heard the term social network (e.g., Facebook), most likely professional network (e.g., LinkedIn), and you may have even heard that Twitter is now referring to itself as an information network. Well, the Open Model Web site is really set up to be an activity network. That is, the majority of the groups on the site are all arranged around documenting and moving forward on active projects. This keeps the focus on the mission: "defining and implementing a new paradigm of communication for citizens and their elected officials."

There's still a lot of work to be done in this arena, but while it has been difficult at times, I'm confident that with each new direction and effort, I've made progress towards accomplishing the goal I set at the very beginning of this journey.

Lessons Learned

I hope that you've found inspiration (or at least entertainment) in reading about my personal trials and tribulations as I've pursued my goal. But I would feel remiss if I didn't provide you with something tangibly useful to apply as you work to implement social media in your specific context.

Strategy

Social media implementation is not about technology. The technology only creates possibilities for change, and the hard part about change is getting people to do it. In reality, what we're talking about with the introduction and adoption of social media is cultural change, and that's never easy to lead.

The good news is that you are probably better prepared to deal with this than you would think. Here are some general guidelines:

1. *What's your end goal?* Be clear about what you're trying to accomplish. It may be grandiose like mine: "enable legitimate and reliable communication between citizens and their elected Representatives," or more down to earth, "improve our customer service." Either way, you'll

---

15 http://om4ce.org/.

need to check back in on this occasionally to make sure you're going in the right direction.

2. *Understand the current culture.* You have to know where you're coming from in order to create a legitimate plan for getting somewhere else. How will people respond to the changes you're presenting? How will it affect their work flow or the way they interact with customers or one another? How hard will it be for them to learn? The answers to these questions vary from person to person and from one situation to the next. Understanding the culture you're influencing will provide these answers, almost intuitively.

3. *Have a vision for what the new world will look like and how it will work.* This gives you the ability to plan where you're going and be excited about it. Enthusiasm is contagious. Share the benefits you see on the horizon, and how things will be better. Don't be shy about dreaming big, but remember to take into account the culture you're working with, as not everyone will be excited about the same things.

4. *Stay flexible.* Wherever you're headed is NOT where you're going to end up. The vision that you have will change when it meets reality. There's always more going on within any organization than you're aware of. When it seems that you've been derailed, just check back in with your end goal, consider your options, and keep moving forward.

5. *Get buy-in wherever possible.* Ideally, you want everyone to be involved and excited. The people at the top have to approve (at least tacitly) of what you're doing, and the people at the bottom are normally the ones that will be most affected by the changes. Anyone in between may be a road block to your progress, so try to be inclusive from the beginning.

With that as a goal, let's be realistic. There's someone you're thinking of right now that you will never get to participate. You have to figure out how to deal with this. You're the expert in this regard (see above #2). Sometimes you can work around them and when everyone else has changed, they'll come along because they've seen the benefits (or they don't have a choice). Sometimes you have to introduce things gradually and show the benefits of each. Sometimes you have to make a stand and be strong in your convictions. I'm not going to pretend that it's easy or that there's a single answer, but I will assure you that it's possible.

One other thing to look out for is that sometimes being inclusive works against you. You may get someone involved who claims to agree with your end goal, but in actuality spends every meeting tearing apart your ideas while not contributing any solutions. Again, how you deal with this will differ depending upon the situation, but you need to get them away from the others. Ask them to stop participating, give them something specific to work on, limit their access to group discussions, or bring them around in such a way that they can be beneficial to your work.

6. *Timing.* I love the old expression, "How can you tell the true pioneers? They have arrows in them." You don't want that to be you, but you may not have a choice if you believe in what you're doing and the culture you're trying to change is just not ready. If you're too early in introducing new ideas, then the ideas will simply not take hold[16]. The difficulty here is telling if you're too early or not. This has to do with your understanding of the culture that you're trying to change, but is also influenced by your own strength of will, desire to make the change, and how much respect you have from the other people whose culture you are trying to influence.

7. *It's going to suck.* This is a complete overstatement, but easy to remember and has really helped me out when things don't go well. Here are some basic truths:

   • Things will not go as you intended. This is why staying flexible is so important.

   • You will fail, repeatedly if you're lucky. This is how we learn. If you're successful the first time, you only learn one means of success and don't have any idea why it succeeded. When you fail, you learn the depth of a topic and are better prepared for difficulties in the future. Remember, it's not over when you fail, it's over when you give up.

   • It doesn't matter if it sucks, at least not if you believe in your end goal. Cultural change is hard, for everybody. Just keep working at it and you'll get there.

Catch-44

Maxine Teller[17] was the impetus for Gov2.0Camp and is a brilliant social media strategist that works with Federal agencies. She refers to adoption of social media as a catch-44. Here's why: effective use of social media requires an understanding of the value of collaboration.

1. In order to understand the value of collaboration, you have to collaborate, but if you haven't collaborated before, why would you want to do this? It's a catch-22.

2. By the same token, you have to use social media in order to understand the value that it brings, but why would you want to use if you don't understand its value? A second catch-22.

Taken together, she calls this a catch-44. Luckily, these parallel catch-22's are not literal, and it actually is possible to introduce collaboration and social media to skeptical individuals and organizations. However, you may want to start by

---

16 This is not quite as complex as the movie Inception, but there certainly are parallels.
17 http://mixtmedia.com/.

introducing them separately, for example, by making meetings more collaborative and finding ways that individuals may engage with social media for their own personal benefits (e.g., if you use Twitter in DC, it's the easiest way to communicate with certain portions of the DC Government or the local cable provider, Comcast).

Barcamps

One in-person collaborative experience that has been significant in the spread and adoption of OpenGov ideas throughout government in Washington, DC, is the use of barcamps. These are participant-driven events that have a specific focus that the attendees are passionate about, and begin with the participants themselves determining the agenda for the day. The events I mentioned earlier are all examples of this (TransparencyCamp, Gov2.0Camp, and eDemocracyCamp), and there have been many more in Washington, DC, since then. These are easy to plan and implement, although there are a few tricks if you're doing it by yourself for the first time[18]. The value of this sort of event is that the collaborative experience it provides is not explicit, but rather a side effect of the participants being able to make significant progress while working on a goal that is relevant to their work or interests.

A final word about government

I grew up as jaded as anyone. I was completely apathetic until about six years ago. I came to DC thinking as much of the world does, that politics here is corrupt, driven by power and money and the desire to maintain them both.

I'm not going to say that's entirely false, but it is definitively NOT the entire story. I have met and worked with a lot of people spread throughout the government and the companies that serve it. This includes people from the Department of Defense to the USDA, the House, the Senate, contractors and vendors, and what I have been most surprised about is their general sincerity for wanting to make government better. A lot of what we on the outside perceive as corruption is nothing more than inefficiency that has been built into the system over 230 years of conflicting rules and regulations from the myriad diverse viewpoints that have run the country and the myriad problems that they have wrestled with, and for the most part, solved.

Please, next time you're angry with the ridiculously inane thing that the government just did, remember that the person on the other end of the phone is most likely even more frustrated than you are. There are many good people who are overwhelmed with information and the demands on their time, who are in many ways hamstrung by rules and regulations that may not make any sense in the modern context.

---

18 See http://barcamp.org/ for basic information and http://www.openspaceworld.org/ for more information about the underlying technology that enables successful barcamps.

If we're going to change the relationship that exists between citizens and their government, it's going to take both sides working to understand the other and find ways to move forward together.

Wayne Moses Burke
wayne@openforumfoundation.org
@wmburke
http://linkedin.com/in/wmburke
http://openforumfoundation.org

Transforming Transportation with Social Media:
A Case Study of the Orange County Transportation Authority

By

Ted Nguyen

In late 2008, the economic recession hit Orange County very hard. Dramatic losses in funding from both federal and state sources left the Orange County Transportation Authority (OCTA) struggling to find different ways of reducing costs while still continuing to deliver and communicate transportation projects. Because of the associated costs of traditional communications tactics, OCTA's team turned to cost-effective social media tools to continue public involvement.

OCTA first took social media for a test drive with a program to garner public support for Orange County to receive its fair share of federal stimulus funds from the American Recovery and Reinvestment Act. Not only did on-the-street YouTube videos, Facebook discussion boards, and a first-of-its-kind interactive Web site help OCTA secure $212 million in federal stimulus funds for transportation projects, but it became increasingly clear that social media was an effective way to engage with the public. Using this first successful experience as a springboard, the OCTA communications team developed a "public e-volvement" program utilizing cost-effective high-tech tools to complement traditional public participation and outreach tactics with an integrated communications approach.

Research

The OCTA team researched social media by attending conferences, participating in webinars, and reading blogs and articles written by some of the nation's leading social media experts. Learning the lingo of social media was one of the first challenges. Online conversations on Twitter include "hashtags," "@ mentions," and even "Follow Fridays." OCTA dove head first into social media by attending the first "tweetup" with the Social Media Club of Orange County.

It was immediately apparent that social media is not just about the online tools, but the vital offline connections. For practical hands-on research, a team of college interns created a Twitter account and began to learn the ropes of digital communications, while others researched the latest online trends and other government organizations using social media. The research showed that it's not really about the individual tools. The one common thread across all social media platforms is the one-to-one human connection with the public. And that it was possible to cultivate and build fans one person at a time by breaking down the walls of bureaucratic communications and literally putting a face on the organization.

OCTA is doing this by building a reputation, demonstrating expertise, sharing information, helping people, and most importantly, listening before talking. Conversations about OCTA, transportation issues in Orange County, and traffic on the I-5 are already happening online, and if team members are not there to engage, the public is losing out. The challenge: not everyone was on board with social media. Executive management was hesitant to grant the public communications department access to Twitter, YouTube, and Facebook. Even members of the team resisted the shift to digital communications.

Planning

• Organize social media panel discussions and hands-on workshops for local government and nonprofit organizations

• Position OCTA as a Gov 2.0 pioneer and a national model for government agencies using social media effectively to enhance transparency and accountability

• Create an online tool kit to help other organizations start on social media

• Develop a social media guide to help other government agencies understand social media

• Integrate social media into OCTA's public communications department's programs

• Share with local universities and professional organizations through speaker presentations

The OCTA public communications team developed the "public e-volvement" program without the use of any consultant help, and all materials and content were produced in-house. While laying the groundwork, a team of three full-time staff and two interns devoted a couple of hours a day to develop the "public e-volvement" program. Now that the framework was created, social media is seamlessly integrated into all OCTA projects and programs on a daily basis, just as any other outreach tactic. The best hearts and minds of social media gathered at OCTA to discuss how to utilize social media to create transparency and accountability, as well as bring a level of authenticity to the seemingly endless and faceless bureaucracy of government and public agencies.

Billed as GOV 2.0, an overcapacity crowd of seventy-five Orange County professionals gathered in the Summer of 2009 to exchange tips and share best practices for popular social media sites like Twitter, Facebook, and YouTube. Hundreds of other people followed the event via live Twitter updates, and others from as far as Lithuania, Germany, and Asia participated via a live streaming video. It was the first event of its kind for government and public agencies in Orange County. Based on the overwhelming popularity of our first installment of Gov 2.0, the team invited local government agencies to attend hands-on workshops led by leading experts in Twitter, YouTube, Facebook, and LinkedIn. A third Gov 2.0 panel discussion with a keynote speaker leading the Gov 2.0 movement, Dr. Mark Drapeau, was held in December 2009 for local governments, public agencies, and citizens, with the goal of encouraging more transparent, responsive, and accountable government.

The communications team also unveiled an online tool for OCTA's new "public e-volvement" program that utilizes social media to complement our traditional mix of outreach and communications tactics. At OCTA, the communications team members are not the experts on social media by any measure of the imagination. But the team has picked up some nuggets of knowledge and garnered success along the way. OCTA also experienced some pitfalls during its social media journey. As a public agency serving Orange County's taxpayers, it can't help but share with others in government and public agencies because OCTA cares about enhancing the community. That's the point of it all—to help each other "get" social media and share it.

Implementation

• Create a robust OCTA Twitter presence with a main account and several project-specific pages

• Develop a main OCTA Facebook fan page with sub-pages for major construction projects and transportation enhancement programs

• Create an OCTA YouTube channel and post weekly two-minute videos highlighting current transportation projects and initiatives

• Communicate the importance of rail safety using social media sites

• Generate awareness of stimulus-funded SR-91 eastbound widening project by inviting southern California social media practitioners to participate in a groundbreaking ceremony

• Create a personalized transportation blog that featured YouTube videos, audio interviews, and music slideshows

• Revitalize CEO's weekly e-newsletter with an improved design and interactive social media tools with the knowledge gained from social media research

OCTA used Twitter as a communications tool for reputation and issues management, media relations, outreach for project studies, and construction communications, with the primary goal of enhancing OCTA's reputation of being transparent. To create awareness and visibility of OCTA's projects and services, the team created a main OCTA Facebook fan page, used to engage with the public by answering questions and sharing relevant and timely transportation information.

By monitoring conversations on Twitter, the communications team intercepted negative tweets and built lasting positive relationships with some of OCTA's critics. Using an inexpensive Flip video camera, the OCTA communications team filmed and edited weekly YouTube segments called "Transportation in 2" (2 for two-minute segments). Not only do these videos enhance the transportation agency's authenticity, but the team also has been able to capture some major milestones on camera, including the unveiling of the Orange County Gateway sign, the high-speed rail press conference, and the SR-91 groundbreaking ceremony.

The communications team is also utilizing the power of social media to discuss a serious issue: safety along hundreds of miles of train tracks in Orange County. A Twitter account and Facebook page for rail safety helps keep community members safe around the railroad tracks. Just days before the groundbreaking, OCTA created a new Twitter account, @91FWY, to provide information about Orange County's largest stimulus project. The SR-91 groundbreaking event was OCTA's first to utilize social media to share instant information via Twitter and Facebook. The @91fwy Twitter account will help OCTA listen to the public and address questions and issues as they are posted.

Evaluation

Social media humanizes OCTA as an agency that's not simply focused on improving roads, freeways, railways, and buses. It's also about effectively communicating with the public and helping provide them with information they need to make their lives better. In these times of greater public accountability and transparency, social media is providing impressive cost-effective results for OCTA. Social media, along with traditional outreach, strengthens OCTA's ability to communicate with residents, businesses, the traveling public, and other stakeholders.

• An overwhelming number of participants agreed that the Gov 2.0 events were relevant, engaging, and well-organized.

• @TedNguyen reached 59,874 people with 94,035 impressions during the first Gov 2.0 panel discussion.

• Tweets containing the hashtag #ocgov reached 43,166 people with 260,845 impressions during the third installment of Gov 2.0.

• As a result of highly successful Gov 2.0 sessions, local government agencies and nonprofits, including the city of Anaheim, the Orange County League of Cities, and the Orange County Sanitation District, have joined social media networks.

• The shared social media guide and "public e-volvement" toolkit with 1,500 people has received positive feedback.

• The OCTA team has led the way with the most Twitter followers for any transportation or public agency with more than 30,000 followers.

• After building a positive relationship through social media with once critic Steven Chan of the Transit Advocates of Orange County, he now frequently posts OCTA project information to his blog with kudos to the OCTA communications team.

• News stories generated by local, state, and national publications provided media credibility for the program.

• The CEO's e-newsletter tripled readership with 4,000 people with 90% saying that it provides timely information.

• OCTA utilized social media exclusively on a transit forum that became the number one trending topic on Twitter in southern California for that time period.

• The OCTA social media program was named California's top communications program by the California Association of Public Information Officers. The program has also won top honors from the Public Relations Society of America's Protos Awards.

Ted Nguyen oversees public communications and media relations activities for the Orange County Transportation Authority (OCTA). Ted has faced and overcome numerous public relations challenges during his more than fifteen years of work in communications. His most recent accomplishment for OCTA includes winning the communications industry's most-prestigious honor, the national Silver Anvil award from the Public Relations Society of America, in 2008 for best issues management program during a ten-day strike of bus drivers. The previous year, the OCTA team won the national award of excellence from PRSA for its community relations program for construction outreach for the Garden Grove Freeway (SR-22). In 2007, Ted was honored as the "PR Person of the Year" by PR News magazine at the National Press Club in Washington, D.C.

Employment

TweetMyJOBS

By

Gary Zukowski

November, 2008. The IT consulting market was at an all-time low. My consulting firm was feeling the heat. The phone rings. A local Hedge Fund owner wants me to evaluate social media technology for a product he's come up with. I had been dabbling with social media for the past few years, but not from a development standpoint. So I spend a couple of weeks researching platforms, languages, trends, and the future landscape of social media. Twitter comes on my radar. It's not a very intuitive interface, and there's not a lot of help on the site as to how to use it for development. But the media seems to be touting it as the next killer app. Business models will start to be formed on this open, real-time search and distribution platform, they say. A few days later, I get an e-mail from a friend in Charlotte, suggesting that I start tweeting out job openings for my consulting firm on my Twitter account. I had been using LinkedIn for a few years for networking and recruiting, with pretty decent results, so why not try another social media channel? So I start tweeting out job openings, saw my follower count increase a little bit, but really didn't get much response. Were my tweets going into a black hole? Were there any people on Twitter looking for jobs? What was the problem?

Then it hit me.

Putting my feet in the shoes of a jobseeker, I realized what was missing. Jobseekers don't want just ANY job opening, they want jobs that are relevant to THEM. Since I was tweeting all my job openings on one Twitter account, jobseekers were getting a lot of jobs that they either didn't care about or didn't qualify for. A salesperson in Chicago doesn't care about nursing positions in Boston. That's just Twitter noise. I needed to be more targeted with my tweets. But how can I do that with Twitter? The answer was simple: Job Channels. Why not create a directory of Twitter accounts for a given location and a given functional job type? Chicago Sales, Boston Nursing, San Francisco IT, etc. That way, a jobseeker can simply select which Job Channel(s) they are interested in, follow them, and then only those jobs will appear in their feed.

There it was. A potential business on Twitter. Why not create a service that allows companies to distribute jobs on Twitter via a network of Job Channels? Corporations get the ability to target jobseekers for ALL their jobs, and jobseekers just get the jobs they want. And the great part is that Twitter is instant. Jobseekers get the jobs in their Twitter feed or on their cellphone within seconds. In an economy that requires jobseekers to look for any competitive advantage, "first to know" might just be the difference between getting an interview or not.

I've had many ideas in the past of new business opportunities, and have gone down the path of some of them, but they had rarely amounted to anything. This, however, felt different. The more I thought about the possibilities, the more excited I got. But maybe that was just me. So I floated the idea past two people who would give me honest feedback on the idea—my wife Lauriana, and my college buddy and good friend Rich Trombetta. Both loved the idea. Traditional job boards like Monster and CareerBuilder had become too large, and jobseekers were starting to feel like a number. This could really be something unique that could give them a run for their numbers. A Monster killer.

It took three weeks to develop the first release. Very basic, but it had the ability for jobseekers to subscribe to Job Channels, and allowed companies to post jobs which would be tweeted to Job Channels. We created around 300 Job Channels for major U.S. metros and prominent job types. A feed was set up with SimplyHired to provide a backfill of job postings until we get companies to post jobs. I asked Rich to help out with marketing, business development, and sales. Lauriana would be our Community Manager on Social Media. February 17, 2009, was targeted for the launch date. E-mail blasts were sent, Facebook and Linkedin posts were made, Google ads were posted. First day: 125 jobseekers. Second day: 150 jobseekers. Third day: I get an e-mail from a recruiter in Canada, asking for Job Channels in Canada. Why not? Then came an e-mail from someone in the UK asking for channels as well. Next came Ireland, Germany, and the Netherlands. I start thinking, "Hey, this thing just might have some legs!"

Within a month of launch, the media started paying attention. I get calls from the local network affiliates, and get to be featured on the six o'clock news for our local NBC, ABC, and CBS stations. PC Magazine puts out a column in March, 2009 of the top 20 online job boards, and we make the list. CNN does a piece on their website about us. NPR interviews me. All without a dime of advertising.

I heard about our first jobseeker success story on March 26, 2009. A jobseeker in NY had been looking for work for six months, had spent countless hours on the traditional job boards to no avail, had paid one thousand dollars for a resume rewrite, and still couldn't land a job. He discovered TweetMyJOBS one Saturday morning, signed up, and on Sunday received a tweet of a job for a local marketing position at a Subaru dealership. He called them up that day, actually was able to arrange for an interview on Monday, and landed the job on Friday. We were ecstatic. We couldn't have asked for a better testimonial, and promoted him to a few reporters that were interested in stories about Twitter and job searching.

For the next couple of months, we continue to build out our Job Channel Network to support the demand. We create Job Channels in every country in the world (even Antarctica). We add the ability for jobseekers to upload a resume, and we'll tweet it out for them. At this point, we were still giving away the service for free. We had to start executing our business model, and see if companies would want to pay for the service. So in April, 2009, we started charging for jobpostings. There was some initial resistance, but given our pricing ($1.99–$19.99 per posting), that resistance eventually went away.

By the Fall of 2009, we had over 300,000 active jobs being tweeted from TweetMyJOBS. We had Partnered with Direct Employers to provide pilots for 500 of the Fortune 1000 companies, and many had converted to paying customers. More success stories were coming in. Intercontinental Hotel Group reports hirings in many of their hotels, and even hired a Finance Director and an HR Director through TweetMyJOBS.

Fast forward to today.

We're the largest Twitter-based job board in the world. 9,500+ Job Channels allow us to effectively target jobseekers in every country worldwide for almost 80 job types. We tweet out 40,000 to 50,000 job tweets per day. 100 of the Fortune 500 companies have selected us for their social media job distribution. Many are using us exclusively for their social media recruiting strategy, and others are using us as an augmentation. Either way, we're adding value and being very effective.We've built in many more features in TweetMyJOBS, including Facebook/LinkedIn integration, Geotagging tweets, a Google TweetMap, and more. We've partnered with all the major recruitment advertising agencies in the U.S., as well as all the major applicant tracking systems. TweetMyJOBS has been featured on CNN, Fox Business News, Wall Street Journal, Good Morning America, and more. Not bad traction for a company that has been self-funded and hasn't spent a lot on advertising. I've been speaking at many career groups about personal branding and social media, and TweetMyJOBS is also active on a grassroots Twitter jobseeker initiative called #HireFriday, led by my good friend Margo Rose, a truly compassionate career advisor.

Companies are seeing results. Some of our largest customers are telling us that their media campaigns are working. (Although many are not as concerned about hires because they recognize that Social Media recruiting is more about branding and attraction rather than applicants and hires.) Our pricing model is also disrupting the traditional job board market enough to make them pay attention.

What's next: Mobile Recruiting. The smartphone adoption rate is laying the groundwork for a whole new frontier of computing, and there's going to be a huge opportunity to engage with jobseekers wherever they are. We're already designing extensions to the TweetMyJOBS infrastructure to build talent communities from these platforms.

Being an entrepreneur and carving out a business out of something that doesn't exist is a very exciting endeavor and potentially rewarding, but it doesn't come without its share of pressures. Sales pipeline, cash flow, customer satisfaction, employee morale, and available hours in the day are everyday issues and concerns. However, the most rewarding feeling that I get is that at the end of the day, we're making the difference in hundreds, if not thousands, of jobseekers' lives, and doing our part to get this economy back on the right track.

Gary is the founder and President of TweetMyJOBS.com, an online job portal connecting employers and jobseekers through social media. A true entrepreneur with a vision, Gary has built TweetMyJOBS from a simple concept to the largest Twitter-based job board in the world in under two years. He received a Bachelors of Science in Electrical Engineering from the University of Massachusetts, and a Masters of Science in Computer Engineering from Northeastern University. Although his education sometimes implies a withdrawn, introverted lifestyle, he's everything but. His last Myers-Briggs exam put him on the extreme end of extrovert. Gary has more than two decades of management, technical, and business development experience, and has worked for large corporations such as The MITRE Corporation, GE, and SeaLand. He also started a successful IT consulting firm, and spent fourteen years effectively recruiting jobseekers for his clients. He continues to push the envelope of social media recruiting via innovation within TweetMyJOBS.

Gary Zukowski
garyz@tweetmyjobs.com
@GaryZukowski
http://www.facebook.com/#!/profile.php?id=629975335
http://www.linkedin.com/profile?viewProfile=&key=414054&trk=tab_pro
www.tweetmyjobs.com
+1-704-544-9370

Solving Unemployment, One Tweet At A Time

By

Mark Stelzner and Robert Fine

What is JobAngels?

JobAngels is a grassroots, nonprofit organization (501(c)3 status pending) dedicated to helping people find gainful employment—one person at a time. That person can be a friend, a family member, a colleague, or a complete stranger. JobAngels is passionate about driving a new generation of talent networking that is both meaningful and results-oriented.

So how did JobAngels get started?

On the morning of January 29, 2009, I was eating breakfast and thinking about the economy. We were in the throes of a debilitating week of job loss announcements and things looked to be worsening in all sectors. I had been spending a bit of time on Twitter and had accumulated about seven hundred followers, a large percentage of whom are experts and professionals in the human resources (HR) sector. So I wondered, what if each of those followers helped just one person find a job? Could we actually make a difference? Here's the original Tweet:

> "Was thinking that if each of us helped just 1 person find a job, we could start making a dent in unemployment. You game?" – @Stelzner, January 29, 2009

And thus, JobAngels was born. It was literally that simple. This was not rocket science and there was no divine intervention. It was one simple idea that somehow tapped into people's desire to stop being victims in a seemingly endless stream of angst, depression, and relentless negativity. When faced with millions of job losses, it's easy to feel overwhelmed and helpless. But if the idea is for you to simply aid one person, be it a friend, a family member, a colleague or a complete stranger, then somehow that not only seems possible, it seems probable.

So how did people respond?

It has been eighteen months since the initial message was sent. We now boast well over 40,000 JobAngels members across Twitter, Facebook, and LinkedIn. In addition, millions of JobAngels messages have been sent across a myriad of online platforms. Our wonderful Angels have donated their time, their networks, their expertise, and their hearts to this grassroots initiative (and we are just getting started).

Before going further, let me be clear about something. JobAngels is not my movement, but it has changed my life. I am absolutely blown away by everyday people deciding to step up and aid those in need of employment. This is a chance to truly impact someone's life and it is amazing to watch the goodwill grow at a time when it's tempting to thrust your head in the sand.

Those first eighteen months were unbelievable. Here are some items that were accomplished:

- JobAngels is effective: We helped over 1,650 people find jobs (that we know of). These represent job seekers who have taken the time to contact us directly to share their story. We are hopeful that the true number is much, much larger.

- JobAngels drives exposure: With tens of thousands of members, we've found that each time we distribute a link to someone's online resume, they get an average of 300–500 views. And that helps trigger the conversations that lead to interviews and opportunities.

- JobAngels is global: We have members in 25 countries speaking 15 languages. That's pretty cool.

- JobAngels is in the news: We were featured on over 250 TV stations (such as CNN), in over 40 tier 1 publications (such as the Wall Street Journal), and thousands of online forums, blogs, and publications. And all of this was without a single interview request or PR campaign.

- JobAngels is offline: Our leaders have spoken to over 300,000 audience members via live events. Since many of these folks will never participate in social media, we believe this is a key contributor to broader exposure and localization.

- JobAngels is yours: You've sent over 5 million messages of hope, support, news, advice, guidance—and yes, venting and complaining. JobAngels does not exist without the support and activity of all of you.

It's amazing what one simple concept can accomplish. The implied contract between employers and employees may be a thing of the past, but one thing is certain—we are all in this together and we can't do it alone. Help someone in need and it will change both of your lives, I guarantee it.

Mark Stelzner serves as the founder and chairman of JobAngels, a grassroots nonprofit dedicated to helping people get back to work one person at a time. JobAngels has been featured by hundreds of top tier media, including the Los Angeles Times, NBC, NPR, and thousands of blogs, podcasts, and online forums.

Mark is also the founder of New Media Services LLC, the single destination for comprehensive virtual, digital, and social media strategies for the career and HR industries. Through its market leading brands such as Voice of HR and Voice of Careers, Mark is driving innovative engagement strategies to current and future stakeholders through new media activation.

In addition, Mark is the founder of Inflexion Advisors, applying over sixteen years of experience in the implementation of internal and external HR transformational initiatives for public and private sector clientele worldwide. Over his career, Mark has brought over $3 billion worth of value to his clients and employers.

A highly sought after voice in the industry, Mark has been featured by the Wall Street Journal, the New York Times, Forbes, CNN, and NPR.

Mark Stelzner
mark.stelzner@jobangels.org
@stelzner
http://www.facebook.com/markstelzner
http://www.linkedin.com/in/markstelzner
http://www.jobangels.org
http://www.thecareersummit.com

Paying It Forward to Build a Community
A Case Study of CPGjobs

By

Neal Schaffer

For many companies, social media marketing efforts are focused primarily on Facebook, and in some cases, Twitter. This makes sense if you are a consumer brand trying to serve your present fan base or develop new business. But what if your business is targeting other businesses (i.e. B2B) or you are a business-to-consumer (B2C) brand trying to gain exposure to a professional or wealthy demographic?

I have seen very niche B2B companies, small enterprise software companies for example, that believe that they are "doing social media" when they create a Facebook fan page. I always think to myself, "Is that really where your customer is? And does your target demographic use Facebook in a way that would make them interested in engaging with you there?"

What I am leading to is this: companies need to be engaging where their audience is, and in a way that is appropriate for that specific platform. LinkedIn is often overlooked as a mere job-hunting site, despite the fact that an Executive of every Fortune 500 company is represented on the site and the average household income of a LinkedIn user is in the six figures. Furthermore, even if you are a B2C company, there are always B2B elements of any business: distributors, partners, strategic alliances, etc. Not only are all of the influential decision makers more likely to be on LinkedIn than any other social networking platform, but many are already utilizing LinkedIn in a professional way as a representative of their business.

LinkedIn Groups

If LinkedIn is an appropriate social media channel for your company's social media strategy, what exactly should you be doing on LinkedIn? There are many ways to utilize LinkedIn, but one of the most powerful ways for businesses to use it is to build a community of present and future customers just like you can do with a Facebook Fan Page. In LinkedIn, this is called a Group.

LinkedIn Groups are communities of people that join them based on similar professional interests or associations. There are more than 685,000 groups on LinkedIn, with the largest group having more than 300,000 members at the time of this writing. Functionality provided by LinkedIn Groups includes a

Discussions board, where it is possible to post a link to a web article of interest, or simply engage in conversation; Group member search; and the ability to directly send a message to someone in the same Group should they be using the default setting that LinkedIn provides.

Why would a business want to engage in LinkedIn Groups as part of a social media strategy? And how would a company go about doing so?

It's best to use a little imagination here and pretend that LinkedIn is a virtual chamber of commerce meeting or trade show. There are more than 70 million participants that you can search out through Advanced People Search that are on the main floor of the exhibition at all times virtually. There are also lots of breakout rooms and sessions for those professionals attending the trade show that have a particular interest. These are LinkedIn Groups, and hopefully thinking about it this way gives you a better understanding of how you can utilize them.

CPGjobs

It's important to give you this background on LinkedIn Groups before I introduce the case study subject of this chapter, CPGjobs, and how they created a group based on a comment from one of their candidates:

"Why don't you start a LinkedIn Group?"

There was no further reasoning given. And CPGjobs had no idea what they were doing when they started their LinkedIn Group, CPGpeople. They understood that LinkedIn was where their target audience was and wanted to better utilize the default social networking platform for professionals. They could not have imagined in their wildest of dreams the business benefits that sprung from creating this group.

CPGjobs is a Consumer Packaged Goods (CPG) industry recruiting company that was founded in 1999. Their clients include Fortune 500 companies such as MillerCoors, Hershey, Sara Lee, and Kellogg's. They are often able to introduce candidates to their clients because they started an Internet job board several years ago where potential candidates can register and have access to a number of job-related resources. Through their original Web site, CPGjoblist was already "paying it forward" by going above and beyond the duty of a mere resume-posting job board and providing informative newsletters, articles on resume writing, and other job-related resources.

One of the motivating factors for CPGjobs to implement a LinkedIn strategy was that it was free. There was never a large marketing budget to play with available, with any funds going either to their Web site development or regular newsletter campaigns. LinkedIn, because it is free to use, would soon be added to this mix, and remain a key component of the CPGjobs marketing strategy to this day.

Like everybody else, Penelope Sallberg-Carrillo, Executive Vice President and Founder of CPGjobs, joined LinkedIn after receiving many invitations to do so. She had naturally accumulated 200+ connections over time. As a lifelong networker and connector, she had an interest in how LinkedIn could help her achieve her own professional networking goals. Little did she know how it could help her business.

Creating a LinkedIn Group

As mentioned before, the LinkedIn Group was created on the recommendation of a candidate. Penny was pleasantly surprised by how easy it was to actually create a LinkedIn Group. She contacted her marketing department and consulted on what they could use the group for, as well as the naming of the group. What Penny wanted to do was to provide an online, virtual networking environment for **those who work** in the CPG industry. Note the emphasis here is on creating an industry-wide resource not just for their own candidates or customers, but for anyone working in the industry. Furthermore, instead of naming the group "CPGjobs," because they were trying to attract CPG industry professionals regardless of their employment status, they realized that the group was about people and not jobs. Thus, on April 12, 2008, the CPGpeople LinkedIn Group was born.

Once the name of the group was chosen, it was important to brand it in a way that would be attractive to the target audience while maintaining consistency with their established brand. CPGjobs did this by using the same image from their logo as well as the "CPG" wording, and replacing "jobs" with "people" in the same lower-case characters and font size. In this manner, both present customers and candidates would immediately recognize the logo image while new potential customers and candidates would immediately understand that this was a group for CPG industry professionals.

Promoting Your LinkedIn Group

Once you start a LinkedIn Group, what do you do next? It's all about promotion, and that starts with introducing your community to relevant professionals in your own LinkedIn network. Active networkers and users of LinkedIn, not to mention LIONs (LinkedIn Open Networkers), will have an advantage here in that they already have a large and potentially relevant audience that they can introduce their new LinkedIn group to. But promotion doesn't stop with just LinkedIn members: Once you begin to strategically engage in social media, you need to optimize your own Web site for social media. For the LinkedIn Group, it can be as simple as posting a logo with a clickable link that leads to your group in a prominent area that gets a lot of views. In this way, your Web site visitors can not only find out about your community, but they can also easily join it. And don't forget if you have an e-mail newsletter to feature the linked logo there as well. CPGjobs did all of that to help promote their group.

Furthermore, Penny reached out by writing personalized notes to candidates that she was already connected with letting them know 1) CPGjobs was creating a new networking community, 2) no recruiters would be allowed in, and 3) that she urged them to invite other CPG industry professionals that they thought might be a good fit into joining the group. There were also professional association members that Penny had not connected with on LinkedIn that she also sent e-mails to. The result of all of this work? About 35 members joined.

Membership growth was slow to begin with, and so was the amount of discussions generated. When starting a LinkedIn Group, group managers need to assume leadership by proactively starting conversations, posting relevant and timely news, and reacting to the discussions and questions of others. Penny still devotes about 1½–2 hours a day to doing this, as well as approving new members. But slowly, discussions began to be organically generated by group members and word started to spread. Soon CPGpeople had crossed a chasm and now was a growing community of 300 CPG industry members.

In social media, relevance matters, but sometimes size helps establish credibility. With 300 group members, Penny now started reaching out to their recruiting clients letting them know that they had created a new online community just for their industry. The objective was not to invite recruiters into their group, but for their customers to start helping them spread the word to their colleagues within the company. Indirectly, this also helped CPGjobs maintain mind share and become perceived as a leader in the CPG industry.

LinkedIn Group Policies

It should be noted that when she created the LinkedIn Group, Penny made the conscious decision at that time to create a highly relevant community, so that CPG industry professionals would not only want to join the group, but also feel comfortable in truly engaging through conversations. Although it is time-consuming, she created the policy that every group applicant would be reviewed and those that did not work in the industry or simply wanted to recruit talent through joining the group would not be allowed in. Only in this way could CPGjobs create the community that they desired and fulfill a promise to their industry professionals.

This strategy had unforeseen business advantages. By personally reviewing every applicant, they could be compared to the actual CPGjobs database to see if they had registered or not. If they had previously registered and were inactive, it created a new touchpoint with their candidates to strengthen the relationship and maintain mind share. If they were not a registered Web site user yet, this created the perfect opportunity to introduce them to the CPGjoblist job board and encourage them to sign up there and at least receive their bi-weekly newsletter regardless of their job status. And jealous corporate recruiters who wanted to join the CPGpeople group in order to get access to the attractive pool of targeted candidates would be prime candidates to develop new business. Penny then created a new LinkedIn Group to foster relationships with these CPG industry recruiters (appropriately named CPG Recruiters), now managed by Michael Carrillo, President and founder of CPGjobs, which helps develop new business while also maintaining mind share with their present and potential customers. She turned a potentially alienating situation into one that brought these "declined" people into a new group and thereby mitigated the sting of exclusion.

The same worked the other way around, too. CPGjobs could now actively cross-pollinate memberships by inviting those who registered on their Web site as a candidate to join their LinkedIn Group.

Daily Engagement Strategy

Almost two hours a day in maintaining a LinkedIn Group sounds like a lot of time to most people. However, CPGjobs began seeing the ROI of their activities and realized that this should continue to be the primary focus of their marketing efforts. Not only did the LinkedIn Group help them to keep in contact with candidates who they had lost touch with, but it helped them find new candidates to fulfill recruiting jobs for because they were now two or three degrees away from a million people in the CPG industry. The value of building networks for the professional on LinkedIn started to take on a new meaning for CPGjobs.

Promoting the group began to become a daily activity. Any conversation with anyone from the CPG industry would always naturally lead to the topic of the CPGpeople group, and since everyone knows that the best way to get a job is through networking, it was a natural for professionals to see perceived value in the group and want to join. It was also a way for these professionals to find and contact old associates that they may have lost track of. In this way they perceived the group to be "theirs" as well.

Penny also continued to periodically target individuals that would be ideal members for the CPGpeople Group, as well as eventually for their recruiting business. If she spotted an interesting profile from someone in the CPG industry when looking at other group discussions, she would reach out to them and invite them into her group. She would then go to their profiles and view the "viewers of this profile also viewed" section to get an idea of other industry people that existed. Although she may not have had access to communicate with these happily employed professionals, she began to build a database of "hard-to-find" people that would come in handy and be a strategic differentiator when performing searches for their clients. In addition to her own LinkedIn network, she could now fall back on her group community to help facilitate introductions to these target candidates.

Find Your Target Audiences

One of the reasons that CPGjobs was successful in creating a LinkedIn Group is that they were on a social networking site where their target audience was located. Through direct marketing to the audience that they were already in contact with, they were able to grow their community and business. Despite this fact, there was still a huge untapped audience of people that were members of other Groups but still did not "find" CPGpeople.

To be at the forefront of their targeted audience and be found by them, Penny joined the maximum fifty groups where she thought her target audience might join. After joining, she could engage in discussions where she could mention that she had a group that others might be interested in an indirect manner. There were occasions where Penny directly posted a "discussion" where the topic was introducing her group. When asked if she ever received complaints from other group managers in doing this, she said, "No. I didn't do it a lot, and it was also done professionally in a way to supplement the value of that group."

Getting back to my analogy at the beginning of this chapter, it's not about just being in your own breakout session. It can be fruitful to step outside of your own session and join those of others. This can only help you and your business get found on LinkedIn.

Group Growth Continues

After some time, as a result of the previously mentioned promotional activities, growth in the group seemed to happen organically and was growing exponentially. With LinkedIn, once someone joins a group, it gets broadcasted in their news feed to allow their connections to be notified and check out the group. The same happens if they participate in a group discussion. The group logo also appears on the profile of every member, so it allows for free advertising of the group. Including the group logo on every newsletter sent out to their CPGjobs database as well as on their Web site ensured that steady growth would continue. Furthermore, all it takes is for a few group members to tell some of their industry friends and colleagues about the group for new membership to increase. Many candidates have told her that they touted the CPGpeople Group to at least ten of their friends.

The group growth also started to work its way back into increasing membership at the CPGjobs Web site. At the beginning of 2009, candidate membership on the company Web site was growing at about 300 new members a week with a total of 35,640 members. As I write this chapter in August of 2010, the membership has more than doubled to 73,766 and membership continues to grow at a high pace of almost 1,000 new members a week.

Simultaneously, the LinkedIn Group has grown from about 1,000 members at the beginning of 2009 to its present 11,647 members in August of 2010. The growth of the group combined with its increasing international membership spurred CPGjobs to create a new CPGpeople International group, which has more than 1,000 members and has subgroups for popular membership countries such as Canada, India, Australia, and the United Kingdom. This folds into their plan to increase their market share of international jobs.

LinkedIn Group Maintenance

The trick to building a community is not only in increasing its membership numbers, but also in the task of getting people to actually visit the group site and participate in discussions. At the beginning, the group manager needed to do a great deal to generate discussions and create a new communal culture for the group. As membership grew, the discussions became mostly self-generated, but Penny still checks the engagement volume on a daily basis and will generate new discussions if she feels there is not enough discussion taking place.

What discussions should one generate? One tactic used by Penny and other group managers is to take an interesting discussion from another group. It could be completely repurposed if it is a general discussion, but if it is a discussion with unique content, the actual person who started the discussion on a different group should be credited. A topic that generated a lot of discussion in a similar group is bound to be similarly successful in one's own.

Utilizing the LinkedIn Announcement Feature

LinkedIn allows group managers to send out an announcement to all of its members at most once a week. It should be noted that this should not be used every week, nor should it be used for purely self-promotional means. Sending out announcements in this manner could be perceived as spam by the LinkedIn community and it could give people reason to leave your group.

With a large group membership, CPGjobs realized that the announcement features were strategic in that CPGjobs could now utilize it to send out a targeted message from time to time, perhaps announcing a new hard-to-find open position with one of their clients on the business development side. It could also be used to announce a new discussion topic to try to engage members who hadn't visited the group recently to come back to the group. With the sending of each targeted announcement, CPGjobs continued to maintain mind share and strengthen their branding.

In such a way, CPGjobs had truly reached a tipping point where they now had a healthy community that they could tap in order to help grow their business. Business development via community creation had been accomplished!

Social Media Success: It's All About Caring for People

Penny explains why CPGjobs was successful in their social media marketing on LinkedIn through building a community the best in this simple statement:

> *"I care about people. It matters to me that people find what I do helpful. We didn't start the LinkedIn Group to make money, but the interactions that resulted from the community created revenue-generating momentum. It just goes to show you that paying it forward, the belief that when you do good things for others it comes back to you, really does work."*

Where does CPGjobs go from here? Potential customers as well as candidates do not spend their time in social media solely on LinkedIn. Since I have engaged with CPGjobs to create their social media strategy, I can tell you that CPGjobs plans to bring their community and resourceful information for the CPG industry to other social media channels and further expand upon what they have been doing so successfully on LinkedIn. Community knows no boundary, and neither should your company's engagement in social media.

Neal Schaffer is recognized as a leader in helping businesses and professionals embrace and strategically leverage the potential of social media. An award-winning published author of *Windmill Networking: Understanding, Leveraging & Maximizing LinkedIn*, a frequent speaker on a variety of social media-related topics at conferences and professional associations, and an avid blogger, Neal is President of Windmills Marketing, a social media strategic consultancy in Orange County, California, and has led social media strategy creation and educational programs for a range of companies ranging from Fortune 500 to Web 2.0 startups.Neal's blog, Windmill Networking, is quickly becoming a powerful online resource for social media strategy and advice.

Neal Schaffer
neal@windmillnetworking.com
@nealschaffer
http://www.facebook.com/windmillnetworking
http://www.linkedin.com/in/nealschaffer
http://windmillnetworking.com
+1-888-541-3429

Roll Your Own – A Case Study of CoolWorks.com

by

Kari Quaas

When I left my traditional human resources job in 2007, and joined the virtual team of five at CoolWorks.com. Working out of my house, I don't think I had any idea of how different my life would be. I certainly knew about, and took advantage of, the obvious benefits like wearing pajamas to work or running a load of laundry, but really I found that by leaving the office, I gained the world. To be a member of a virtual team, one must have access to the Internet. Without it, ironically, I cannot do my job. Being a social person, the most difficult adjustment I had to make was the lack of direct human contact. However, I found early on that social media filled some of that void, and now I have gained friends, colleagues, and connections all over the world. I do also leave my home to go to the gym, support my community through volunteer opportunities, and have lunch with friends. Face-to-face contact cannot and should not ever be replaced by virtual connections, but I feel blessed with a strong online network of folks who I can tap into when I need an ear, an opinion, a distraction, or education. All in all, the move to CoolWorks.com and my working from home has been one of the best things I have ever done.

To set the stage for how all of this relates to my job and to the job seekers we serve at CoolWorks.com, here's a look back at our humble beginnings.

Cool Works was founded by Bill Berg, who first experienced and began to appreciate seasonal employment after a summer job pumping gas in Yellowstone National Park in the early 1970s. He was a young college kid from Minnesota with dreams of the West. That summer job lead him to find his home, his wife, and a life that included all kinds of outdoor adventures and fun. Eventually he moved up the ranks and became one of the lucky ones to either grant a summer spent in the park or not. He got to know many of the human resources managers from across the Parks System, and was an original member of SHRA, the Seasonal Human Resources Association, a group of HR professionals who network, support, and console one another regarding their challenges working in the parks. Then, in 1994, Bill decided to pursue his MBA at the University of Washington in Seattle. During one of his Information Systems courses in January 1995, he was introduced to Mosaic. A light bulb went on. He knew all of these folks who put forth a great effort each spring to hire thousands of summer seasonal employees who, if they're lucky, will stay five months, sometimes less. Then, the summer season ends, the employees go home, and they have to start the hiring process all over again for the next year. There had to be a better way. Bill decided at that point to leave the MBA program, return to Yellowstone, and start a job Web site. He purchased the domain CoolWorks.com (after much deliberation about cool being cool) in September of 1995. On November 1, 1995, the site launched. And 15 years later, we're still providing a place for job seekers to come and find those seasonal opportunities that just might change their lives.

My first interaction with Cool Works occurred in the fall of 1998, when I was responsible for hiring Drivers/Guides to operate motorcoaches and give tours in Alaska for the cruise line Holland America. We opted to use CoolWorks.com for our employment advertising, and Kathi, my now coworker at Cool Works, was my representative. She and I built the first advertising Web site for Gray Line of Alaska—brochureware as they call it now, but back then, it was beyond cool, it was the right price, and it worked.

Eventually I moved on to Princess Cruises and into their Human Resources department, where I met other members of the Cool Works team, including Bill and Patty, who I then saw at least once a year at the SHRA conferences. The connection between me and Cool Works was growing. At the 2006 SHRA conference in Seward, Alaska, after meeting the final member of the Cool Works' team, Eric, Bill asked if I wanted to be a "Cool Worker." Let me just say for the record that I remain in awe of that question and the faith he had, they all had, about adding me to the team. I'm not a math whiz, but going from four to five employees is a big deal. So now when you see my bios on the various social networks, you'll understand the "one-fifth of CoolWorks.com" reference. We all make it happen and consider ourselves to be partners in its common success.

Going way back to 1999, Cool Works engaged their job seekers in forums designed to swap stories and get user feedback, but much of it was driven by anonymous posters, which can be tricky at times. Cool Works has also been publishing blogs since August 2004. I always remember when Bill would present at SHRA, or once at the Princess post-season meetings, and he would always wow the crowd with the latest and greatest technologies. When Ning announced the ability to start your own social network, Bill signed Cool Works up right away. So when I joined the company in March 2007, I quickly went from a fairly straight and narrow human resources manager to a Web 2.0 and social media student. This evolution continues today.

2007 was also the year that I was finishing a certificate course in photography through the University of Washington. Although photography was the reason I was taking the classes, one major benefit to Cool Works was the fact that I could join the then closed collegiate Web site Facebook because I had a verifiable student e-mail account. The irony here was that when I was truly a collegiate at Washington State University during the early 1990s, e-mail as we know it today didn't exist, and certainly none of us had our own personal account provided by the school. So armed with my u.washington.edu e-mail address, I got in at least a year before it was opened to the rest of the world. Facebook now claims to have over five hundred million users and, in my humble opinion, is taking over the world. I firmly believe that if Facebook isn't a part of your social media strategy, you and your company, organization, or nonprofit, are missing out. People will always turn to their friends first to find out what they should like and not like. A personal recommendation always carries more weight than an advertising campaign.

Although Facebook (http://facebook.com/coolworks) is huge for us, I think our real success has been our Cool Works branded social network called My CoolWorks (http://my.coolworks.com), which we treat as a mini-Facebook with a seasonal job twist. When it was launched in February 2007, we initially created it as "invitation only" and we peppered it with blog posts, quotes, and forum topics to set the tone and make it as wholesome as possible. Our tag line is, "A social network for those who want to compare and share their work and life experiences in great places." It's grown from a few hundred in that first year to almost 5,000 members today. We now also have over 1000 discussions, over 15,000 photos, 867 blog posts (not all written by me!), 60 groups, and a live chat that ramps up in the fall through late spring with curious job seekers and our seasoned veterans from what we affectionately call our tribe. People say that they keep coming back because they have friends on the network, people keep asking them questions, and honestly, they're looking for the next great gig.

From our humble beginnings, this is quite an accomplishment and has honestly taken quite a bit of time and work. You cannot just set it and forget it. It takes constant attention, nurturing, encouragement, and a moderator (that would be me) to keep out those who don't play well with others and who don't follow our rules. All in all though, I wouldn't trade the last three years of tending our network for the world. I've met some incredible people, seen generosity and caring from our members to others across the country and the world, and selfishly, I get to live vicariously through these people doing cool jobs all over the planet. I have a pretty cool gig.

The last tool I really believe to be a major component of our social media strategy is Twitter. We jumped on this one early too. In April 2008, I joined Twitter as myself (@kariquaas). In July 2008, I couldn't help myself and signed up my cats (@cats_of_kari). Finally, in August 2008, we began tweeting as Cool Works (@coolworks). The benefit that I have always seen from Twitter is finding people (cats) with common interests. As my coworker Eric paraphrased, "Facebook is for those people you used to be friends with, and Twitter is for those you *should* be friends with." I've also heard Twitter described as the ultimate coffee shop where you can eavesdrop on thousands of conversations, pick the ones you like and join in the fun. I think it's great.

Each of the Twitter accounts has a different purpose. We use the Cool Works account to publish all new listings and job postings on our main Web site, as well as some of the wonderful blog posts from our social network. Personally, I use my account to stay connected to like-minded people, my community, and my many interests. And the account I have for my cats, well, that one is just for my entertainment. If done right, Twitter is a powerful tool for connecting with people/entities that share a common interest and desire to connect. Beyond that, if you get some champions for your product, idea, or whatever, the power of the RT (retweet) and the compounding ability to share are unmatched since tweets are now indexed by Google.

To wrap up, my only suggestion for anyone jumping into the social media fray is to remember the golden rule: don't say anything on the Internet that you wouldn't say to someone's face. Other than that, I'm a dyed-in-the-wool, true believer, in the power of social media. Where it goes from here, and what the next greatest tool will be, I don't know. But, the desire for individuals to connect with each other on common issues, desires, and interests will only continue to grow, and I assure you that Cool Works and I will be right there riding the wave.

Kari Quaas is a Washington State native and lives in Seattle. She graduated from Washington State University, and her career, mostly in travel and tourism, has included a variety of job titles including day camp counselor, office assistant/receptionist, driver/guide, safety, recruiting and training manager, benefits coordinator, human resources manager, photographer, employer support, and community manager. Since 2007 she has worked for the niche job web site, CoolWorks.com, which focuses on jobs in great places. Kari authors the Seasonal Human Resources Blog and moderates Cool Works' presence in social media. She also would be more than happy to photograph your cat or dog.

Kari Quaas
kari@coolworks.com
@kariquaas
http://facebook.com/kariquaasphotography
http://linkedin.com/in/kariquaas
http://coolworks.com
http://kariquaas.com
+1-206-962-1345

Nonprofits

Changing Our View of Medicine with Pixels and Paint

by

Regina Holliday

"If you are serious about changing the world, you must get on Twitter and you must have a blog." — Christine Kraft

"It is not the technology, it is the community." — Dave DeBronkart, referring to ACOR[1] at the board meeting of NeHC[2] on June 2, 2009

June 29, 2009, was a beautiful day. It was sunny and warm with a slight breeze. I wore my blue Easter dress, the blue dress I would soon wear within a monumental mural called *73 Cents*. I was going to a seminar downtown to the JW Marriott in Washington, DC. I heard about this event through my Twitter friend @ePatientDave. Known in real life as Dave DeBronkart, Dave had spoken at the board meeting of NeHC on June 2. He had carried my husband's medical record with him as an example of why patients need access to data. After hearing his speech on epatients.net[i], I began to subscribe to the NeHC newsletter. A few weeks later I received an invitation to attend the NHIN[3] Connect 2009 seminar via the NeHC subscribers list.

This was my first medical conference. I had created some simple business cards using my home computer. I entered the luxury hotel and began to descend to the lower floor. Amongst trays of breakfast muffins and silver coffee decanters stood a large, milling populace. Arrayed before me were two groups. My artist eye caught a sense of division within the crowd. I saw small huddled groups of men with longish hair wearing matching polo shirts and talking with an isolated intensity. I saw other groups in expensive business suits conversing within loose circles. As I walked around the hall I never saw the two distinct groups talk to each other.

I felt out of place among the business suits and polo shirts in my bright blue Easter dress, but I took a deep breath and began to introduce myself. I would say, "Hi, my name is Regina Holliday. I am a medical muralist. I paint about

---

[1] Association of Online Cancer Resources.
[2] National eHealth Collaborative.
[3] Nationwide Health Information Network.

healthcare." I would explain that I was inspired to paint murals that would promote change within the U.S. medical system. I would hand them my flimsy business card and tell them to contact me via Twitter, Facebook, e-mail, or my blog. I would continue speaking, sharing that my medical advocacy mission was a response to the horrific things I had seen during my husband's eleven-week hospitalization at five different facilities during his short battle with kidney cancer.

Soon it was time for the morning program to begin, and we filed into the large ballroom. That morning I would hear David Blumenthal, National Coordinator for Health Information Technology, give the first keynote. During his speech, I was introduced to the ramifications of a HITECH[4] legislative term: "meaningful use." He concluded with saying, "I want to bring us back to what we are here for. We are here for the millions of patients whose lives can be improved by the work we do."

Aneesh Chopra, Chief Technology Officer and Associate Director of Technology, gave the second keynote at 9:45 a.m. After he finished speaking about the power of technology within medicine, he opened the floor to questions from the audience. Two lines began to form of those who wished to ask questions. I got in line and slowly moved forward. Quite a few people asked their questions before Mr. Chopra said, "Last one, Vish, before we get hauled out of the room. Yes, ma'am?"

It was my turn. I stated, "Hi, my husband received his diagnosis of renal cell carcinoma on March 27. At that point, I began to e-mail, do Internet research, try to find every resource I could to help him. I began to Facebook—Facebooked every night daily, stating his status, developed over 200 friends, and then began to Twitter, and ended up speaking to a doctor from Boston, Massachusetts. Did everything I could as a caregiver to support my husband using the Internet. Developed a blog. Also asked for Internet data. Prior to this I did not (often) e-mail, nor did I use a cell phone. During a three month period (I) became a complete caregiver and a walking PHR[5] for my husband. I am asking you how will the patient and patient advocate be allowed to access the information of (the) EMR[6], to have that a standardized form, that we all as advocates of our spouses or loved ones, and (can) provide the best level of data and catch all kinds of errors in the medical record?"

Applause echoed in the hall. Mr. Chopra began to answer. He said he had a downer observation. He said that the technology in medicine in no way matched the technology in the world of retail. He went on to say, "I applaud you for what you (are) doing with limited resources to try to help your family, but I am committed to making sure we have a foundation available so that clinicians on

---

[4] Health Information Technology for Economic and Clinical Health.
[5] Personal Health Record.
[6] Electronic Medical Record.

their own and by themselves and amongst themselves can start to have those kinds of transactions captured."[7]

I did not see patient access to the EMR addressed within his answer. I thought about it through the rest of the seminar. I pondered his answer as I left the building and began my descent on the metro escalator. My blue dress billowed slightly from the warm breeze escaping the metro tunnel. The metro tunnel was filled with beautiful music as a transgender man sang a soaring falsetto aria on the lower platform. I was filled with hope that I would be able to address this lack of access. June 29 was a beautiful day even though it was twelve days after my husband had died.

I would spend the next year using every tool in art and social media to address the need for patient access to the EMR. I would speak about meaningful use and testify before the ONC[8] about why the HITECH legislation would not be "meaningful" without patient access. A little over a year later I would sit on the stage with David Blumenthal at the Department of Health and Human Services. It was July 13, 2010, at the announcement of the final rule of Stage One meaningful use. The speakers were Secretary of Health and Human Services Kathleen Sebelius, David Blumenthal, Director of CMS[9] Don Berwick, and Surgeon General Regina Benjamin. I was the fifth speaker and represented the patient's voice in HIT[10].

That day patients everywhere got a standing ovation.

A little over a year ago I was a sales associate in a toy store and also taught art part-time at a local preschool. I was happily married for over 15 years. My husband Fred and I had two wonderful sons, one of whom had high-functioning autism. We were just a family getting by from day to day. In early March of 2009, I had no idea what the term "social media" meant. I had recently learned Twitter was some kind of Internet thing, and not just a noise a bird makes. I had been on Facebook for less than seven months and had fewer than fifty friends. I could have easily been termed a technophobe. I did not even own a cell phone or drive a car. There were so many things I did not know.

And I didn't know that an oncologist was a cancer doctor.

In late March, my husband was hospitalized for tests. On March 27, Fred's oncologist told him, while he was alone, that Fred had "tumors and growths." Fred called me at work crying; he was unsure what the doctor had meant. I rushed to the hospital and got there within thirty minutes, but the oncologist had left town for four days to attend a medical conference. I scurried around the

---

[7] Recorded by USGOVHHS on June 29, 2009, uploaded onto You Tube on August 6th 2009.
[8] Office of the National Coordinator of Health Information Technology.
[9] Centers for Medicare and Medicaid Services.
[10] Health Information Technology.

hospital for days asking everyone questions, and I wasn't providing hands-on care to my husband.

I would spend each night researching Fred's disease on medical Web sites and through patient stories. The Internet was filled with honest answers if you knew how to look for them. I bypassed the sites that were blatant advertisements from pharmaceutical companies and found data from actual clinical trials. I studied medical outcomes on UK sites and found hospice and palliative care mentioned again and again. The information I was reading was very grim. Fred's chances of survival were almost non-existent.

It is very quiet researching at 3 a.m. There are no distractions—no children to feed or phone to answer. It is just me in the darkness that is dimly lit by a computer screen. It is just me and a few thousand of my online friends on the worldwide Web. Those friends would be there for me as I researched kidney cancer online. They would pop up and quote Shakespeare on Facebook and share my grief. When I could not sleep for weeks due to shock and sorrow, they would be there represented by a blinking placeholder. I was not alone. I would post into that binary darkness, and they would respond.

At the hospital, I got very few answers to my many questions. After four weeks of no access to a written record, I went down to the medical records department and asked for a copy of his record. They told me it would cost seventy cents a page, and there would be a twenty-one day wait. I was astounded. This was a state of the art hospital, yet they were asking us to wait twenty-one days and spend hundreds of dollars just to see Fred's record. The very next day, Fred was told he was being sent home. On Saturday, April 18, Fred's oncologist entered his hospital room. Let me paint you a picture of that day and that room.

Fred lay in his bed. We were quietly talking about our little boys. I was wrapping small presents that Fred could give the children when they visited. This was our quiet little domestic island in such a sea of sadness and confusion. This was a picture of Fred and me trying to be good parents. Then the oncologist walked in. He stood across the room about ten feet away. I looked at Fred. We had a list of questions taped to Fred's bed just in case the doctor came by. The questions were things like: "When will we get surgery?," "When will we get a pain consult?," and "When will we get an orthopedic consult for the hip that is so painful?" The doctor brushed aside our questions and told us they were sending us home on a morphine pump. He was sending us home to die without even having the bravery to use those words. He abruptly left, and we cried. I cried with great tears dropping onto my sons' wrapped presents. My husband rolled his head toward me. Tears ran down his face as he said, "You go after them, Regina, and try to get me care."

Fred had been a good patient. He had rarely complained even though he had been in so much pain. Each time I questioned the decisions of his doctors based on my research he would defend their actions. He had trusted them. They had betrayed that trust. I fought for the next five days to get transfer to another facility.

Upon transfer, we were sent with an out-of-date and incomplete medical record and transfer summary. Fred went without pain medications for six hours as the staff of the new hospital tried to recreate Fred's medical record using a phone and a fax machine. The next day, Fred's new doctors sent me back to the old hospital to get a complete copy of the medical record. It took them one and a half hours to print it out. I brought the record to Fred's new doctors, and they read through it briefly and gave it back to me. They said the record would be safest with me. They said Fred may be treated at many facilities, but if I kept the record of his care it would always be accessible.

I read the record in about three hours. It was filled with errors as well as data that would have affected our choice in treatment options if we could have only seen it sooner. Here was the first time I could see that the "3 cm tumor" Fred had told me he had on March 27 was really a 9 cm tumor in his right kidney and a 6.6 cm kidney in his left. The 3 cm tumor was referring to his sacrum, but with the shock of hearing a verbal diagnosis while he was alone, Fred had been unable to process the things the oncologist had told him. I was outraged that we had been given so little access to information.

I wished to vocalize my outrage at a medical system that would treat my husband and our family with so little honesty or respect. I wrote an e-mail to everyone I knew on May 2, 2009. I proposed that I would paint murals about the state of health care in the United States on the walls of Washington, DC.

On May 3, I worked a short shift at the toy store. It was a "sanity" shift. For a few hours, I left the hospital and went back to working retail in order to reclaim some semblance of normalcy. As I sold toys to parents and answered questions about art projects, my heart thudded within my ear and I could find no peace. At closing time, a customer whom I had helped for many years came in. It was Christine Kraft. I told her about my husband's cancer and our journey thus far. I had no idea at the time, but Christine is what one would call an Internet maven. She connects people. She said I must find @ePatientDave [11], a stage four kidney cancer survivor, on Twitter. I told her I did not know how to use Twitter. She told me I had better learn how that night.

On May 4, at 3:10 in the morning, I sent my first tweet: "I am trying to talk with Christine Kraft and epatient Dave." I am amazed they found me because I had no idea how to use Twitter. On May 5, Dave contacted me, and I spoke with him and his doctor. He also connected me with ACOR. The kidney cancer listserve was instrumental in our decision-making process. On May 6, I started my blog: *Regina Holliday's Medical Advocacy Blog* at http://reginaholliday.blogspot.com. On May 27, Christine Kraft invited me to attend a small Health 2.0 meetup that

---

[11] E-Patients are patients that are equipped, enabled, empowered and engaged in their health and health care decisions as defined by The Society for Participatory Medicine.

had no agenda. I presented our medical story to Cindy Throop, Susannah Fox, Claudio Luis Vera, Nancy Shute, Dave DeBronkart (by phone), and Ted Eytan, MD. Within days this group of wonderful people would blog about our patient story. On May 30, at 4:30 in the morning, I would place the first mural in the medical advocacy series called *The Medical Facts Mural*. Within days, the work would be written about on *The HealthCare Blog*. An advocacy movement was born.

We called the movement 73 Cents, as that was the name of the second mural in the series. On June 2, I wrote to my new Health 2.0 friends: "Speaking of paint. I have two more walls lined up, and one is quite big, so I sort of want to do a Picasso's *Guernica* meets David's *Death of Marat* set in the modern American medical world." I sat at my husband's side as he lay in his bed in inpatient hospice and then home hospice designing *73 Cents*. Fred would look over at the work and occasionally give me a comment or critique.

On June 17, Fred died. On June 21, I would send out another mass e-mail called "The Battle Begins." I told everyone I knew I was going to do battle against an uncaring medical system that does not respect patients' rights. I began painting on June 23, and I painted until September 30. Each night I would promote the cause on Twitter and Facebook. On August 6, Dana Milbank wrote about the painting in *The Washington Post*. The piece had 485 comments and 358 Facebook shares. Just a few years ago this would have been just a local story, but due to the Internet it was spread throughout the nation within days. Most of the comments were negative, but they taught me a valuable lesson. Working with Cindy Throop, we created a time line of my advocacy to dispel the comments "that I was made-up, a fiction of the Democratic Party." That time line advocates 24 hours a day at http://www.open-health.us/topics/reginas-advocacy-timeline.

The painting became part of the health care reform debate and was covered by the FOX, BBC, CNN, CBS, VOA[12], NPR and the BMJ[13]. In addition, it appeared online in AOL, Yahoo, Salon, and numerous online blogs. On Saturday, October 3, 2009, I woke up to find sixty messages and friend requests on my Facebook account. Three days before, reporter Andrea Stone had profiled my patients' rights advocacy on the AOL splash page. The 73 Cents movement was growing, and I had many new "friends."

On the night of October 20, the *73 Cents* mural was dedicated. There were over forty people shining their flashlights at the mural singing songs from the *Buffy the Vampire Slayer*[14] musical episode "Once More, With Feeling." We wrapped up the dedication with the song "Where Do We Go From Here?" That night I said, "That is my question for all of you: what do we do next? Thank you so much for coming tonight, thank you so much for being part of Fred's life and my life and

---

[12] Voice of America.

[13] British Medical Journal.

[14] *Buffy the Vampire Slayer* was a television program that aired March 10, 1997, through May 20, 2003.

spreading the word. And please go out tonight and Facebook and blog and post and tweet, and do not stop. Do not give up until we get change in this nation, until people get taken care of and we all have the right to see our own information."

The medical advocacy using art continues to this day. I now have 620 friends on Facebook and 967 Twitter followers. My blog has over 250 followers, and my complete profile has had over 2,600 views. The advocacy art I do is promoted on all of these social media platforms. The art has diversified as well. I paint on jackets that are worn to medical conferences, as my Twitter friend Jen McCabe suggested. I paint on canvases that can be shown in local medical offices. I paint *en plein air* in front of hospitals and talk of data sets and patient satisfaction scores. I then enter such work in online competitions, such as the Ashoka Changemakers: Patient Choices and Empowerment, and BodyShock the Future from The Institute for the Future. As I said when this all began, "I will stand up. I will not be silent. I will not give up the fight." Thank God for art and social media; with their power combined, I think this is a war we can win.

Regina Holliday is a DC-based patient rights arts advocate. She is currently at work on a series of paintings depicting the need for clarity and transparency in medical records. She placed her first mural in the series in May of 2009. After the death of her husband, Fred Holliday II, on June 17, 2009, she began a large Mural Titled *73 Cents*. This piece can be viewed at 5001 Connecticut Avenue, Washington, DC, 20008. This piece depicts the Holliday family's nightmare journey through the medical system during Fred's cancer care. The painting became part of the national healthcare debate and was covered by the BBC, CNN, CBS, AOL, The Washington Post, and the BMJ.

Regina Holliday
reggieart123@yahoo.com
@ReginaHolliday
http://www.facebook.com/regina.holliday
http://www.linkedin.com/profile/edit?id=28731480
http://reginaholliday.blogspot.com/
http://www.open-health.us/topics/reginas-advocacy-timeline
+1-202-441-9664

Did You Say Festival? Or Twestival?

by

Perri Gorman

Social media for social good has become a prevalent theme within the online space. From incredible philanthropists that use their celebrity like Alyssa Milano (@alyssa_milano) raising money for a good cause, to not-for-profit managers like Jonathan Wilson, who tweets for @OperationSAFE, whose passion and persistence attract people to help him spread the message of children affected by trauma, to the way the world came together to raise money faster than ever before for Haiti. Everyone with access to a phone or the Internet has the ability to participate and do something.

The world is full of good causes that need our attention and one can get overwhelmed by all there is to do. Tools like Twitter have the power to take someone in even a small town and put them right in the middle of a global event, allowing them to have impact. One special event that arose through people's connections on Twitter and their desire to give back is Twestival.

The brainchild of visionary Amanda Rose (@amanda), Twestival began on a snowy day in Vancouver in 2008. A tweetup turned into gathering clothes and blankets for the city's homeless. It was the first step to Twestival becoming a global event, simultaneously occurring in over two hundred cities in nations clear across the map. The first global Twestival in March of 2009 was dedicated to raising money for Scott Harrison's charity : water. Over $150,000 was raised on that one night. September of 2009 was the first Twestival Local where each city chose a local organization to raise funds for in the Twestival spirit. People, many times meeting for the first time, came together through the power of Twitter to create community events that were not only for a good cause, but were also where real lasting friendships were made.

I had the honor and privilege of being part of the 2009 local Twestival, led by Jay Oatway (@JayOatway) in Hong Kong, and then leading the organization of Twestival Global for Hong Kong in March of 2010. Of all the activities I have been a part of in my life, it was truly special to be part of Twestival. The March 2010 event was dedicated to a wonderful charity called Concern Worldwide

(@concern). There are over 72 million children all over the world who do not attend school because they are too poor, too sick, or because there is simply no access. The impact of not having an education is profound. The statistics show that these children are more likely to end up as victims of child labor or the sex trade and will have a shorter life expectancy than those children that are given the opportunity to go to school. Concern Worldwide addresses education holistically and looks at the unique issues of each community and how it can best be helped to facilitate education. Each city that participated in Twestival was able to select how they would like to designate their funds: to building schools, providing meals, hiring teachers, or providing clean drinking water. Hong Kong chose to help build schools.

For those who have never been to Hong Kong, it is a pretty special mix of East meets West. There are a large number of expats living in the former British colony and financial hub of Asia. You can get by with some basic Cantonese as a foreigner, and socially, except for certain pockets, there tends to be a real separation between expats and local Hong Kongers. Twitter helped bridge some gaps and brought people together over common interests. Though people tweet in Chinese, there was plenty of tweeting in English as well. On Twitter, there are people that bond over coffee and food, and others that connect over their passion for gadgets, social media, and technology. The nice thing was that Twitter combined with events like @WebWednesday (by Napolean Biggs) and iPhanatics (by Casey Lau - @hypercasey), and created opportunities to really get to know new people in real life with common interests.

When it came time to put together a team of volunteers for Twestival, we did it almost entirely through Twitter. Some team members I had already met in person, but all the relationships originated with Twitter, including many of our largest sponsors including Coca-Cola, Intel, Yi-Yi.hk, and the Four Seasons. We had a dynamic, multinational team of talented helpers working on marketing, fundraising, video, photography, design, technology, PR, and of course Twitter.

With Hong Kong's mixed passion for technology and luxury we wanted to create an event that captured the essence of the city, while bringing together different communities and demonstrating that social media is a powerful tool that local businesses should be familiar with. Our event was held in the heart of Hong Kong's SOHO (South of Hollywood Road) at a rooftop bar. Our team set up flat screen TVs that showed live photos and a tweetwall, and a video connection to stream our event out to the rest of the twitterverse. All in all we were able to raise over $13,000 from our efforts.

We became creative when discussing sponsorship packages with our potential donors. We offered custom Facebook page tabs with embedded video dedicated to our top level sponsors, and custom tweets with sponsor designated content distributed by a team of influential Twitter accounts. In particular, sponsor designated content worked very well for Intel. The sponsorship was a good fit for them because their Corporate Social Responsibility Program is geared towards education. One of the issues with securing large corporate sponsors, especially when suggesting non-traditional forms of brand exposure, is guaranteeing visibility and clicks. We tweeted out links about different programs they ran from their website, and used the #Twestival hashtag to enhance distribution and visibility. We used Hootsuite's scheduling feature to space out the tweets over the week leading up to the event, and for the night of the event as well. We wanted the sponsored tweets to show up on the tweetwall the night of the event, but we were too busy with the event itself to focus on tweeting links, so pre-scheduling was a terrific solution. We had a post-event follow-up with the people at Intel and they presented a Radian 6 analysis of our work, and were extremely pleased with the outcome. This was a fantastic result that demonstrated that Twitter can be used successfully in exchange for sponsorship. This is a model that other charities and events can learn and replicate.

One of the highlights of working on Twestival was coordinating with many of the other city leaders around Asia and the world. Together we managed to secure a regional sponsorship for Hong Kong and Malaysia from Coca-Cola, fix a last minute venue situation with Sydney, and make friends in Singapore, Shanghai, Beijing, Kuala Lumpur, Tokyo, Sydney, Melbourne, New Delhi, and Mumbai, all while helping a good cause. Huddle, an incredible online organization portal, sponsored Twestival, giving us access to their tools, allowing for a level of communication between cities and continents that would not have otherwise been possible. PayPal waived its service fees and channeled money directly into the hands of Concern Worldwide. All in all, Twestival Global raised over $460,000 and had more than 14,000 participants. The spirit of Twestival is to hold an event to bring people together from Twitter with 100% of the money raised going to the charity. Even the simplest events can accomplish Twestival's main goal: Tweet, Meet, Give.

Perri Gorman
@bethebutterfly
http://LinkedIn.com/in/PerriGorman

Small Nonprofit Wins Major League

by

Alane Anderson

This case study looks at the chronology of a one-woman nonprofit organization that put into play a social media strategy which, resulted in her attending the Major League Baseball All-Star Game, meeting five United States presidents, and having her organization featured on the big screen prior to the game. There will be several strategies and tips unveiled as we move through our step-by-step process that can be applied to all organizations, big or small.

Warm Up

While attending an Anaheim Angels game in April of 2009, People Magazine and Major League Baseball (MLB) announced a contest: they wanted to know about everyday all-stars who were doing great and inspirational things in their local community. Game attendees visited the MLB or People Magazine Web site in order to nominate their candidate.

TIP: A contest can work for any organization, and this particular contest resulted in an immediate increase in subscribers for MLB and People Magazine. As an example, I had a client offer the latest technology device as a prize, which resulted in a 12% increase in orders and 36% increase in subscribers over a one-month period. Their business had nothing to do with technology, however, it's a high demand promotional item that gets attention.

A nomination for Knots-of-Love, a one-woman nonprofit organization founded by Christine Shively that's dedicated to providing cancer and trauma patients with hand crocheted caps, was submitted via PeopleAllStars.com.

The goal for entering the contest was to boost their amount of volunteers and cap volume, increase geographic reach, help non-cancer patients, and increase financial donations for production and overhead support. Since the organization was rather small and underfunded, challenges to winning the contest included size, limited resources, overhead costs, unknown new business, and poor economic conditions.

Recruiting

The next step was to reach out to the Knots-of-Love social media contacts to spread the word. Since the CEO and Founder, Christine Shively, was not yet a subscriber to various social media sites, we brought in her husband, Rob Shively (a beginner to social media), to reach out to his contacts. Using LinkedIn, Rob asked twenty of his friends and supporters to consider nominating Christine, and also requested their support in spreading the word.

TIP: Be specific about what you want followers to do and make it easy for them. Provide the contest Web site link, your Web site link, and any data necessary for your subscribers to implement the request. Remember, they are following you for a reason and they believe in your professional capabilities—they will support you, so don't be afraid to ask.

With only twenty LinkedIn subscribers and a clearly stated call to action, Christine was notified in June of 2009 by MLB contest officials that she had been selected as one of three finalists to represent the Angels.

Game On

Using myriad social media platforms, we let several people know that she was one of the three finalists. Moreover we let them know that a link to the voting page would be coming on June 8th and that we would appreciate their support. We sent out evites and meeting reminders for that date.

TIP: Think of any platforms you can use to spread your message. In this case we used an Internet-based event planning and invitation tool, Evite (www.evite.com). This format allows you to design an invitation and send to contacts with a variety of options. Since we wanted the process to be as interactive as possible, we decided to allow everyone on the invitation list to see who else was invited and all yes/no/maybe responses, all with invitee comments. Most of our invitees responded YES and added comments, which included their ideas, willingness to forward to their contact list, wishing us well, and much more. It was truly a way to get the conversation flowing and allowed everyone to participate. If you are running a contest, this is also a great way to get feedback from contestants. Their information will help you adjust your contest to be successful for you and the contestants. There is also a built-in function that allows you to "take a poll," and you can ask contestants a question and get their immediate feedback. As an example, "Would you rather win an iPod or a gift certificate to Apple.com?"

In addition to the evite, we also sent our contact list an e-mail with the June 8th date and link, invited our growing LinkedIn contacts to vote with the link and posted the link information on our status, and began tweeting the request for voting support with links to our followers.

On June 8th at 12:01 a.m. EST, the voting page for the three finalists for all thirty teams went live. We posted the link to the voting page on the LinkedIn profile page as well as added it to the end of the narrative profile on LinkedIn. We also sent it to the myriad groups we were members of and asked supporters to do the same.

A Knots-of-Love volunteer had just setup Twitter a few weeks earlier and had approximately fifty followers before this contest. As a result of the initial tweet (and retweets) about this campaign, we suddenly saw the volume of followers rise to over 2,100 in a matter of two weeks. Hundreds of Twitter and LinkedIn followers tweeted and retweeted the link to thousands of people with the news that she was a finalist and a request for votes, and asked that people also retweet the message.

Various Knots-of-Love volunteers added the company's link to their LinkedIn profiles, should someone want to go deeper into Knots-of-Love. As a result of these efforts, the "join my network" request volume increased by 30%. We also submitted "request for vote" to LinkedIn contacts along with a link to vote.

We developed a social media strategy to immediately post, repost, and ask others to spread the news to the voting link through:

- the articles she was receiving in the Orange County Register
- the blogs
- her public appearance before 44,000 fans before the first game of the Angels vs. Dodgers LA rivalry
- the Angels web site
- online polls
- her Flip videos of trips to cancer centers delivering hats

We encouraged people to let their corporations know that this charity existed and that it was nominated to represent the Angels at the All-Star Game in St. Louis. We asked them to spread the word and the link for votes. Through LinkedIn, Twitter, and Facebook, we received messages that people were voting for Knots-of-Love multiple times. Several LinkedIn members reported voting as many as 150–250 times each. Since its inception, several corporations had become involved in helping Knots-of-Love by supporting their efforts to help them grow and be able to provide more chemo caps to cancer patients, who can so desperately use kindness from a stranger. By using LinkedIn, we accomplished the goal of letting those businesses and corporations know about the contest and solicited their support.

Twitter is more about quick hits; mass exposure similar to broadcast television, while LinkedIn is more akin to targeted direct marketing. We used Twitter to spread the word to the masses. For those who wanted to know more about Knots-of-Love, they could go to Facebook and LinkedIn specifically to find out information about the charity and the people behind it before going to the Web site Knots-of-Love.org.

Via the various platforms, we answered many questions from people who were touched by Knots-of-Love, and who subsequently voted and got others in their social networks to vote. We heard that people who heard about this contest via social networks had gathered for voting parties. We received feedback and posts of support, and votes from all over the world including India, Thailand, Singapore, the UK, Scotland, Italy, and Australia.

A final push-to-get-out-the-vote strategy using social networks exclusively went into effect during the final voting weekend of June 19–21. On Friday June 26th, Knots-of-Love's Shively was notified by the Major League baseball contest officials, letting her know she won and was going to be the Angels' representative at the All-Star game in St. Louis. Later that day, Knots-of-Love received another call from MLB saying that a video and photo crew would be coming Monday morning at 8 a.m. They arrived, all ten of them, and stayed until seven that night, with a quick stop by a local cancer center where they filmed and interviewed a few patients who had received caps. We thought all thirty nominees were going thru the same thing.

On Tuesday, contest officials announced the thirty team contest winners, one per MLB team. We posted, tweeted, and blogged to everyone and thanked them for their support.

A few days later, after fielding hundreds of congratulatory postings, tweets, emails, and calls, MLB held another press conference where they announced that five of the thirty winners would be presented in a pre-game video by the five living presidents.[1]

During the All-Star game ceremonies, Christine Shively, Founder and CEO of Knots-of-Love, and her son, were treated like real all-Star VIPs. They participated in press conferences with the Commissioner of MLB, and with some of the players competing in the game. They rode in cars for the All-Star parade and felt as if they were truly the all-Stars for the day. Interestingly, fans knew Christine's name as she traveled around town and rode through the parade that 250,000 attended. We could only assume that people got to know her from the exposure she received from all the voting activities and visits to the social networks like LinkedIn and her Web site where fans could dig deeper.

The presentation of the People All-Stars Among Us on the field prior to the game was uniquely special. All sixty-four players came out to greet them. They received a chance to talk to every one of them and share their respective joy at being selected by their fans and peers.

---

[1]http://mlb.mlb.com/news/article.jsp?ymd=20090714&content_id=5874014

Since the All-Star game, some of the following things have occurred:

1. Several articles and blogs from around the world have spoken of Knots-of-Love and Christine.

2. The Web site received so many hits the day after the All-Star game that it was knocked out of service.

3. The MLB Go Beyond Web site that the five living presidents promoted during the game has received millions of hits.

4. The front page of President Obama's Serve.gov Web site presented the video that featured Christine (Knots-of-Love) and the four other All-Stars.

5. Several businesses from around the world were touched by what Knots-of-Love does and were inspired to donate money to help defer some of the charity's expenses.

6. One business, a jewelry manufacturer in New York, decided to make a line of necklace jewelry based on the Knots-of-Love logo (a heart). The line will be gold with diamonds and will be sold to retailers like Zales and Kay Jewelers. Knots-of-Love will receive a percentage of all sales.

7. *Meet The Press* host David Gregory did a segment on the show where he gave credit to MLB for "nailing it" with the All-Stars Among Us campaign and pre-game video.

8. Supporting posts were sent from people all over the world. One post said the following to Christine's husband: *"Congrats Rob, what a special moment for the Shively's. You have one special woman there and she had my whole office in tears during that video!!!"*

9. Knots-of-Love has seen the single largest increase in the number of volunteer members since that video presentation. The member base of 250 women who knot and crochet chemo caps for cancer patients has grown to over 400. That represents a 60% increase in less than two weeks. It took Christine two years to get the first 250 members, resulting in an increase in the number of chemo caps to cancer patients of about 10,000.

Another result of the contest is people from all over the world and the United States now know about Knots-of-Love. Volunteer numbers are up, new chemo caps are higher, and new donations have increased.

Everyday we receive thank you letters from patients, their loved ones and the nurses who treat them. The following is a sample:

"Seeing new caps in the basket are a little slice of heaven when the patients check in for their treatment. I've helped one of my favorite male patients pick out one that's 'the most masculine.' I've helped women find the perfect one in their favorite color. You are truly an angel. I thank you...on behalf of all of the patients I see who wear your darling caps. You have no idea how much of a difference you make in their lives. May God bless you in everything you do." — Amy, RN

"Dear Knots-of-love,
I am currently a patient at the Mayo clinic in Phoenix, AZ. I was diagnosed with non-Hodgkins lymphoma and I have been undergoing treatment for four months. I have been coming to the outpatient section for three months now and the room is always cold and the blankets here don't seem to do the trick. There was no way to stay warm...well that was until today. A box of hats arrived at the Mayo OPIV and because of your kindness and caring I now have something to wear that will keep me from feeling cold for the several hours that I am getting treatment here. There is however, one benefit of it being so cold in here...when I leave treatment the 105 degree temperatures outside become a welcome. On behalf of myself, and all the other patients, as well as the Mayo Clinic OPIV ward, I want to send a heartfelt thanks for your gift as well as your time. Thanks again!" — Nathan Day

"On behalf of the patients at Cedars Sinai Outpatient Cancer Center, I want to extend our sincere appreciation for your very thoughtful donations of hats. We gave them to our patients who were receiving chemotherapy, and they loved them! You can't imagine the joy a gift like this brings to the patients. Today in the midst of our busy schedules, most of us fail to take the time to think how we can help others. Your simple act of kindness exemplifies how one company, or even one person, can make such a difference to so many. Very truly yours." — Diane Gabay, RN, MN

"Some people have a special gift for making sure that everyone is taken care of. They always remember the little things that make others feel loved. What a wonderful organization you have put together. It is quite uncomfortable to be bald, you are either too hot or too cold. Having to deal with wigs, scarves and hats is an undertaking all on its own. Much love to you."

"Dear Christine,
Being diagnosed with ovarian cancer four months ago was one of the toughest things I have ever gone through. But when you get a bag of the cutest, warmest, made-with-love hats passed around the chemo room, what a joy. What touches me most is that people who will never even know me cared enough to take the time to make something that makes me feel better because my head is warm and I look cute. I need to look cute right now; it's good for my heart. What you do is even better for my heart. Thank you again from the top of my cute, warm head to the bottom of my heart. God's blessings to you all."

"Thanks for allowing us to be a part of KOL and the opportunity to perhaps bring a smile to someone's face who is going through the fight of their life. Thank you!" Carol, Knots-of-Love member

Alane Anderson is the Founder and President of Vision Project Management, LLC, an e-marketing and social media firm. She is an award winning professional and graduate of the University of Irvine's Executive MBA program. After leaving IBM, she decided to combine her experience in technology, marketing, and sales to help others bring their business into the new era of Internet marketing and social networking. She formed Vision Project Management, LLC, in 1995. Since then, Alane and her team of professionals have worked with many clients to build their unique online and offline presence, including Virgin Unite Foundation, Indian Wells, Avery Dennison, Weyerhauser, Trus Joist, and Mitsubishi. As a consultant, speaker, and trainer, she demonstrates how to harness the power of the Internet using Twitter, Facebook, LinkedIn, blogs, and YouTube, along with specific examples to stimulate the imagination of her audience. She has spoken at various universities and corporations throughout the country.

Alane Anderson
Alane@AndersonWWW.com
@AlaneAnderson
http://www.linkedin.com/alaneanderson
http://www.facebook.com/AlaneAnderson
http://www.marketingmavin.blogspot.com

The Artists

"*Mad Men*" on Twitter: Drama in 140 characters

by

Carri Bugbee

The story of @PeggyOlson and the rest of the *Mad Men* on Twitter is filled with as many plot twists, mysterious characters, and questionable motives as a well-crafted drama. It was "written" by fans who helped shape it every day with their passion for the story *and* the medium. For many (certainly for me), the medium was even more important than the message.

The saga started for me on Monday, August 18, 2008. I was tweeting from my personal account, @CarriBugbee, when something in the twitterstream caught my eye: "@Don_Draper is on Twitter." It was like a slap upside the head. I was a big fan of the show, I was a marketer, and I was already managing multiple Twitter accounts. The idea of tweeting for television characters seemed like such a great marketing idea, my initial reaction was "Wow....why didn't I think of that?!"

I immediately clicked through to see what @Don_Draper was up to. He was tweeting in character to @Joan_Holloway, but not to any other *Mad Men* characters. I crossed my fingers (figuratively since they were flying over the keyboard) and raced to see if anyone had nabbed Peggy Olson as a character on Twitter. My heart was literally pounding the way it does when you're dialing into a radio contest and you desperately want to be first. I certainly felt like I had "won" when I discovered @PeggyOlson was available and grabbed it before anyone else could.

I began tweeting to Don and Joan right away. To my delight, they tweeted back! I initially thought tweeting for Peggy would just be a fun way to role-play my favorite *Mad Men* character. I figured I'd tweet at my friends for a couple of weeks, we'd have a good laugh, and interest would fall off. However, from the first tweet, I realized many people thought the characters were part of an actual marketing campaign for the show.

> "*Love how AMC integrated Mad Men into Twitter—taking a character beyond the tube.*" – @tjeffrey

> "*'Mad Men' characters on Twitter take us right into the show - http://tinyurl.com/6ykt3r*" – @mediaphyter

"Would love to meet the clever PR agent behind the Mad Men tweets... ;)" – @SarahJaneMorris

"I don't know what's up with all these Mad Men Twitter handles...but I sure am excited to see what they have to say." – @susqhb

"I am loving the Mad Men Characters twittering. So fun." – @stephaniemar

As soon as I saw that, I deleted my first few tweets from Peggy, which were a bit on the snarky side and dedicated myself to making Peggy's Twitter persona accurately reflect her on-screen persona. I got an immediate charge out of entertaining the "fans." It was a little like being on stage. I'm a professional singer with an acting background, so this was right up my alley. As a marketing pro, I also recognized that this little experiment could provide a great case study about creative ways to use Twitter for marketing, so that became my primary motivation. I started treating @PeggyOlson like a real job—to the extent this was possible while not having any interaction with AMC.

Proof Point: Twitter Can Sell *and* Entertain

Peggy picked up nearly two hundred followers that first evening, which shocked and delighted me. Gaining two hundred followers in a few hours may not seem like much now. Celebrities add thousands of followers a day, but in August 2008, there were no celebrities on Twitter.

Mad Men on Twitter went viral over the next few days. Nearly all the Sterling Cooper characters (those who worked at the ad agency on the show) were grabbed up within the next forty-eight hours. Marketers and fans of the show were gushing about this "genius" campaign and/or speculating about who was behind it (many of those blogs and articles are archived at delicious.com/peggyolson).

Home Profile Find People Settings Help Sign out

Mad Men characters on Twitter are the future of grassroots movie and TV promotion. Seriously ahead of the curve. @adage You listening?

10:31 PM Aug 21st, 2008 via web   Reply Retweet

aziari
Amy Ziari

Each time someone raved about the "campaign," it gave me a little thrill. It also convinced me to stay anonymous. I hadn't initially planned to be incognito, but once I saw that people enjoyed analyzing the tweets and speculating, I didn't want to spoil the fun. Plus, most people thought the *Mad Men* tweets were quite authentic. I was worried their perception of that would change if they knew the tweeters had nothing to do with the show.

The other thing I did was attempt to meet the people behind the other *Mad Men* characters on Twitter. I wanted to convince them to stay anonymous as well. Even though I didn't think any of the tweeters were connected with AMC, I was very cautious through this process. It occurred to me that once the mad tweeting had taken off, someone from AMC or its agencies may have jumped in to "manage" it—overtly or surreptitiously.

I started with @Don_Draper and @Joan_Holloway, since they were the first characters I found. Joan played coy—she didn't want to coordinate or reveal her identity. Don and Peggy began exchanging direct messages in character, but quickly dropped the façade and started messaging each other out of character, but we still didn't exchange our identities. I met the people behind other office characters right away. @Sal_Romano, @Paul_Kinsey, and @Bertram_Cooper all had started up within forty-eight hours after I did and were happy to share their identities and ideas.

One thing was clear: we all got a kick out of the interaction and the publicity—even though we were anonymous. It inspired us to increase our followers and continue engaging authentically with fans of the show. While it was big fun, it was also *very* time-consuming. I put in about fifty hours during the first eight days I was on the "job."

Brandjacking or Fan Fiction?

On the evening of August 25, 2008, just a week after I started @PeggyOlson, I was busy following people talking about *Mad Men* on Twitter when it just froze. I hit "home" to refresh my page and was horrified to see that my account had been suspended for "strange activity."

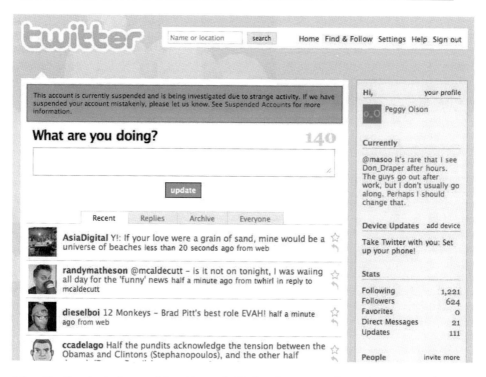

I frantically started searching through Twitter's terms of service to see if I had accidentally violated any rules. A few minutes later, I received a vague e-mail from Twitter with the ominous subject heading: "Trademark Infringement." My heart leapt into my throat.

In just a week's time, I had already invested a great deal of time and energy into @PeggyOlson and I'd become very attached to her. I loved the role-play. I liked the challenge of writing in Peggy's voice. I was competitive about increasing her followers (I really wanted to beat @Don_Draper, who had a six-day head start). I was especially giddy about all the blog posts that said this was the new way to do marketing, since that was exactly what I wanted to prove.

I swallowed hard and started looking at all the other *Mad Men* tweeters to see if their profiles had been taken down. Only @Don_Draper, @Joan_Holloway, and @PeggyOlson had been suspended. I was mystified.

Until that point, it had never even occurred to me that what we were doing could be construed as trademark infringement or brandjacking. Using fake names and avatars, even celebrity names or approximations on Twitter and other social media platforms was quite common. I was stunned that Twitter had targeted us. But that was the just the first in a series of twists and turns on a crazy roller coaster ride that provided me with a fast-track education about crisis communications, fan fiction, entertainment marketing, and savvy brand management.

When a Character Falls on Twitter, Everybody "Hears" It

Just moments after @Don_Draper, @Joan_Holloway, and @PeggyOlson were suspended, the twitterverse (that's what many of us refer to as the universe of people on Twitter) erupted with curiosity, helpful information and commentary.

> *"... and one by one, @don_draper, @peggyolson, @joan_holloway... suspended and gone."* – @neilkleid

> *"Hmmm... the @peggyolson and @don_draper Twitter accounts were suspended for suspicious activity."* – @kessler

> *"Whoa, was @don_draper not an officially sanctioned account? Whoever it was knew what was going to happen in the newest episode. Epic sad"* – @cinevegas

> *"If @don_draper didn't exhibit suspicious activity, none of us would actually watch Mad Men."* – @Armano

I was riveted by the tweetstream for the next few hours as the story picked up steam. This is how I found out *why* @PeggyOlson and the other Mad Med tweeters had been suspended:

> *"Update: Twitter blacklisted the Mad Men characters due to a DMCA takedown notice http://is.gd/1UYy"* – @parislemon

VentureBeat (now SocialBeat) managed to contact Biz Stone (co-founder of Twitter) to determine that AMC had sent a DMCA (Digital Millennium Copyright Act) take-down notice to Twitter. My first thought was "Oh my god, I'm going to get sued by a network!" I immediately composed an e-mail to a lawyer friend who specializes in intellectual property and trademark issues.

I was also indignant. We were doing a great job of promoting AMC's program for *free* and we were all very respectful of the show and the characters. I thought if AMC actually cared about their characters conversing on Twitter, they would have done it themselves. Moreover, if they wanted to know what the *Mad Men* tweeters were up to, all they had to do was reach out and ask.

Since my indignation was stronger than my fear, I pulled something out of my back pocket: @Peggy_Olson. I had reserved several versions of Peggy's name and decided I wasn't going down without a tweet! This is the only thing I ever wrote for Peggy that was somewhat out of character. It ended up being widely quoted:

I worked hard. I did my job. But the boys at Twitter are just as churlish as the boys at Sterling Cooper. Such a pity that they're so petty.

about 6 hours ago from web

Peggy_Olson

People started following the new Peggy and furiously tweeted about the take-down. I was up until 4:00 a.m. reading the twitterstream. I couldn't sleep anyway. I was worried I'd be shot down by a posse of Hollywood attorneys the next day. When I woke up a few hours later, the story had spread like wildfire with east coast tweeters catching wind of what was happening. Most were outraged that their Twitter "friends" from 1961 had been taken away from them.

> Oh AMC TV...how could you be so dumb. Everybody loved the **Mad Men** Tweeters, regardless of whether or not they were real. – @jpgardner

> Goodbye **Mad Men** on Twitter? http://twurl.nl/p8of0o Bad move on AMC's part in my opinion. – @stevehall

> ☐ Looks like **Mad Men** was Twitterjacked. And AMC doesn't like it. I hope you staff up the accounts, AMC. http://snurl.com/3jydk – @ScottMonty

> V. bummed that Twitter suspended @peggyolson, esp. since she was more interesting than a lot of "real" twitterers. – @jonnodotcom

> Let the **Mad Men** Tweet!!!!! – @adtothebone

> **(Mad Men**) - hopefully AMC will resurrect the Twitter accts now that they've "retrieved" the usernames. If not it's a huge opportunity lost. – @uniquevisitor

> @pdxmama twitter is removing **Mad Men** tweets?? No!!! I love being tweeted by fictional characters! – @pdxlilly

A number of bloggers had offered more detailed perspectives on the takedown. Most railed against AMC for taking such a hard stance against people who were essentially doing their marketing for free—often with funny headlines and graphics. I appreciated the levity.

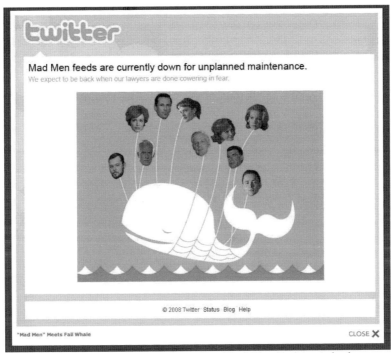

One of my favorite images from the *Mad Men* Twitter takedown.
Alas, I never knew who created it.

By midday, the Hollywood Reporter wrote about it. Reuters then picked it up, and within hours it was international news. I was stunned, to say the least. Reporters were reaching out to @Peggy_Olson (my back-up character) and the other *Mad Men* characters who were still functioning. They were eager to find out the identities of the fan fiction outlaws.

I was busy on the back channel (e-mails and direct messages) trying to convince the other *Mad Men* tweeters not to reveal their identities and not to give up on the grand experiment. This was no small feat. It was very tempting to give an interview to a big news organization—especially if our time as *Mad Men* was over anyway. As a PR gal, I sensed that the story would be a flash in the pan because we had just gotten started. Some of the characters had only been on board a day or two. It was definitely too early to glean any actionable insight for a white paper.

However, the tweeter behind @Paul_Kinsey was extremely worried that AMC's lawyers would come knocking. In an effort to mitigate future legal problems, he wrote about his identity in a blog post (no longer on the Internet) the morning after the takedown. I understood why he did it, but I was still crushed. I felt like he'd given people the answer to the mystery while we were still in the middle of the story.

By now, the drama of the tweeters was just as riveting as anything that had ever happened on the small screen with *Mad Men*. A big corporation had us running scared, people were scurrying to take cover, the loosely assembled "team" could not agree on a course of action, the press was eager to report on it, we already had a leak, there was rampant speculation by on-lookers, and I was extremely worried about anyone discovering my real identity (sounds like a *Mad Men* character we know, eh?). All I could do was read the tweetstream and write cryptic messages (in character) as @Peggy_Olson.

> @*dabitch* *Thanks for the advice. Unfortunately, I don't seem entirely in control of my own career.* – @Peggy_Olson

> *Pleased to discover it's not hard to make friends in advertising after all. But the guys in legal are humorless, and frankly not too bright.* – @Peggy_Olson

> @*CatWeaver* *There is a lot of confusion in the office today. Nobody at Sterling Cooper seems to know what's going on. Mr. Draper isn't here.* – @Peggy_Olson

Suddenly, at 3:15 p.m. the day after our profiles were taken down, our accounts went back up! I received an e-mail from Twitter saying AMC wanted them to restore the accounts and asked us to contact AMC's digital agency, Deep Focus. Of course, I immediately started tweeting as @PeggyOlson again.

> @*saleandro* *After a long, exhausting day in meetings, I'm finally free.* – @PeggyOlson

> @*bryanfuhr* *I've chatted with* @*Don_Draper*, *but he's got a lot to handle at the moment. He'll be back in the office very soon.* – @PeggyOlson

> *I don't think I've spent so much time in meetings as I have in the past two days. I just want to do my job. I'm glad to be back at my desk.* – @PeggyOlson

I felt a little uneasy about reaching out to the folks at Deep Focus, but after thinking about it for twenty-four hours, I was more curious than cautious. I dialed in as "Peggy" and eventually told them who I was. Since I was a marketer and was mostly interested in @PeggyOlson as a case study, I think they were convinced I wasn't going to do anything to damage the AMC brand.

Later that evening, I had a long phone call with the creator of @Don_Draper as well. We finally revealed our identities to each other and it was fantastic to connect. He felt much the same way I did, that this was a great marketing experiment, and that's why he created @Don_Draper in the first place. It was the first of several long phone calls over the next few weeks in which we discussed plot lines, character motivations, marketing, social media and the *Mad Men* tweeter backchannel (which is another saga).

Fan Fiction Wins Out

Ironically, the DMCA takedown provided a tremendous amount of publicity for the *Mad Men* tweeters, and actually encouraged many more to join the *Mad Men* Twitterverse. Over the course of about ten days, at least one hundred and fifty news and blog articles were written about the fan fiction drama. It was covered by the New York Times, the Wall Street Journal, the UK Guardian, BusinessWeek, and publications in at least five other countries, including Brazil and Germany.

Every available character name was snapped up, including the remaining office characters, peripheral characters, people from Don Draper's home and neighborhood, even inanimate objects! @Dick_Whitman and @Betty_Draper showed up the day of the takedown, with a second @BettyDraper accompanied by neighborhood gossip @Francine_Hanson arriving the next day. @Harry_Crane, @Ken_Cosgrove, @Midge_Daniels, @Sally_Draper, and many more came on board. @Jimmy_Barrett was particularly brilliant. He nailed the obnoxious humor of the second-string rat-pack comedian on the show. His cheating wife, @Bobbie_Barrett, was true to form as well.

Over the next few weeks, whenever a new character appeared on the television program, that character would show up on Twitter the next day. Even the new-fangled copy machine that was installed at Sterling Cooper received a Twitter account: @Xerox914 (one of my personal favorites).

Just as interesting, a lot of fictional accounts were created specifically to interact with *Mad Men* characters, though they weren't *Mad Men* themselves. The first was @FrankAdman, who joined right after @Don_Draper did and was clearly a send-up of the Sterling Cooper era of ad guys. Mailroom boy, @Bud_Melman, joined us the day before the takedown. He was very helpful in delivering inter-office memos while Don, Joan, and Peggy were "indisposed." @HullaballooGirl was a '60s-era jet-setting fashion model who exhorted @PeggyOlson to break out of her conservative rut.

Then there were characters based on real people of the era. @David_Ogilvy, @Frank_OHara, @Dick_Nixon, @BarryGoldwater, and others jumped into the fray to engage *Mad Men* tweeters in relevant conversation about ideas and events of the period.

Later, a crop of commentators arrived on the scene. I think of them as the tweet tabloids. Those included @OnMadMen and @MadMenTalking. Those accounts are now silent, but new tweeters have popped up to take their place: @MadMenTweets, @MadMenFodder, and @MadMenWiki.

What's most fascinating to me is that the people behind every one of these characters stayed anonymous for months. Most of them still are. The tweeter behind @Don_Draper revealed his identity a few weeks after season two was over (then went dark until season three when he passed his character on to somebody else), but the rest of us stayed the course.

Other characters went dark as well, and new versions of those characters popped up to take their places. Some of the new characters were even better than the originals. In 2009, @_DonDraper surpassed anything @Don_Draper had done, in both writing and followers. @_PeteCampbell, @BertramCooper, and @HarryCrane have long since superseded their originals as well.

In some cases, the original tweeters just didn't want to put in the time to do their characters justice, so they handed them over to me. Yes, I tweet for multiple *Mad Men*—new and old! Those other characters shall remain a secret for the time being.

Engaging The Passion Of @PeggyOlson's Fans

In December 2009, a small start-up in New York City had an idea that blew up into a star-studded event dubbed "The Oscars of Twitter." Of course, I'm talking about *The Shorty Awards*.

Sawhorse Media launched the Shorty Awards thinking it might end up being nothing more than a few dozen people toasting their favorite tweeters in a bar. Yet, thousands of people participated and twenty-six winners were named. True to the spontaneous nature of Twitter, people were allowed to make up their own categories and voters were *required* to tweet unique reasons why their favorite tweeters deserved to win. This inspired lots of great content as people became creative with categories and nominations.

@PeggyOlson was nominated in the advertising category. I was surprised by all the spontaneous, unsolicited votes that she received initially. However, it became highly competitive very quickly, and I realized I was at a huge disadvantage. People (and brand accounts) wrote numerous campaign tweets, sent out e-mails, put badges on their Web site, called their friends, wrote scripts to auto-populate text for voting, got their employees to help out—you name it.

I was still clandestine, so I couldn't use *any* marketing tools besides Twitter. I couldn't even ask my friends to vote! Plus, I had to stay in character as a copywriter from 1962 while campaigning. What I did have on my side was a community (that I'd worked very hard to cultivate) and a bank of good will. This came in handy. Fans of @PeggyOlson not only showed up for her in a big way, many of their tweets were quite inspired.

> *I vote for @PeggyOlson in the Shorty Awards Finals for #advertising because she can slay an anachronism in 140 characters! – @ProfOrganizer*

I vote for @PeggyOlson in the Shorty Awards Finals for #advertising because...I love when my virtual reality worlds clash! – @SheriWhitt

I vote for @PeggyOlson in the Shorty Awards Finals for #advertising because of the fabulous, innovative role playing. – @Sidney_Williams

I vote for @PeggyOlson in the Shorty Awards Finals for #advertising because she revolutionized the way to market tv! – @annawhitlow

I vote for @PeggyOlson in the Shorty Awards Finals for #advertising because she was my first 2-way rel with a show. – @redw0rm

@PeggyOlson ended up with the second most number of votes across all categories in the preliminaries and went on to win the Shorty Award in advertising.

The year's best producers of short* content

*140 characters or less, on Twitter

The first annual Shorty Awards Ceremony was held on February 11, 2009. Read what the press had to say about it and watch video from the night. Get news about next year's awards and who to follow on Twitter by joining the email list, subscribing to the blog, or following @ShortyNews on Twitter.

More about the Shorty Awards

The 2008 Shorty Awards Winners and Finalists

advertising

 Sponsored by Porter Novelli

PeggyOlson	madmain	girlinyourshirt	tedmurphy	rdeal1
Vote!	Vote!	Vote!	Vote!	Vote!

Since the Shorty Awards were to be broadcast live on YouTube, I realized I would finally have to reveal my identity. I didn't want to give it up without a little fanfare though, so I planned to do it *on stage* during the awards show. Not only did the promoters of the Shorty Awards use the promise of this revelation to help promote the show, I was also able to offer the scoop to a Wall Street Journal reporter who was interested in covering the event.

The story was covered by numerous other media outlets as well, including BusinessWeek.com, NYTimes.com, and Wired.com. Michael Duff, a writer with LubbockOnline.com, even conducted a live "twinterview" that started with

@PeggyOlson and segued into an interview with @CarriBugbee (archived with the other stories at delicious.com/peggyolson) right after the show.

As Twitter Grows, So Does The *Mad Men* Twitterverse

In 2010, the *Mad Men* Twitterverse is more robust than ever. The original tweeters are still active, but there's a whole new crop of *Mad Men* tweeters as well. Since the character names were already taken, many of the new tweeters have appended their names with SCDP for Sterling Cooper Draper Pryce (the agency where Don and Peggy work in season four of the AMC TV program).

@PeggyOlson continues to received many tweets from fans who are thrilled to discover her. As in years past, they often believe it is part of an AMC marketing program. They are almost always thrilled to engage with Peggy, so I don't disavow them of that notion.

I never tweet from @PeggyOlson to @CarriBugbee or reference anything about me from Peggy's account. I like to maintain the mystery for Peggy's fans, as much as that's possible. Some marketers and friends know I have multiple identities. I also tweet for @CarriBella (my jazzsinger persona), @JazzCrowd (an account to promote jazz music and events), and accounts for clients, nonprofits and experimentation. Quite often, though, people know both me and @PeggyOlson but don't know we're the same person. When they find out, they say "Oh, *you're* @PeggyOlson? I love her!"

There's more of the story to tell of course, including the insights I've gleaned about Twitter marketing, fan fiction, crisis communications, even group social dynamics—but that would require a lot more space. If you'd like to learn more, please follow @CarriBugbee on Twitter. If you're a *Mad Men* fan, engage with @PeggyOlson and the other *Mad Men* tweeters. They're the modern wave of advertising, don't you know?

Note: I didn't provide the identities of any of the *Mad Men* tweeters because many are still anonymous, but this changes all the time. Sometimes characters are even handed off to other tweeters. Instead of inaccurately reporting any *Mad Men* tweeter's identity (or leaving someone out), I'll leave it to readers to discover them. I actually prefer it to keep most of it a mystery, which is why I haven't revealed the other *Mad Men* characters I tweet for.

Carri Bugbee is a social media marketing strategist, writer and PR pro. She won a Shorty Award for tweeting as the *Mad Men* character, @PeggyOlson, and has spoken about social media methodologies at many conferences and events. Bugbee owns Big Deal PR, which helps clients get ramped up on social media platforms and integrate them with traditional marketing. She teaches a class in social media marketing at Portland State University and is the founder of Social Media Club Portland. All her social profiles are listed at CarriBugbee.com.

Inventing Twitterature:

How I released my debut novel via Twitter and landed a book deal

by

Matt Stewart

On a fog-soaked morning in 2005, I sat down to write a short story. I'd recently run off some photocopies at a forgettable copy shop on San Francisco's Market Street, and was struck with a vision of this innocuous locale thrown into upheaval by fictional staffer Esmerelda Van Twinkle, a woefully obese wannabe chef who wound up becoming the fastest cash register operator in town. My imagination started pumping and words poured out of me—I gave Esmerelda a massive wool bag that functioned as a portable closet/utility belt, worked in a love interest with an itinerant coupon distributor, and described Esmerelda's morning with the most blisteringly evocative descriptions I could conjure, her "gumdrop-shaped body quivering like a landed bass" with "the permanent bun containing her once-silky chestnut hair bobbing like a buoy in a tsunami" on her "uneasy shamble" to work.

Over the next few years the tale blossomed into a complete novel, a brassy, multi-generational San Francisco family saga loosely structured on the historical French Revolution. Some said my whimsical style reminded them of *A Confederacy of Dunces*; others compared the writing to Junot Diaz or even Jonathan Franzen. After an eternity of rewrites, I landed an enthusiastic agent, and we sent the book to publishers in the fall of 2008.

It was all coming together, I thought.

My timing couldn't have been worse. Amid an imploding economy, the slow-moving publishing industry was facing rapid technological changes; fear was in the air. My novel is bold, ambitious, gutsy, from a debut novelist with no track record—I posed a significant risk. Over the course of four months, the novel was rejected by thirty publishers.

But I believed in this book, and so did my agent. I analyzed feedback from publishers, consulted with my inner circle of literati, and spent another three months rewriting. Freshly polished, my agent sent the manuscript to another batch of publishers in spring 2009.

By the end of June, rejections were trickling in again. The economy still stank, as did publishing industry morale. I considered reaching out to small niche publishers, or self-publishing, or even giving up. None of those options sat well; my agent and I truly believed this was a good book, and I didn't have the time or expertise to self-publish. I needed—and felt the book deserved—a professional launch into the world.

This was a real dark point. As a writer, I've come to enjoy total control—over characters' lives, over plot arcs and zany twists, over choosing the word "zany" instead of "wild." Forced to wait for the publishing gods to pass judgment, I felt handcuffed, subverted, stripped of my writerly independence. And I've never been a patient person.

It hit me in the shower just before the Fourth of July: why not release my novel on Twitter?

I'd been using Twitter increasingly for work, and knew it was a snappy way to communicate. I could interact with readers on an unprecedented scale, sparring over word choice and soliciting feedback on plot direction. I recognized that Twitter's much-mocked brevity is actually its underlying strength, that people actually read 140 characters—once you've looked at it, you've already read it— and checking out a few of my zippy snippets could entice readers to learn more. Moreover, Twitter was hotter than an Atlanta sidewalk in August, the latest media darling. Maybe I could be that wacky sign of the times news story, build a market, and boost the odds of a book deal. A round of Googling indicated that nobody else had done this before; the title of First Twitter Novelist was mine for the taking. If my gambit didn't get any attention, I'd be right back where I started—nowhere. And if it did, maybe it'd help launch my book, and my writing career.

Why the hell not?

I called my dad, who's a lawyer and has never ever used Twitter; not only did he confirm that my plan wouldn't forfeit any copyright claims, he thought it was a terrific idea. I called up my agent, who signed off on the plan so long as I didn't register for an ISBN number, which is used to track sales. As she put it, the only thing harder than selling a first novel is selling a second novel when the first novel tanks.

Logistically, I had neither the time nor hand-eye coordination to sit by a computer all day, cutting and pasting my novel into 140-character chunks. I raised this problem with a friend who works at Pandora Internet Radio, and he casually mentioned that it'd be pretty easy to automate the process. Three days later, he'd engineered a web script that sliced and diced my book into tweetable form, complete with hashtags and links and publishable on a schedule of my choosing. I put together a basic Web site. I posted the entire ISBN-free novel in the Kindle store and on Scribd for purchase. It took about two weeks to cue everything up for Bastille Day—the natural launch date for a book titled The French Revolution.

I anticipated a major objection to my plan: who's going to read a novel on Twitter? Nobody, I conceded on a Q&A posted on my Web site—it's a huge pain in the ass to reverse engineer a coherent story from 140-character segments. Rather, Twitter's job was to capture attention and build an audience by showcasing my razor-sharp wordplay, maybe even persuading readers to buy a digital book—like watching a few minutes of a TV show before ordering the whole season. Also, this was an experiment. Bear with me, please.

On July 14, 2009—Bastille Day—I hit go.

I told all my friends; I alerted online celebs; I digitally flagged it with anybody I thought might care, and plenty that didn't. And, most importantly, I told the tech and publishing media. My day jobs for the past six years have all involved some aspect of PR, and I know a few tricks to attract a journalist's attention and guide them along to publishing a piece. Through a mixture of connections, hard work, good timing, and Irish luck, I landed the best media coverage of my life: The New York Times, Wall Street Journal, CNN, Techcrunch, Le Figaro, AFP, and dozens more around the world covered my Twitter escapades. Publishing insiders circulated the story; social media barons chimed in; even @GuyKawasaki tweeted about it. For a couple of days there, I was somewhat notorious.

Amazingly, the media coverage and social media buzz was overwhelmingly supportive. Admitting the limited thrill of reading a novel on Twitter submarined some objections, certainly, but I also tapped a deeper zeitgeist about books and how we read. Many were frustrated with the sluggish pace of innovation in publishing, how the book industry seemed resigned to succumb to the same structural disruptions that shattered the music world, even with a ten-year head start. I represented a welcome attempt at evolution, a step at stumbling toward some sort of progress.

Six weeks later, I landed a book deal; the hardcopy was officially released on Bastille Day 2010. My plan pretty much worked out perfectly.

A few lessons:

1. Some derisively called my experiment a gimmick or publicity stunt. So what? **Gimmicks and publicity stunts work.** Consider the Old Spice Guy video campaign, which drove a doubling of sales; @shitmydadsays, now a NY Times best-seller and Shatner-starring TV show; or Pepsi Refresh, the crowd-funding platform which has made brand advocates out of thousands of organizations. Social media is still very much the Wild West; if you create a fresh-faced, interesting angle, you can invent your way into a whole lot of attention.

2. **Social media success doesn't automatically validate your work.** *Snakes on a Plane* rode one of the greatest social media initiatives in

history, but the movie wasn't that good (I'm still teary-eyed over that one), and it tanked at the box office. I could tweet my novel until the end of time, but it won't change how readers are rightfully reluctant to fork over twelve dollars to spend eight hours reading anything unless they're reasonably sure it's a good investment. Like any other novelist, I've had to earn literary street cred through the long haul of book reviews, readings, events, and interviews. Social media can hook a few eyeballs, but after that your product has to deliver.

3. **Social media lets me influence my own destiny**, and while that sounds basic, it's extremely hard to pull off when you're a no-name working to stand out in an entrenched, old-school industry like publishing. I wasn't hemmed in by the traditional publishing process; I made my own way. What a tremendous thrill.

4. **Go for it.** The world is hungry for new ideas. With persistence and a few breaks, your billion-dollar concept could very well start earning out. Even if it doesn't work, people will respect you for trying.

Matt Stewart's debut novel, The French Revolution, is a San Francisco family saga loosely structured on the historical French Revolution. It's been called "wildly imaginative," "brilliant," and "an excellent achievement," and was named a Notable Debut by Poets & Writers. Matt's mildly infamous for releasing The French Revolution on Twitter first, and you can grab his free FrenchRev iPhone app on matt-stewart.com.

Matt Stewart
matt@matt-stewart.com
@mjfstewart
facebook.com/mjfstewart
matt-stewart.com

Don't Dream It, Be It

by

Colleen Crinklaw

I've always been one funny broad. I grew up on the stage, a theater geek, a choir rat. I'm used to being the center of attention and entertaining crowds. It's who I am, and what I love to do. As I grew up, I began to dream of fame and fortune by staying up too late to watch @ConanOBrien on *Late Night with Conan O'Brien* and @JimBreuer on *Saturday Night Live*, among others. When my sister got married in 2002, I spent weeks writing my "Maid of Honor" toast in order to make it as funny as possible. When my mother told me I should be a comedian, I began to dream of that too. Instead of pursuing my wild dreams, I got married at 18, went to college, got a job, and became a shadow of what I wanted to be.

Six years later, I got divorced, changed cities, changed perspectives, lost weight, and dusted off some of the dreams I had carefully packed away with my wedding dress (which I most certainly did *not* burn in effigy in case my mother reads this). I promised myself to indulge in every creative whim in order to find my passion should the opportunity arise. In February 2009, bored at work, I began surfing the ads on Craigslist looking for theater auditions or independent films to try out for. And there was my opportunity:

Stand-up Comedians needed for Amateur Comedy Night! *(Anchorage)*

Being the neurotic freak that I am, I consulted all my friends, including my ex-husband @ikantthink, all of whom insisted I should really sign up and I should really do this. So I did. I signed up and experienced a mixture of excitement and fear when I was told that I was the only female in the show—a trend that would continue throughout my career in Alaska. But, as iconic drag queen Dr. Frank-n-Furter declares moments before his death in the *Rocky Horror Picture Show,* "Don't dream it, be it." I spent a week writing my set, drawing from my experiences growing up as a bowhunter in Alaska, exaggerating stories based entirely on random thoughts that crossed my mind at doctor's appointments, and poking fun at the adult toy industry. @ikantthink listened to all my preliminary jokes, helping me tweak my delivery style and laughing out loud when something really struck him. I'd often call my friends and say, "Tell me if this is funny." As the date grew closer for the show, I began to wonder how to promote myself. The flyers for the show promoted the headliner with "special guest comedians," but didn't mention anyone else by name. I took about ten minutes at home one night, drinking wine and watching the @eddieizzard "Circle" DVD for the millionth time, and created my homegrown marketing plan:

1. Log in to Twitter.

2. Post the following tweet:

   @onefunnybroad: is performing stand-up comedy for the first time EVER @ Player's House of Rock this Thursday at 9pm! Please come out and laugh! RT plskthnx!

3. Log in to Facebook.

4. Post an event invite talking about the comedy show. Invite everyone over 21 in Alaska that is on friends list. Post to wall daily until date of show.

5. Hope people show up.

6. Hope you don't suck.

7. Drink beer either way.

My first show was, for lack of a more modest word, amazing. Facebook friends came out in droves and over twenty people with less than a week's notice came to watch me try my hand at something I'd been dying to try for most of my adult life. The headliner requested I come back to open for him every week for his six-week engagement. I quickly became drunk off the applause and the beer and the shots purchased for me by friends and new fans. In a rousing fit of narcissism, I created a Facebook Page for my comedy, and identified myself as a comedian under my occupation on Twitter. Then, I promptly forgot about it.

Within a week, I had 13 fans and almost double the Twitter followers. Watching the shaky video @ikantthink shot for me, I realized—I *can* do this. I revamped my Facebook page, redesigned my Twitter page, got some headshots taken by a professional photographer, and began writing more jokes and improving on my old ones. I went from performing 5–7 minute sets to doing 15–20, working my way up to a good 30 minutes of solid comedy.

Don't dream it, be it.

Months passed, and my reputation grew, as well as my group of fans. After the six-week engagement opening for Ken Lewis, I performed in a weekly open mic night set up especially for comedians. People were talking about me, and the news was good. I was given the opportunity to open for comedians @_TomRhodes and Carl LaBove at @koots. My fan page grew as I promoted myself at the end of my sets, and the more humorous my tweets were, the more followers I obtained. I built a static Web site for myself and linked my Facebook and Twitter pages to a contact page. I would get into Twitter banter-wars with real life friends like @redrummy, increasing each other's follow count so readers could get the whole conversation. An example:

@onefunnybroad: Passive-aggressive tweet.
@redrummy: Sarcastic response.
@onefunnybroad: Overly sensitive reply with ubiquitous "your mom" joke.
@redrummy: Scathing insult followed by winking emoticon to show levity.
@onefunnybroad: Tentative reconciliation on the condition that beer is involved.
@redrummy: Agreement.

Okay, so maybe it's only funny to us. Or maybe you just had to be there. (Follow us both and you can be there, too!)

In the fall of 2009, more new comedians came out of the woodwork when local radio station @movin1049 sponsored the *Make Alaska Laugh* competition, and almost twenty local comics competed for a $500 dollar prize and a paid private gig. I placed second in the finals, edged out by a veteran comedian transplanted to Alaska from NYC, me with less than a year of stage time under my stilettos. The arrival of the new interest in Alaska's comedy scene meant a number of my fellow comics created their own Facebook fan pages, their own blogs, and their own podcasts. My Facebook wall was soon full of self-promotion, and I noticed a distinct difference between myself and my peers. For one, I'm a chick and they're all dudes, but that's entirely irrelevant.

The majority of my posts from my fan page were interesting things I found at the store that I took a picture of with my phone and uploaded with a funny caption or hilarious tags. Event links for upcoming shows were posted to my wall once a day, not once an hour. I didn't send any messages to event attendees the day of the show reminding them to come. I wasn't...*annoying.* And I firmly believe that is the key to my social networking success. I don't have to advertise that I'm funny. I just have to be funny—and friendly. That's the second key to my success, what's made me pseudo-famous. I'm approachable in my online personas. I try to respond to all the fan letters I've ever gotten (and I've gotten at least three, so...you know...I'm not overwhelmed if you want to write one), and I interact with my Facebook fans and Twitter followers. I retweet when something is funny and makes me snort (@oatmeal, I'm looking at you) out loud at work. I post not only inane and funny things or information about my upcoming shows, but I also post links to news articles that are relevant or information about causes I hold dear to my heart, like advocating for the GLBTA community and raising funds for scholarships for local students. Because, according to the media, celebrities who do good things with their fame are better celebrities. Isn't that right, @BPGlobalPR?

Finally, in January 2010, I decided it was time to set up my first solo show. I perform in a drag/variety show every Friday at @MadMyrnas, Alaska's finest gay cabaret nightclub, and since I'm friends with the owners, managers, and employees, I was given the opportunity to do my own show. I purchased an ad— the first ad I've *ever* paid for—in the @anchoragepress, posted a Facebook invite, tweeted about it often, created flyers thanks to @ikantthink's graphic design skills, and performed my first ever 45-minute set, titled "Soul Searching," and actually made money doing the thing I love the most in life.

Don't dream it, be it.

Two weeks later, I reprised my "Soul Searching" act when I opened for *(the extremely talented)* comedic hypnotist @jjhawj at the University of Alaska Anchorage's largest auditorium, the same stage where columnist @Dan_Savage performs a live version of his nationally syndicated column once a year. In March, the loving crew at @MadMyrnas lifted me up and encouraged me to fly to Los Angeles to audition for @LASTCOMIC7 on NBC—which I did. I didn't make it on the show, but the experience was fantastic and made me recommit myself to my future career and the eventual goal of real instead of pseudo-fame. I plan to return to Los Angeles this winter and show them what Alaska's only female stand-up comedian has to offer. And trust me. It's a lot.

Don't believe me or want to see for yourself?

Follow @onefunnybroad on Twitter. Let's have some fun.

Since early 2009, Colleen has built her reputation as Alaska's premiere female stand-up comedian. Like a hobo or a televangelist, she thrives on undeserved attention from strangers, soaking up the stagelights and the laughter from the crowd. Colleen has headlined and performed in several venues in the city of Anchorage and has made guest appearances in the city of Palmer. Her comedy is deeply personal, letting the audience get an intimate look into her life as an Alaskan woman. Colleen's often-provocative topics include her involvement in Alaska's vibrant gay community, childhood memories of bowhunting with her military father, her own quest for her sexual identity, and her consistently entertaining love life. Booty calls, drag queens, bad sex, and a lot of soul searching make up a hilarious time with plenty of "I can relate to that" moments.

Colleen Crinklaw
onefunnybroad@gmail.com
@onefunnybroad

An Interactive Fiction: The Making of a Participatory Literary Reality Show

by

Constantine Markides

You are about to read an account of an online reality show. The first of its kind, in fact. A blog-based reality show. A *literary* one, no less, so please don't let your high standards and sophisticate's crap detector put you off. And please don't make too much of my paternalistic tone, phony civilities, and gaudy italicizations. I'm the Host, you see, so a patronizing, second-person address of chummy affectation is required of me. It's all part of the reality show pizzazz. I'm merely assuming that special mélange of personable chattiness and affected verbiage one would expect from the host of a *literary* reality show.

Don't mind the sarcasm. I can't deny some embarrassment at introducing myself as a reality show host. I should explain.

I once was full of Byronic zeal-and-brooding over myself as the Next Great Writer. I spent the better part of a decade living the archetypal rambling writer's life cliché: skipping about among a motley assortment of abandoned, makeshift, and illegal structures from Maine to California while working a string of transient, part-time odd jobs, during which I devoted myself to the maxim "Work Little Write Much," which as any unpublished Serious Writer knows, consists of round-the-clock unrecognized work that is exponentially more gratifying and vile than its moneymaking counterpart. When I discovered no publisher or agent was all that interested in discovering me, I launched a Web site on July 4, 2005—*www.FourthNight.com*—where I began posting essays on the fourth night of each month. It soon became apparent that trying to attract a wide readership by writing 5,000-word essays once a month was comparable to hawking Russian fur hats in the Caribbean.

Sometime in 2008 I recognized I had to take emergency remedial action. Already marginalized by virtue of being a writer, and sensing a future of nothing but increasing isolation and alienation from mainstream culture, I decided it was time to shelve my 20th century secluded writer impulses and step up to the crass, self-promotional, voyeuristic, reality-show-glutted 21st century. It was the right time for it. A young black upstart candidate had recently skyrocketed (steamrolled, Hillary might add) his way to becoming the 44th U.S. President on an oratorical platform of change. The spirit of the new and the fourth was in the air. For months I'd been planning an online writing project that integrated fiction with new interactive technologies and lining up participants, most of whom I'd encountered through my travels over the last decade; so shortly after Obama's inauguration I announced my plans that on July 4th, the four-year anniversary of my Web site, I would host a blog-based, literary reality show:

"The premise is simple. As in elimination-style reality television, there is a host (me), contestants (twelve writers), and judges (you, the readers). Each of these twelve writers will begin a novella that will be published in installments online for as long as that particular contestant remains in the competition. Three times a month—every 4th, 14th, and 24th—I'll announce in a YouTube video the guidelines for the next installment, which the writers will all have to complete before the readers vote to eliminate one of them. In every video I also name the newly eliminated contestant. On December 4th, the competition ends, with one writer having survived all twelve rounds, thereby completing a novella.

This blog-based reality show—called Fourth Fiction—will launch, as I mentioned, on July 4th. However, the actual competition, with its rounds of literary challenges and elimination voting, won't begin until August 4th. Over July the twelve contestants will only post on one Twitter page, indicating themselves by a capitalized four-letter name at the beginning of each tweet. This pre-competition warm-up month gives readers an opportunity to acquaint themselves with the writers. As a text-only medium amenable to anonymity, Twitter is ideal because the identity of the contestants, who've all pledged secrecy, will remain hidden until the end of the competition. The anonymity is so they're judged not on appearance but writing.

I won't pretend at munificence. I struggle enough with supporting my own writing, let alone pitching it, so I'm obviously not hosting this literary competition out of charitable impulses to bring recognition to other writers. I'm primarily doing it to drive traffic to my Web site and elevate my profile. A former roving luddite, I've come to learn the hard way over the past decade that if you shun your inner Paris Hilton and aren't a reputed writer like Pynchon or Salinger, you destine yourself to literary obscurity."

This project put a swift end to any lingering remnants of my "former roving luddite" life. Whereas I had once lacked running water, plumbing, heating, refrigeration, and electricity, let alone a social media presence, I now had a Blackberry[1], an iPod Touch, two Facebook pages, two Twitter accounts, a LinkedIn network, a YouTube channel, and a loaded, self-hosted Web site. Whereas I'd once ducked out of frame anytime a camera focused my way, I was now filming myself. Whereas I once scoffed at Twitter, I was now a Twitter

---

[1] A possession that would have disturbed me several years earlier. I didn't get my first cell phone until July 2007 while reporting for the English language daily Cyprus Mail. CNN's Anderson Cooper and his team were flying into Cyprus to cover the evacuation of refugees during the Lebanon War and they needed a stringer [local guide who serves as driver, go-to man for info and contacts, coffee grunt, etc.]. Since I was covering the evacuation, our chief reporter referred CNN's team organizer to me. When she asked for my cell number, I said I didn't have one. She shot back: "If you want to do this, you better have one by tonight."*

> *It should be obvious by this unnecessary digression that the possession still disturbs me and I need to hedge/justify/hem and haw, etc. to prove to myself I'm still more of an au naturel free-range reporter than a slick Crackberry user.

Conference speaker. I'd entered the lower ranks of the social media elite—the Twitterati—embracing the plugged-in, self-promotional lifestyle I once abhorred. I figured if I wasn't going to howl and protest at our exhibitionist, technologic era, I may as well try to trailblaze in it. Better the ends of the pack than the congested middle.

The transition wasn't easy. My first video required countless retakes: the footage bogging my hard drive from those two days of filming testified to my on-camera discomfort. Even when the filming ended, I was unable to get my video up[2] due to a technical glitch. At midnight, July 4th, when the Twitter phase of the contest was to launch, my Web site was dysfunctional. On top of that, one contestant— Fyor—was incommunicado, unresponsive to my outreaches from recent weeks. Another contestant, Igor, nearly withdrew from the first pre-competition month, fulminating that Twitter was a "global wankfest of the wankers, by the wankers, for the wankers." His invectives against social media reminded me of my former self.

After much sweating, I managed to post the video. At midnight I e-mailed the contestants the Twitter account password. And at 12:03 a.m. on July 5th, a contestant, Tess, posted the first tweet. My metamorphosis from reclusive technophobe writer to online reality show host was official.

After the pre-competition month on Twitter, the readers had a vivid sense of the contestants' personalities and writing styles. From July 14th to July 24th, I assigned the contestants a daily literary dare every midnight. They then had 24 hours to tweet a response. For example:

DARE 2 – *Tweet a story that involves an act of cannibalism.*
UTAH: Stranded in the Arctic, he killed himself so she wouldn't starve. "I ate you," she sobbed over his gleaming bones. "I ate your guts."

DARE 5 – *Write a sex scene that incorporates a Michael Jackson song title.*
UTAH: To thrill her, he decided to try talking dirty. Diana wasn't used to it. So when he said "Beat it," she got up and left.

DARE 6 – *Make a rhyme that includes the words "Obama" and "Osama" without using any vowels besides "o" and "a" (no "y"s allowed).*
UTAH: Knock, knock. Who's that? Obama and Osama. Obama and Osama who? O Sam a' took to AfPak to attack a pack of Afghans.

The chain story—which ran from July 24th to July 31st and consisted of contestants writing in a relay, one tweet at a time—received a tepid response from readers. Like the Telephone Game in which short sentences are whispered from ear to ear, collaborative writing over a soundbite medium like Twitter is good for little more than sniggering at the ensuing absurdities. Even in the literary dares and the chain story, the personalities of the contestants still

---

[2] One way techies experience impotence.

seemed to trump their fiction. For example, few readers following the Twitter portion would have had trouble identifying the authors of the responses below even if their names hadn't been attached:

DARE 4 – *Write an alternate ending to the fairy tale "Three Little Pigs."*
ISIS: Pig opened the door, arms outstretched. "Peace, brother." Wolf was moved to tears. No one had ever before opened their heart to him.

TUCK: Pig opened the door, arms outstretched. "Peace brother." Wolf paused then tore him to pieces. There was just no challenge with hippies.

It wasn't always easy for me to stomach the voting results. For example, in the second round, where the challenge was to write about interactions over the web, the eliminated contestant, Fido, had the strongest opening in my view. Through a peculiar transitive logic, the rejection of his writing felt like a rejection of me. I initially thought it might be due to a recent spike in Brazilian visitors—over 700 in one day alone—after Fourth Fiction [FF] was profiled in *Folha de São Paulo*, the largest circulation newspaper in Brazil; I assumed Fido's puns and street jargon came across as ungrammatical gibberish to non-English speakers. Here is part of his Round 2 response:

French bulldogs, rottweilers, chow chows, lend me your floppy ears, cuz gone are the days of lonesome ramblin'. I'm itchin' with fleas to guide you around my turf, the fenceless dogyard where i roam, the digital colosseum where our gladiavatars are crowned and wined and dined and chewed up and shat out, the new new york of the dubya dubya dubya where the rags to riches hopeful strut their wuff for their 15 million hits of fame, the electronic jungle with ten thousand talkers whose tongues are all dangling, the betweenthenet bedsheets where there's ten thousand whisperin' with nobody listenin'.

But after hearing from friends who voted him off, I realized it was just that most readers, regardless of country, just didn't share my appetite for Fido's hermeneutic wordplay. As host, I influenced the reality show's trajectory, but it was the readers who ultimately dictated the outcome.

Towards the end of the contest I gave a presentation on FF at Bob Fine's "Cool Twitter Conferences" Brooklyn venue. Though I had to make my PowerPoint relevant, even if only in some vague conceptual sense, to the earnest social-media-aspirant businessmen who'd come for tips on how to "monetize" and "leverage" on Twitter, my role was really just as Token-Young-Guy-Who-Founded-An-Amusing-But-Pointless-From-A-Monetizing-Perspective-Project   to serve as light A&E relief between the Sit-Up-Straight-It's-The-Finance-&-Marketing-Industry-Gurus who could offer precisely those Strategies for Maximizing Influence and other Key Concepts that their companies had sent them to learn about. I decided, therefore, to focus on how our new DIY real-time interactive age had ripped the hinges off literature and opened a new era in fiction[3] just as it had in journalism[4], where readers/consumers were now active participants rather than passive recipients; the concept, I noted, could be extrapolated to any business model in this new Gold Rush age in which those who adapt, make rules, and take risks are the ones who'll strike gold (even if it's Fool's Gold, a nugget of unnecessary cynicism I left out of my presentation).

The subtitle of my presentation was "Reinventing Literature for the Interactive, Real-Time Reader." Indeed, what distinguished FF from other reality shows was its real-time interactivity with the public. The commenters infused a vivacity and metafictional richness that only an interactive fiction allowed. The contestants and readers were in constant dialogue, sometimes friendly, occasionally hostile. The interactivity also crossed over into the fiction. One of the more truculent contestants, Tuck, incorporated the readers in his fiction, often malevolently, as when three readers who'd been critical of him made it into his story as a brothel overseer, a human trafficking scout, and a pimp. Another contestant, Rhae, always integrated a current online news story, including the link, into her writing. The most astonishing instance of this was her same-day integration of an August 28th report on a *Science* article called "Fido's Fur Fated by 3 genes" in her response to the Round 3 challenge which, in honor of Fido's departure, was to incorporate the death of a dog.

Readers also dictated elements of the contest. In one round, they assigned the literary challenges to the readers; in another they assigned me "video challenges," i.e. climb the Statue of Liberty, visit a sex store, do Brazilian Jiu-Jitsu grappling, etc. I also recruited readers (and their children) to film themselves opening the rejection letters, which included a five-year-old Australian boy fetching the Round 7 rejection letter from the bottom of a swimming pool, a London PhD student in Human Evolution surgically opening the Round 8 letter with tweezers, and a Maine lobsterman hauling from the seafloor a lobster trap containing the Round 11 rejection in a ziplock.

With contestants dropping away, with my acclimation to the contest, and with the technical glitches ironed out, I assumed FF would demand less of me as it progressed. But while the first month or two may have been markedly more chicken-with-its-head-cut-off than in later months, in some ways the workload only increased. By the final rounds, for example, filming and editing the videos kept me up for days on end.

---

[3] Of course, in some ways it's not all that novel: the main difference between hypertext and "Choose Your Own Adventure" gamebooks of the '80s, or between blog feeds and Dickensian-era serial fiction, is an improved distribution model. Not that this should dispirit us, considering we've all known since Solomon that there's nothing new under the sun.

[4] I.e. people "on the ground," breaking stories before major news outlets (tweets of US Airways jet crashing in Hudson River), online networking as new protest media (Iran's "Twitter" Revolution), or Oprah beating People Magazine to the news by sharing in a tweet her instruction to her assistant to order her a Reuben sandwich.

But aside from its sheer physicality, FF was also emotionally overwhelming. A "crazy posse," as one reader put it, of dedicated readers had formed. Some readers even had a personal stake in it as they were responding to the challenges in parallel to the contestants, writing a novella as outside participants on their personal Web sites. One commenter later told me that FF inspired her to start a blog, to share her writing in public, and to show her face to the world; another told me that had it not been for FF, he'd have given up on life outside of his family and cloistered himself for good; yet another reader, who was living in a remote place and who once detested all things technological, began online dating after FF (with no minor success); yet another had a darker response, as FF had dredged up some painful unresolved issues and left her feeling like she were, as she told me in an image that haunted me for some time, staring at a beautiful vista from behind barbed wire.

The winner was announced on December 4th, 2009, and the reality show ended four days, four hours, and forty-four minutes later. As a result of the new real-time technological platforms and the interactive format of the contest, something new and raw emerged over the course of the contest. Another story found conception in the fecund commentary between contestants and readers, a story impossible in earlier decades. Within the twelve interlaced novellas and comments, an unexpected act of alchemy took place as the readers took stage, becoming characters in their own right as reality mingled with fiction.

In many ways, the commenters outshone the contestants, who were purportedly the idols. In fact, a godhead metaphor isn't so far from the truth, at least not if we go back to our old gods. The Olympians were always pettier, bitchier, and more human-all-too-human than the mortals. The stories we remember and cherish and suffer are not those of Apollo and Artemis, or of Aphrodite and Ares, but of Odysseus and Penelope, of Achilles and Helen. The Olympians just happened to be the privileged royal family who got to write the history books. Of course they'd place themselves center stage.

From the beginning, the ostensible grand prize was potential publication. But the real winner was not the contestant who survived all the rounds. The winner was the spectacle itself, the lusty brushing up of fiction against life, the messy eruption of discourse and ribbing and banter, of which the commenters were as essential as the contestants. Without them, Fourth Fiction would lack its most essential dimension, the fourth one.

In the summer of 2011, Constantine Markides will launch a new interactive real-time project at www.FourthNight.com—this time not a reality show, but an innovative, continent-spanning experiment in online journalism.

A cynic with crypto-idealist leanings and a highly variable moral fabric, Constantine has formerly worked as a bartender, book reviewer, brain study subject, busker, caretaker, carpenter, caterer, conscript, counselor, editor, explorer, farmhand, fashion executive assistant, fish market packer, foreign correspondent, garbage compactor, gardener, grip, harmonica teacher, high school tutor, house painter, human rights researcher, lawn mower, library aide, lifeguard, literary agent assistant, mover, music teacher, newspaper reporter, office aid to Rabbi, proofreader, publishing intern, reality show host, recycling inspector, road worker, sternman, stock analyst, stringer, substitute teacher, swimming instructor, technology teacher, trail maintainer, transcriber, translator, tree planter, tunaboat crewman, waiter, and Web site consultant. As of this writing he resides in Buenos Aires, although as of this reading he is probably somewhere else because he moves around a lot.

Constantine Markides
fourthnight@gmail.com
@FourthNight
http://www.facebook.com/FourthNight
http://www.linkedin.com/in/ConstantineMarkides
http://www.FourthNight.com

True Crime Author Offers DIY Publicity

by

Cathy Scott

You don't need a public-relations or marketing expert to blitz your new book. You can do it yourself with the advent of social media. Most publishing houses have marketing departments that will publicize your book. Gone, however, are the days of publishers paying for book tours. And publishers, because of a downturn in book buying and less money to put behind books, now expect authors to do a large part of their own publicity. No problem. Today, because of more and more social media outlets, the sky's the limit. That includes, with a little bit of ingenuity and social media know-how, being able to put a book in front of the public. You just have to tap into it. Best of all, aside from the cost of the Internet, it's free.

And if you want to increase traffic to your blog or website, you can do that too by connecting social media sites. What you post on one appears on the other with one push of the "send" button.

On Twitter, I started out very simple. I learned about Twitter from my lifelong friend Victoria Pynchon (@VickiePynchon). When I joined her on an election-day walk of a precinct to get out the vote, we headed on foot that afternoon down a quiet neighborhood. Out of the blue, Vickie said just one word: "Twitter."

"What?" I asked her.

"Twitter," she said.

"What's that?"

"I can't really describe it. Just try it. Twitter.com."

And so I did. I've been on it ever since. And it has paid off in different ways. One of my first followers on Twitter was MC Hammer (@MCHammer). I wrote the book *The Killing of Tupac Shakur*, and Hammer was a friend of the fallen rapper, who was gunned down near the Las Vegas Strip in 1996.

I was hooked on Twitter. And I thought, especially with M.C. Hammer following me, along with about 100 others, I was off to a great start. The problem was, I had no idea what I was doing. I learned about Twitter the first week in November 2008. A week later, I was scheduled to travel to Santa Fe, New Mexico for a book signing with Ali MacGraw and photographer Clay Myers. Ali, an actress and lifelong animal activist, had written the foreword to my book *Pawprints of Katrina*, which had been released a couple of months earlier. With my new found knowledge of Twitter, my followers were quickly increasing. I hooked up my tweets to Facebook and hit the ground running with short and quick blurbs about the event. The key, I've learned, is not to appear overly aggressive in marketing your book or events. It turns people off. I try and find a news hook. When I saw that a friend's book, which had been released a few weeks earlier, was still a top seller in the true crime category, as shown in the sales ranking on Amazon.com, I tweeted that too. I included a shortened URL at the end, taking readers to the book's Amazon page: "Author @KathrynCasey's SHATTERED in Top 10 for #truecrime on Amazon," I twittered.

Twittering about other people's books is an example of another key activity on social media I wanted to bring up, and that's about not being stingy with your posts. I have no problem helping publicize friends' books in my blog or on Twitter. In fact, Twitter garners a generous community environment and a camaraderie with an almost pay-it-forward atmosphere. I'm happy to play a small part in that.

Connect social media platforms -- Twitter, Facebook, LinkedIn, My Space, your blog, website and whatever else has that capability -- and you've got yourself a formula that works. Because I didn't have an enormous number of fans early on, I posted the news about my San Fe book signing with Ali MacGraw by going to other people's Facebook pages and posting the event there. On Facebook, I have a "Like" page (formerly called a "Fan" page) for my website of the same name (CathyScott.com), plus a Killing of Tupac Shakur page. My tweets are linked there as well.

The key for tweets that advertise your book is to come up with a news angle. When my book *Pawprints of Katrina* was picked up by Kindle, I immediately posted it on Twitter and used the hashtag #LI, which also sent it to LinkedIn (I'm already automatically set up for all my tweets to go to Facebook). The message was simple: "Great surprise 2day. I learned Pawprints of Katrina is now on Kindle," and I included a tiny URL. That, too, is key. If you do not include the link to a the book's page on a bookseller site (as in Amazon.com or BarnesandNoble.com), you are missing potential sales. On August 29, 2010, the fifth anniversary of Hurricane Katrina making landfall in New Orleans, I twittered about *Pawprints.* And on the 14th anniversary of the shooting of Tupac Shakur, September 7, 2010, I put my *Tupac* book on Twitter as a reference for his fans.

When *Pawprints* continued to sell in the Top 10 in books in the disaster category, I tweeted with a link of course to the online bookseller. I can tweet about one of my books, or a fellow author's. After tweeting, a few minutes when I then go to Amazon.com to check the sales ranking, it invariably has gone up -- an immediate positive response to putting a simple post on the Web. In August of 2009, when my last book, *The Rough Guide to True Crime*, was released, I tweeted the heck out of it. The Women in Crime Ink blog, which I contribute to, ran an excerpt, so I tweeted that too.

Thus, I slowly figured out how Twitter, besides being a place to converse with friends, could be used to publicize my books and articles. It took about a week for it to make sense to me, but longer to get a really good feel for it. Figuring out how to link Twitter, Facebook, LinkedIn, and my blog came later too. I know some authors who have their assistants do their social media for them, but I like to keep a personal eye on it, not to mention knowing that it's been done the way I want it.

One thing I did from the start was use my name as a brand, because it's my pen name for books and byline for articles. The trick is to remain consistent.

And don't underestimate the power of Twitter. It has a domino effect. The followers of those you follow, and vice versa, see what you tweet. And that's exactly how a story about a pair of would-be lawyers made it inside the pages of the prestigious *ABA Journal* -- the American Bar Association's online news outlet.

I noticed two relatively new IDs on Twitter identifying themselves as lawyers and law partners. They were @BeatriceBitcher and @RichardPrickman. I thought the names odd (I figured they were British) but that was about it -- until I noticed what they were tweeting, about tricking judges and taking advantage financially of clients. Their avatars looked like cartoonish renditions of their photos, but that's not uncommon on Twitter. Beatrice's tweets caused a lively banter with other twitterers, so I followed her. And then I followed Prickman. More interesting, however, was the attorneys who were responding to the pair, including an exchange of tweets between Prickman and lawyer-turned-celebrity Star Jones. The result was a post on my personal blog, also picked up by Law.com's "Legal Blog Watch" column. "The more Scott followed Bitcher, however, the more suspicious she became. When she also found out about Prickman, she looked into this firm of Bitcher & Prickman. What she found was a cartoon, Bitcher & Prickman, drawn by lawyer and cartoonist Charles Pugsley Fincher."

Law.com, a leading legal news and information network for attorneys and legal professionals, quoted from my blog: "Now, it seems, they'd jumped off the cartoon page and into twitterland, where they were -- and still are -- being taken seriously some of the time."

Before I wrote my blog post, I tweeted something to the pair about being "comic characters". Beatrice responded with, "Ha. I'd expect a crime writer to come down on the side of truth and justice. You have exposed Beatrice's denial. Caution".

"It's the skeptic in me -- and the reporter", I responded.

Beatrice added in her next tweet, "And I thought women stuck together".

My answer? "We do. Do fictional cartoon characters stick together too? (Or are you based on a true character?)"

And so, Beatrice Bitcher and Richard Prickman were outed and exposed on Twitter for the cartoon characters they are.

Next, *ABA Journal* picked up the story after reading Law.com's article.

"True crime author Cathy Scott solved her own mystery when she investigated two tweeting lawyers from the law firm 'Bitcher & Prickman', reporter Debra Cassens Weiss wrote in the *ABA Journal*. "Lawyers 'Beatrice Bitcher' and 'Richard Prickman' may have raised some eyebrows in their posts on Twitter, but nothing they said was 'exceedingly outrageous,' according to Legal Blog Watch."

"There was this post, for example", Weiss continued, "from Bitcher: 'I'm giving Edward, an associate, choice. 1. Work on brief all weekend. 2. Be my weekend servant. He's thinking'.

"Scott noticed that some commenters, including some lawyers, took the posts seriously. But Scott became suspicious and checked out the Bitcher & Prickman law firm. She learned it was the creation of Texas cartoonist and lawyer Charles Pugsley Fincher."

The *ABA Journal* picked a different quote from my blog, CathyScott.com: "A funny thing just happened in the world of Twitter", they reprinted from my blog. "Reality and fantasy crossed over."

My personal blog about the pair was retweeted a few dozen times in just a few days. To me, writing about cartoon characters being mistaken on Twitter for real people was a blast. The icing on the cake was that it got noticed.

Months later, in the midst of writing a true crime book about the Barbara Kogan murder case out of New York in which Kogan was accused (and ultimately confessed to) of paying for a hit man to kill her husband, I tweeted about spending a Sunday working on the manuscript. I probably tweeted about the case a handful of times. Then came a direct message from a relative of George Kogan, Barbara's husband who was gunned down in broad daylight on the Upper East Side of Manhattan. That relative, who prefers her name not be used, attended the sentencing of Barbara Kogan. Because of that contact, I was able to include in the book her close relationship with the victim. Other family members, some of whom lived in San Juan, Puerto Rico, of George Kogan contacted me via e-mail after I posted a story about Barbara Kogan on the Women in Crime Ink blog (WomeninCrimeInk.com), for which I'm a regular contributor. They too were a huge help in fleshing out George Kogan's background.

I also, because of a post I wrote on Women in Crime Ink about a high-profile murder case, was invited to cover the story for *The Daily Beast* (I was on deadline and unable to do it). The invite came about because I was seen on a blog, showing once again the exposure power of social media sites.

Besides writing books and blogs in my spare time, I write full-time for Best Friends Animal Society's magazine and website. And through the Best Friends' site, the power of social media proves that you can fight City Hall. With a bit of effort, I helped a story go viral. It was about a 6-year-old boy named Anthony and his treasured pot-bellied pet pig, Lupe, separated because the local city council ordered his pig out of the home based on a several-decades' old ordinance. The boy, who is autistic, was devastated without Lupe. He couldn't sleep, and he wouldn't eat. I wrote about the pair at BestFriends.org. Then, I blitzed it on Twitter, Facebook, Digg, StumbleUpon, and DEL.ICIO.US, and I included the link to the mother's petition. I also went to the local newspaper and TV news sites, looked up reporters' names and their Twitter IDs (most news outlets include them on their sites), and posted the link to the story on their Twitter pages. As a result, the online petition that had been getting little attention took off. Local media as well began reporting the sad quandary the boy and his pig faced. His mother was able to present several thousand signatures to the City Council when she went before them, asking that council members reconsider their decision. The issue was tabled. In the meantime, while the mother continues fighting for her son and his pig, Lupe lives temporarily at a pot-bellied pig farm, where Anthony and his mother regularly visit.

In the Fall of 2009, I was scheduled to speak at a Cool Twitter Conference in Orange County. I planned to drive the four hours each way to and from Las Vegas. But I was fostering a new tiny puppy and I couldn't leave her home alone all those hours. So (after getting permission) the puppy accompanied me to the conference. Attending, coincidentally, were a bunch of animal lovers, including veterinarian Annmarie Hill (@VetLovingPetsHB), who let the five-pound Papillon pup sit with her. During a break in the conference, some attendees started calling the puppy the "Social Media Dog". "Make a Twitter page for her", they said. And I did. While I no longer have the pup (she was adopted to a great home), I still have an avatar of her on my @SocialMediaDog Twitter page.

And that is what makes social media not only effective, but also enjoyable. It's difficult to explain, as my friend Vickie Pynchon pointed out when she introduced me to Twitter, but Twitter and other new media sites don't feel like work. They're just plain fun. And, at the end of the day, it's free publicity for your book, or article, or website, or blog, or business, or nonprofit organization. Social media is a vehicle with endless possibilities for spreading the word.

Cathy Scott's work has appeared in The New York Times Magazine, New York Post, San Diego Union-Tribune, George magazine, The Christian Science Monitor, The Los Angeles Times, Las Vegas Sun and Reuters news service. Known for her books, The Killing of Tupac Shakur and The Murder of Biggie Smalls, Scott was a journalism instructor at the University of Nevada, Las Vegas until she left to cover the largest animal rescue in U.S. history for Best Friends Animal Society following Hurricane Katrina. Her most recent TV appearances include Investigation Discovery and VH1. Her eighth book, about Barbara Kogan who was convicted in the murder-for-hire of her husband, is set for release in Spring 2011 by St. Martin's Press. In addition, she's a contributor to Women in Crime Ink, a lineup of criminologists, profilers, legal analysts, TV commentators and authors.

Cathy Scott
@CathyScott
@SocialMediaDog
@WomeninCrimeInk
http://www.cathyscott.com
http://CathyScott.blogspot.com

Global Perspectives

Twitter Evolution in India: Case Studies

by

Shrinath Navghane

I am writing this as a part of the study of few chosen brands who are experimenting with the whole social media trend, and hence being perfect early adopters. They should be awarded for their bravery; as more and more corporations remain clueless, these are the pioneers who are taking the plunge, or leap of faith, which can make or break their brand image severely. India as a country offers diverse experiences and an uneven playing field where people are not swayed by advertising, but still depend largely on the word of mouth which is usually backed by community seniors who in turn become influencers for any brand.

Now with the rising middle-class in India, the influence factor is being challenged by the youngsters who are increasingly adopting social networking as a way of life. As compared to the United States, India's dominant social media presence comes from 18–32 year olds. This means its students, company executives, and the majority of singles are testing new lifestyles, pushing cultural boundaries, and adopting the tech age faster than any other country in the world.

Brand: SkodaAuto India

A Volkswagen Group company, Skoda came to India ten years ago and quickly became the preferred luxury car brand for the rising middle-class. Faced with some technical and management issues, Skoda also soon became one of the most untrusted brands in India with a couple of dealerships being canned in the press, and Skoda issuing public announcements in newspapers warning people against fraud with the servicing of their car.

My interaction with them began when they "found me" on Twitter talking about my Skoda. I am also the founding member of an unofficial Skoda owners club called "Skoda Buddies," which is a nationwide group. We meet once a year and last the meeting was in Goa in January 2010. It was interesting to note that

Skoda India actually was on Twitter, and this intrigued me on what could be the potential reason for them being on it.

Skoda risked a lot of negative feedback by jumping onto Twitter before any other VW Brand in India, given their customers' bad experiences with dealers, myself included. But Skoda proudly called me "one of their biggest fans" and announced this on Twitter.

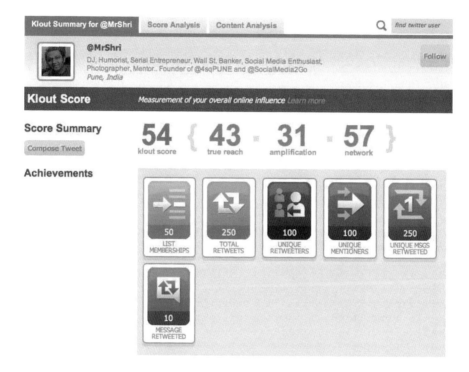

On interacting with the Twitter account, I realized that Skoda India was on a serious brand-building mission and was addressing customer complaints, taking feedback, and making sure that complaints were answered.

Their strategy was unique from other Indian brands, as they made sure that public opinion of their brand could be changed into a positive if they "heard" what their loyal or new customers were saying about their cars and after-sales service.

Skoda also filtered out positive Twitter reviews of their vehicles by using searching tools and then retweeted these from their own account to further build the trust factor. This is what I like the most about them and consider them very brave indeed.

The real test of their "Connect With Customer First" strategy came after my car had a nasty accident when the front air bags were deployed. The cost of this was being challenged by our insurance provider, who said, "airbags were considered as accessories and hence not covered under insurance." This would mean a whopping cost of Rs.120,000.00 (approx. $2,600.00 USD) to me directly.

I decided to tweet about it and Skoda picked it up instantly. They relieved my woes when their senior executive called from the head office and said that they would instruct the insurance company to cover the cost as this was supposed to be under the agreement.

Got a call from @SkodaIndia HO backing up my call on insurance claim for the Airbags... Thank you!

12:52 PM Jun 16th via web
Retweeted by 1 person   Delete

MrShri
Mr. Shri

This can be considered a perfect example of the most effective use of Twitter by an automobile brand in India. Not only have they pioneered in the space, but they have also setup a concurrent system to make sure that communication between their social media channel and company management remains flawless. I did not need to make a single call, they picked up my tweets, got in touch through DM, and voila.

Although I might not buy a Skoda again, it's reassuring to know that someone out there is listening when it matters the most. Other car companies can learn a lot from this, and although now we have @VolksagenIndia on Twitter, they seem to be following the blind "we're here too but have no idea" path. As opposed to their sister brand, the @VolkswagenIndia account is managed by an independent PR company (Hanmer India) and seems to be doing less in terms of real service to its customers.

Bottom line: Skoda is a perfect example of how Twitter can help change opinions, make a lasting impact, and build a strategy around customer satisfaction in India.

Brand: Hippo

Hippo is a new "snacks" brand which is being launched in a market dominated by Lays and other large established corporations, who control the distribution networks of the majority of the FMCG (fast moving consumer goods) brands. Their Twitter strategy is unique in the sense that it's not related to their main products at all, and is centered around using broken English to tweet news and make comments on current affairs.

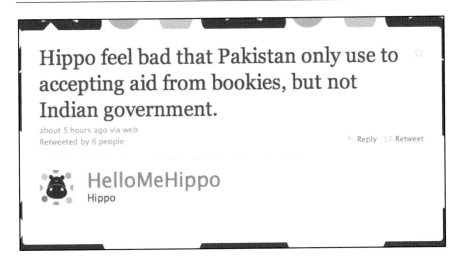

Hippo feel bad that Pakistan only use to accepting aid from bookies, but not Indian government.

about 5 hours ago via web
Retweeted by 6 people

Reply   Retweet

HelloMeHippo
Hippo

I was very impressed with their @HelloMeHippo account and contacted them for more information on what the purpose was and how it was helping in a market where the odds are clearly against it.

The following is an interview with their Twitter Community Manager, Mr. Huzefa Kapadia:

1. Why is @HelloMeHippo on Twitter?

Simple. To connect with the consumers more effectively. Second, Twitter is a platform where you'll find influential people. People who are peer leaders. So, there are even strong chances of spreading awareness about the brand and its activities exponentially. Third, you can't just exist on the basis of conventional media. You have to explore new mediums, and also new ways to communicate.

2. How has your community (followers) grown and how do they influence you?

Hippo's objective was clear: Don't sell the munchies, sell the philosophy. "Hunger is the root of all evil." The tweets are nothing more than a jovial comment on hungry (evil) people out there causing unnecessary trouble. Hippo marries the current affairs with hunger and simply urges people to not go hungry. Constant and casual conversations (unlike pre-programmed bots) help Hippo to establish a bond that goes beyond a brand-consumer relationship. Hippo also randomly picks his followers and sends them surprise Hippo Hampers with a personally handwritten note.

Unlike other social networking sites, people (at least in India) are an informed bunch. Catering to them requires a lot of discipline and consistency. Every tweet needs to be well thought-out, well said, and more importantly, honest. It is actually the followers that bring out the best in Hippo. You also need to remember that Hippo is a brand who is tweeting and not a common guy. You have to be politically correct, not get too carried away, and yet be consistently interesting and entertaining.

If you lose focus, followers lose focus in you.

3. Any experiment(s) you as a brand have done specifically on Twitter?

Hippo actually used Twitter to do something that no brand has ever tried doing before: get the followers to work for the brand on something as technical as inventory tracking.

Hippo is still new to the snack market and has a nascent distribution system. In India, distribution and stock availability plays a vital role. If a new brand is not seen on the shelves after its launch phase, it is considered to have failed. So, to tackle competition and inventory tracking and supply, Hippo simply asked his followers to tweet him whenever they couldn't find Hippo packs in the stores.

And surprisingly, Hippo's followers without any hesitation responded. This activity not only helped Hippo identify empty shelves, but also new markets.

Here's the case study: http://bob.vg/hippoindia.

4. The story behind Hippo?

Hippo thinks "empty stomach is the devil's workshop."

He believes hungry people fight more. And that no matter what or how big the problem is, it could be solved with food. Hippo, very innocently yet with a lot of conviction, also shares his philosophy in detail on every pack of each variant.

When was the last time you took time off from work or studies and did a favor for your stomach? When was the last time you asked yourself whether you are hungry? Exactly. We humans tend to give work so much importance that sometimes, well, we forget why are we actually working. That's why we have Hippo—a Hippo who cares and doesn't want us to go hungry. Who reminds us to not go hungry, but eat. Coincidentally, no animal opens its mouth as wide as a hippo does. This means it can put more food in its mouth and eat more!

The job for Hippo's packaging and design was clear: establish itself in an overly cluttered market where brands were fighting a world war for eyeballs, and also to survive in this cutthroat market without a single piece of communication until the distribution was set up in 200,000 outlets across India.

Thus, the idea was to create a packaging design that in itself became the piece of communication for the brand. A bright and bold look, a witty and humorous tone, a soulful thought (kill hunger—kill evil), and the most unexpected name to carry it off, HIPPO was born, and began to fight the market with packaging alone, until the distribution was wide enough to invest in media.

Hippo did better than expected. It caught the eyes, charmed the country, and established itself in the market (against stiff competition from Frito Lay and ITC Foods) without a single piece of communication for the first six months until the distribution was optimized. The unique packaging also generated a lot of PR and social media buzz for the brand.

5. Any direct sales figures via Twitter or any relation between these?

The Twitter-Inventory Tracking activity led to a whopping 76% increase in sales during the early days. Since Hippo had a nascent distribution system, through followers, Hippo managed to identify not only empty shelves but also identify new markets at zero cost and with faster turnaround time than any of its competitors.

6. Challenge of being an early adopter in India? Any lessons, insights, or discoveries you would like to share?

Social media in India can be used ingeniously. It has an unbelievable potential in our society. It's totally different than compared to the west. It's only in India where you will find 90% of the retail market unorganized. Though it might be extremely diverse and complicated, it provides ample opportunities to come up with innovative sales, marketing, and communication solutions. Hippo's problem was unique. And through Twitter, Hippo managed to come up with a unique solution. The activity has seen an overwhelming and effective response. This has encouraged the makers of Hippo to set up a core cell that monitors the stock updates received. The information is then passed on to the distribution teams and the stock is sent to the respective locations.

Bottom line: The success of the @HelloMeHippo account can be summed up as a brand which is being built upon a philosophy with a great story, and setting a new benchmark for Twitter in India.

Shrinath Navghane is the founder of Social Media 2Go, a boutique social media solutions company based in Pune, India, which specializes in running product specific campaigns for clients around the world. Shrinath puts his passion for social media to work for his clients, and he regularly speaks about community building and crowdsourcing at social networking events in India. He maintains a blog at http://www.mrshri.co.cc, and is described as "approachable and friendly" by both friends and colleagues. Sharing and helping are second nature to him.

Shrinath Navghane
mrshri@sm2go.com
@MrShri
http://linkd.in/shrinath
http://www.sm2go.com
http://www.mrshri.co.cc

"#TeAmoEcuador. I love you Ecuador."

by

Alfred Naranjo

A beautiful country with snow capped mountains, exotic beaches, tropical rainforests, and the famous Galapagos Islands, Ecuador is South America's hidden treasure.

With an area slightly smaller than Nevada, Ecuador is bordered by Colombia on the north, Peru on the east and south, and by the Pacific Ocean to the west. Ecuador is one of the countries with the highest levels of biodiversity in the world. One hectare of Ecuadorian rainforest can have as many species of frogs and birds as the whole of North America.

I live in Quito, the capital of Ecuador, and the first city to be declared a World Heritage site by the United Nations Educational, Scientific, and Cultural Organization (UNESCO). A gorgeous city surrounded by mountains with the largest and best-preserved historical buildings and churches in Latin America.

Historically, Ecuador's economic growth and development has been concentrated in the two main cities, Guayaquil, the largest city in population and economical power, and Quito, the capital and the house of the political power. For years there was an internal fight between cities and the regions where the cities are located to accumulate more power and become better than the other city.

Comments and critiques about the other city were something we were getting used to reading. Complaints about the economic situation and endless pessimistic messages were, as expected, reflected in Twitter too—and is a situation that many Ecuadorian twitterers want to change.

Twitter Magic

Even though I still don't have too much time to spend on Twitter, I have become addicted to it. It's like a perfect world: all the news you want to read, all the interesting things that are happening are compiled for you by someone else. The news is there as it's happening. No need to turn on the TV or read the newspapers. Interesting discussions about politics, economics, and sports are there too, and all of it is for free.

You can express your opinion and make your comments to people you could never reach in any other way. And sometimes these people reply to your comments. This is wonderful I thought. Social networks and Twitter give you power.

Then we had the terrible earthquake in Haiti and obviously Twitter was a good source of information. Everybody was talking about Haiti and how devastating the earthquake was, and for the first time in history the whole world put their eyes on Haiti. Twitter was no exception. Haiti was a trending topic (one of the most commented on topics) in Twitter for a long time.

A few months later, Chile suffered the same situation. Again, a natural disaster put an emerging country in the news. Chile was a trending topic in Twitter. Live coverage from hundreds of thousands of Chilean twitterers provided us fresh news in our hands almost every second.

Jonathan Klein, President of CNN, mentioned in a media conference a few days after the earthquake, "The competition I'm really afraid are social networking sites. The people you're friends with on Facebook or the people you follow on Twitter are trusted sources of information. Well, we want to be the most trusted name in news."

I thought to myself, if there isn't a natural disaster, an armed conflict, or a very serious political issue, most places will never even be mentioned in the news. Have you ever heard about Ecuador before?

According to Byron Mayorga, @bmayorga, Twitter started to grow in Ecuador at the beginning of 2009 mostly because of Barcamp events organized in several cities of the country. At that time most users were geeks or early adopters. A second wave of new Ecuadorian twitterers came with Facebook popularity.

If It Is Not Happening, It Is Because You Are Not Doing It

Thomas Friedman, in his book The *World Is Flat*, describes several facts and forces that made the world flat. In one of the chapters, Friedman talks about all the power the Internet gives you. He says if it is not happening, it's because you are not doing it.

With a population of about 14 million inhabitants, just about 16% of the population of Ecuador has Internet access. Very low compared to other South American countries: 64% in Argentina, 52% in Uruguay, or 50% in Chile.[1]

Even though you can find Internet access almost everywhere in the country, mostly in business offices or Internet cafes, most people still cannot afford Internet at home.

---

[1] http://www.internetworldstats.com/stats15.htm#south.

Like many other Twitter users, most of the time I just share information that I think might be as useful to others as it was for me. I still have a lot to learn about social networks; as a casual user, most of the time I tweet on my free time, during lunch, or while a cup of coffee allows.

I was in my office after a long day, and while waiting for my wife to pick me up, it was Twitter time. I had an idea in my mind for a few days and it was time to research it. My friend Google was just a click away, but unfortunately I didn't find what I was looking for. I needed to ask someone about it, so I decided to contact the oldest and most respected Ecuadorian twitterers:

> *Has Ecuador or something related to Ecuador ever been a Trending Topic on Twitter?@bmayorga @palulo @coberturasms @cjumbo @pitonizza @earcos*

@bmayorga replied almost immediately saying that some time ago there was an earthquake in Peru very close to the border with Ecuador and that was the closest to a trending topic he can remember.

Some others mentioned that it was impossible because we don't have enough users to become a trending topic. Nevertheless, I had decided to say what I had been thinking for days.

August 10th is a special date for Ecuadorians. According to our history, our first independence attempt from Spain occurred back in 1809 in Quito. There is debate on the way the people at that time tried to obtain liberty, and that has been questioned by many people. But it's still a very special day for Ecuador. It was on July 29th that I replied to my friend's tweets saying, "What if we all together try to have #Ecuador as a trending topic on Twitter this coming August 10th?"

Why don't we let the world know about our country and all the wonderful things that we have?

In a matter of minutes the idea received almost a hundred retweets. Many people started suggesting ways to do it. In general, comments about Ecuador's situation are not very positive, so it was nice to hear from people ready to help and waiting for the day to arrive.

With all the excitement, it was difficult to read everybody's messages; we needed to define a temporary hashtag that could help us coordinate our efforts. After some time, we finally agreed on #QuieroEcuadorenTT—that means IwantEcuadorTT (TT—Trending Topic).

There was a lot of work ahead and time was running short. With @bmayorga, @pgarzon, and @pitonizza, we started a small group trying to coordinate the idea. We needed to define what hashtag to use during our chosen date and at what times of the day to tweet. Once again, people started suggesting hashtags, and many good ideas were shared. It was going to be a difficult decision and we didn't know who was going to make it. A twitterpoll was launched by @pitonizza, which was a great move that facilitated the discussions.

While the poll was running, some twitterers started to criticize the idea:

> *A trending topic is something that must flow, not something prepared.*

> *Don't waste your time. Because of the language, the number of users and time zones, you **won't** be able to do it.*

> *If you become a trending topic, which I don't think will happen, the idea **will** stop there.*

There were some disputes about the date. Some thought that we have some other celebrations with more meaning that August 10th, and I think they are right, but it is not every day that we have all these people willing to collaborate.

After the poll was closed, we analyzed the results, and the hashtag selected was #TeAmoEduador, which means I love you Ecuador.

Pablo Garzon, @pgarzon, mentioned that the idea was to allow everybody to express their love to the country and all the important things that we have: food, traditions, words, so why not also some things that we need to improved? Pablo was crucial on the initiative and one of the key players.

The selected hashtag didn't need explanation for the rest of the community. @palulo, @bmayorga, and @incom joined the core team; the jet set of Ecuadorian twitterers were supporting the idea. I haven't personally met any of these people in the group. We had some virtual meetings and exchanged several Direct Messages (DM) with other users. The idea was growing and growing. Suddenly we had a Web site to collect all messages and inform people about the initiative. There were several discussions about the best time of the day to concentrate our tweets, based on typical Ecuadorian behavior. I was amazed at people that have never met in person, working towards a common objective.

OVNI (UFO)

A few days before August 10th, several people reported an OVNI (UFO) in a neighborhood in Guayaquil. Several twitterers started to tweet about the situation. Several hours later, #ovni became a trending topic on Twitter. The first time that a discussion started in Ecuador made the list.

The UFO was a kite with lights that someone decided to fly that night. I received some Direct Messages from people asking me if after the OVNI trending topic we were going to cancel #TeAmoEduador. No we won't, was my reply. I had mixed feelings. It was a shame that #TeAmoEduador was not the first Ecuadorian

Trending Topic, but it also showed that we were enough users to achieve a second Trending Topic.

Several newspapers and TV stations reported the issue; most of the largest media groups in Ecuador are present on Twitter and their number of followers is growing every day. They seem to understand the importance of being on social media.

The day was getting closer and people started to send their tweets attaching the hashtag #TeAmoEcuador. The night before the event, it was crazy. Hundreds of tweets were filling my timeline. It was like a group of children saying out loud how much they loved their country.

Si Se Puede (We Can Do It)

During the qualifying games for the World Cup in Japan and South Korea in 2002, Ecuador was having a great performance. For the first time in its history, Ecuador had real opportunities to qualify. Soccer is by far the most popular sport here. In one of the most difficult games, people started to support the team by yelling: "Si se puede!," which means "We can do it!" It became very popular. The phrase had a real impact: our team defeated Brazil, Argentina, and other very important South American teams, and qualified in second place for the World Cup. If you ask an Ecuadorian what is the single thing that can bring all Ecuadorians together? The obvious reply will be soccer.

That is exactly the same feeling I had when I was reading the #TeAmoEduador tweets. People proud of being Ecuadorians. Trying to show the world the beautiful landscapes we have. Our most traditional food. The words and phrases we use and that only Ecuadorians understand. There were some others that were using the same hashtag and were against the idea; in any case, at 11:45 a.m., just forty-five minutes after the agreed time, #TeAmoEduador became a Trending Topic.

A few tweets I want to share:

- The Twitter whale was born in Ecuador, #TeAmoEduador referring to humpback whales that come to the coast of Ecuador from June to September

- The US invented Twitter, but they have not had an "I love you USA." #TeAmoEduador

For the first time in a while I was not interested in the latest Apple news or what new technology is coming. I discovered that Ecuador is the country I love and the place where all my dreams can come true. Pride and patriotism seem to be universal values. However, on August 10, 2010, I felt more Ecuadorian than ever before.

I received a DM from the official Twitter account for the President of Ecuador, @presidencia_ec, congratulating all the people for the idea.

Almost every major newspaper and television station in Ecuador mentioned something about #TeAmoEduador. Several editorial articles talked about the positive lessons the initiative created.

A Google search shows now about 200,000 results for the hashtag. According to @incom, almost 10,000 tweets were sent from 2,300 different accounts.

Andres Santos—@asantos, who originally didn't agree with the idea—mentioned that in his opinion, a trending topic needs to be organic (like the wave in a stadium, where people that feel identified with it participate) and that organizing a trending topic might sound like forcing someone to do something. I don't think we forced anybody to do something, but I understand what he means. Andres actually contributed with good ideas for the initiative.

Diego Rivadeneira, @millacta, is an Ecuadorian. Like many that have left the country, he currently lives in Santiago, Chile. Diego has always tried to stay connected with Ecuador and certainly Twitter has helped. For him, #TeAmoEduador was a way to show thanks to social networks and that a national feeling can become global.

Twitter is changing the way we live. Weeks later, after the event, we have seen that negative messages and pessimism, while still there, have less presence than before. #TeAmoEduador was built entirely out of 140 character messages, but the sum total of those tweets added up to something important that made a difference in many Ecuadorian lives that day: positive mindset and optimism are a value that all of us need to cultivate.

P.S. While I was writing this article, a third Ecuadorian trending topic showed up on Twitter. This time not organized.

Alfred Naranjo is a systems engineer and father of three, who enjoys nature, computers, gadgets, and reading. He's a dreamer of a better world and an entrepreneur.

Alfred Naranjo
anaranjoc@yahoo.com
@anaranjoc
http://www.facebook.com/anaranjoc/
http://ec.linkedin.com/in/anaranjoc/

Political Crisis As The Lever-Effect to the Expansion of Social Media:
A Case Study of Madagascar

by

Haja Rasambainarivo

Known for its rich biodiversity and natural resources, Madagascar is also one of the ten poorest countries in the world, with a gross domestic product (GDP) at purchasing power parity (PPP) per capita of only $932.00 USD[1].

With nearly twenty million people and a couple of Internet service providers owning bandwidth[2], only a very limited number of Malagasy have the opportunity to browse the web.

A vast majority of these users receive Internet through the use of cybercafés or mobile devices. Recent statistics from the Ministry of Telecommunications show that the total number of subscribers has only reached 36,000. By taking into account all these mediums, the total penetration of Internet usage would be 350,000 users,[3] accounting for only 1.75% of the total population.

This is much lower than the average of the contiguous continent of Africa, where the Internet penetration rate has reached 8.7%.

You can see that the digital divide in Madagascar is huge.

Social Media in Madagascar

Social media in Madagascar has initially been used to share personal interests and activities among local residents. It's also used to maintain links and relationships between the Malagasy diaspora members in Europe and North America with their family and friends back home.

Like their foreign counterparts, Malagasy users have quickly embraced the use of the Internet platform to voice their interests and opinions.

---

[1] Source: World Economic Outlook Database, April 2010, International Monetary Fund.
[2] Telecom Malagasy and DTS; Orange Madagascar are the only ISPs which are connected to the internet via an underwater fiber cable.
[3] In 2008, The World Bank estimated the number of Internet users to 316,100.

Several initiatives have been used by early adopters to help their compatriots promote the usage of Web blogs. Among them, we can cite the Best Of Malagasy Blog contest, a.k.a BOMB[4], that appraises the value of Malagasy blogs in several categories.

With high deforestation, the loss of endangered species, and poverty issues plaguing the country, blogs have also become very popular among Malagasy environmental and humanitarian activists. Some expatriates such as Peace Corps volunteers or foreign corporate workers launched personal blogs to share their insights about their daily life in their host country.

Besides blogs, with nearly 90,000 users in Madagascar[5], Facebook is the most dominant social media network used by the islanders.

Crisis as a Lever Effect

Regularly hit by a series of deep political crisis every seven to ten years, Madagascar has not been able to break the cycle and is currently scrambling to get out of the state of disagreement in which the country has been plunged since January 2009.

Madagascar's president Marc Ravalomanana has been pressured by opposition rallies initiated by Mr. Andry Rajoelina, a young businessman and former mayor of the capital.

Successive weeks of extreme tensions and violence in the country's capital led by Mr. Ravalomanana led to his being overthrown in March 2009. Mr. Rajoelina swore himself in as the transitional head of state of Madagascar and is still struggling to receive the recognition of his political peers and the international community. At the time of this writing, election dates, which would end this long crisis, are not yet scheduled.

What's the peculiarity of this crisis? While in the past, newspapers, radio, and TV broadcasting have been the focal point, 2009 was the first time social media has played an important role in Madagascar's political scene.

In February 2009, at the peak of the crisis, several factors have contributed to the rapid growth of Internet and social media users:

The failure of traditional media:

- o Although the constitution of Madagascar states that the freedom of opinions and expression is insured, human rights

---

[4] http://www.bestofmalagasyblogs.com/.
[5] Facebakers: Facebook Statistics for Madagascar, http://www.facebakers.com/countries-with-facebook/MG/.

organizations have pointed out that several journalists have been pressured or sentenced while they were covering topics that were contrary to the ruling party's interests.

o The vast majority of traditional media such as radio, television stations, and newspapers are owned by political parties and broadcast ill-informed information.

o Some media stations have been shutdown during the political crisis—whether they were state owned or from the opposition party.

In this situation, the Malagasy population has been facing a dilemma: on the one hand, some journalists were putting their life at risk while doing their job; on the other hand, the traditional media were not receiving a very good level of trust from the population.

Up-to-date News:

Where do I get updated and real time information? In a time where speedy delivery of information has become very important (compared to the last crisis of 2001-2002), Madagascar does not have the press agencies that are able to produce written real time information to the public.

Internet as the only space of freedom:

To my own knowledge, and according to several sources such as Reporters Without Borders and the OpenNet Initiatives[6] (which monitors the use of Internet filtering and surveillance practices by nation), Malagasy authorities do not have the means to control the country's cyberspace. Therefore, nobody could use the state's intelligence services to shutdown the Internet or censor traffic, in a similar manner as seen in Iran or China.

I am almost certain that this space of freedom has contributed to motivate Malagasy to become "connected." Between 2007 and 2008, the number of Internet users in the country has seen a growth of nearly 265%[7].

How Social Media Was Used During The Crisis?

Social media has been found to be the answer to many of the issues above, and all these factors have contributed to the rise of social media in Madagascar. To

---

[6] http://map.opennet.net/filtering-IT.html.
[7] Source: World Bank; World Development Indicators: Internet users.
http://data.worldbank.org/indicator/IT.NET.USER?cid=GPD_58.

illustrate this statement, I will try to provide a few examples of how social media has been used during the current political crisis.

At the peak of the crisis, mass gatherings and unrest occurred in Antananarivo, the capital of Madagascar.

Facebook users have used their status to update their friends and networks about the ongoing events in their respective cities, and more specifically in their neighborhoods. In several cases, users have expressly relaxed their privacy settings to allow users that are out of their network to see their wall updates and pictures related to these events.

Some users took enormous risks to tape videos of pillaging and shootings, which were posted on YouTube or Dailymotion within a few minutes.

Twitter has been used in a similar manner to share useful and life saving information.

I recount that a Twitter update from one person I am following allowed me to run away from a neighborhood in which I was located before protesters showed up breaking car windows and destroying several businesses.

With the wealth, diversity, and most importantly the objectivity of the information, some tweeters and bloggers have become the local correspondents of major news networks, such as the BBC and CNN, which in turn relayed the updates on their front pages.

The crisis has been lasting for more than eighteen months, and although topics have changed and foreign reporters have left the country, social media is now the most common way for foreign press agencies to verify whether some information is valid.

To illustrate this, a great deal of information has been relayed about the trafficking of rosewood timber. Taking advantage of the state of civil disobedience, illegal logging has surged to meet the demand in China. Various high-level officials and notorious businessmen are involved in this very profitable, illegal enterprise. Made aware of this, several news agencies are asking social media users to report facts and pictures about this issue. Thanks to the response of the citizen media and the efforts led by other organizations, a great deal of evidence has been collected to build a case against these traffickers and reports have circulated worldwide.

With a non-negligible proportion of political activists located abroad, Malagasy politicians and parties have begun to create blogs, Facebook pages, or Twitter profiles to share their ideologies or projects. To date though, this approach doesn't seem to be successful at reaching the mass population because of the huge digital divide.

Conclusion

Facebook, and more recently Twitter, became increasingly important in the life of "connected" Malagasy in the past years. The political crisis has helped a large number of them to understand that social media can be used to transmit quick and reliable information when traditional media fail to accomplish their mission. In a crisis which is lasting too long, these tools are helping to maintain the flow of information and communication between my compatriots and, most importantly, lobby the international stage for a return of good governance in Madagascar. Unfortunately, only a handful of Malagasy can take advantage of this technology. Once this crisis comes to an end, I strongly hope that Madagascar's economy will finally improve so the digital divide can be overcome in my country.

Holding a postgraduate degree from HEC Montréal, Haja Rasambainarivo has specialized in the deployment of IT infrastructure projects in developing countries. He works principally with non-governmental organizations and their partners in Asia-Pacific, Sub-Saharan Africa, and South America. In his spare time, he is involved in the promotion of Madagascar as a main tourism destination.

Haja Rasambainarivo
@rashaja
http://ca.linkedin.com/in/rashaja
http://www.hungry-travellers.com

Worlds Apart

By

Noaf Ereiqat

Like many people of this day and age, I have been fortunate enough to have lived a very metropolitan life. Being of Palestinian origin, I grew up between Germany and the UK.

With friends and acquaintances all over the world, any kind of network to facilitate staying in touch was a welcome relief. Over the years from 2001 onwards, I had my share of failed experiments with initial social networks such as Hi5 and BeBo (God they were awful!). And after a lot of trial and error and endless "ASL" messages ("age, sex, location" for those who are fortunate enough not to know), I eventually decided to stick to Facebook to stay in touch with friends and family, and LinkedIn for work-related networking.

In 2008 I left Europe and moved to the Middle East—Dubai to be precise—to take a job that had been offered to me via LinkedIn. Here social networking took on a new importance for me, as I was in a country where I knew no one and all my friends and relatives were miles away. For my initial three months in Dubai, Facebook was my best friend, and I was so busy socializing online that I neglected socializing offline. This included a personal blog and Skype.

The difference I noticed though is that, whereas my UK peers were like-minded and very net-savvy, my peers in Dubai did not share the same passion. Here, networking was something people did in coffee shops and restaurants as well as over the phone. Many considered it a waste of time; you have to log on to a computer, then access your profile all just to type a message or post something on someone's wall and then wait for your reply. Everyone just picks up the phone and it's much quicker and easier!

That was only the starting point though, in which the adoption of a new trend was considered with large skepticism by a generally more conservative society than Europe. Despite much talk about "online marketing on the rise" in the Middle East since 2004, and some of the most advanced companies of our region coming from the Arab world, I watched as both marketing departments and agencies all but closed their eyes to online and social media marketing. In 2009, even the few who started adopting new media into their plans still initiated their campaigns with no mention of their social media activities anywhere, be it in print, radio, or even their Web sites.

With the rise of "Facebook Pages" as well as the gaining popularity of Twitter, things changed in the middle of 2009, which was strongly driven by the adoption of social media applications on mobile phones. According to data released by the Telecommunications Regulatory Authority (TRA), the smartphone market grew by 47% from 2009 to 2010, and mobile applications for social media drove their popularity immensely.

From there on, it was a constant upstream. The number of UAE Facebook users reached 1.69 million users in May 2010 and grew to 1.75 million users by the end of August 2010 according to www.facebakers.com. This means that 35% of the UAE's population are active Facebook users. Furthermore, the majority of the UAE's Facebook users are aged between 25 and 34 years, and using Facebook for a mix between personal and professional purposes with a large number of local and regional Facebook pages growing both locally and regionally.

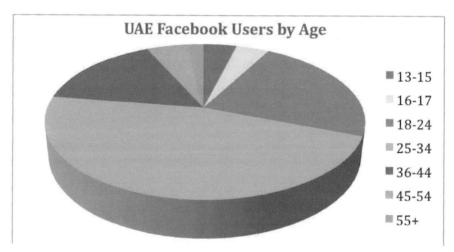

I myself have only been on Twitter since March 2009, as one of the early(ish) adopters locally. Twitter, unlike Facebook, grew very quickly and suddenly, and while I was one of the doubters, it looks like it is around to stay. The UAE's Twitter community matured from around 5,000 users at the end of 2009 to about 15,000 by August 2010, according to www.twopcharts.com. The interesting fact is that the UAE alone amounts to 37.5% of the number of an estimated 40,000 Twitter users across the Middle East and North Africa.

That said, the UAE may not be one of the early adopters of social media compared globally, but when comparing it against the Gulf Cooperation Council (GCC) or even the Middle East, it has proven to be a market leader in the field, giving a lot of room for social media networking both online and offline. There are numerous agencies now offering social media training and management doing a great job approaching local and regional companies to integrate social media into their marketing efforts, and we are seeing more and more interesting and useful social campaigns implemented.

It's funny to look back; although I have only been here for three years now, the progress made is immense. I have made a number of new friends through both Facebook and Twitter and make them one of my prime sources of reference when I'm on the search for anything. Just a few months ago, I broke my heel at a conference in Deira—an area of Dubai I am not very familiar with—and posted my annoyance on Twitter (which also feeds onto my Facebook profile). Within ten minutes I had received numerous replies not only to cheer me up, but with locations of nearby shoe repairs!

So now, less than three years later, when I whip out my Blackberry to access Facebook or Twitter, I am no longer looked at as unsociable, but more often find my friends and colleagues doing much the same. It's a funny little thing this social media.

Noaf Ereiqat has been active in the online marketing field since 2005. Her early career started with eBay UK, as part of the online marketing team to launch a German version of Shopping.com, an e-commerce Web site, then progressed to manage partner development in both the UK and Germany. In 2007, she moved on to Buy.at UK, an affiliate network that was bought out by AOL's "Platform A," again managing online affiliate and partner growth. Noaf shifted to Dubai in early 2008 to join Maktoob.com, the world's largest Arab online platform heading up the marketing team, and then joined THECONTENT|FACTORY in October 2008 as a Business Development Consultant with a key focus on online and social media campaign development.

Noaf Ereiqat
nereiqat@gmail.com
@noaf_e
http://www.facebook.com/noaf.ereiqat
http://ae.linkedin.com/in/noafereiqat

A View From The Very Deep South

by

Nicholas Evans

The adoption and usage of social media facilities in South Africa has rapidly grown in recent years. This is a surprising phenomenon given the lack of cheap, readily available internet access. Due to the small percentage of the population who have Internet access, usage of social media facilities is still considered a luxury, a play thing for geeks and the wealthy within some circles in South Africa.

Adoption of social media such as Facebook, Twitter, and MySpace has been rampant with the 16–25 year old middle class demographic, and has provided an entirely new and unique method of interaction with peers. Adoption within the 25-year and older following is at a slightly lower pace but is growing consistently at an ever increasing rate.

Although adoption within South Africa is strong, the high costs of Internet access and limited availability prevent the majority of South Africans from experiencing the social media revolution. Over time, with increased availability and decreased cost, it is expected that there will be a dramatic surge in usage.

The Rise of Facebook

With well over a million South African members, Facebook is the social media tool of choice and has permanently altered the way South Africans interact with friends, family, and clients.

A few years ago, text messages were the preferred medium for non-invasive interactions, e.g. wishing people happy birthday, etc. Now this has been almost entirely replaced by Facebook posts and messages. This represents a significant paradigm shift and must be troubling for the South African mobile cellular service providers, as it inevitability impacts their bottom line.

The number of friends one has on Facebook has become a source of tremendous pride and something of a status symbol within South African society, the notion being the more friends you have on Facebook the more popular you are. This has resulted in many people sending friend requests to people they don't know all that well or, in some instances, complete strangers, in order to boost numbers.

I myself have received friend requests from complete strangers trying to build a large set of contact or develop a "mailing list" of sorts for marketing purposes. This phenomenon of people and businesses sending out mass friend solicitations via Facebook is very much on the rise and is extensively used for marketing and awareness reasons.

Many South African companies are creating Facebook user groups that typically serve a dual purpose, as a team building facility for staff, and as an awareness/marketing medium for clients. Companies often include pictures of their staff, their offices, and promotional videos on their groups, creating a public intranet of sorts. User involvement empowers and motivates both staff and clients to get involved and creates a sense of ownership, which ultimately helps build longer lasting relationships. This has become so popular that several local television stations have established their own user groups to advertise their shows, post clips, and build followings.

Rocking Robin (Tweet Tweet Tweet)

Twitter adoption within South Africa has been slow but is rapidly growing in popularity. Initially many people struggled to comprehend the concept of a microblog.

Many individuals use Twitter to share information about their work, social activities, and opinions. From a self-promotion perspective, Twitter has become the medium of choice for local politicians and public figures who want to be more visible and build closer contact with the public or fans.

Some local municipalities are even using Twitter to update the public on road works, traffic conditions, maintenance schedules, and service interruptions.
Many South African companies have adopted Twitter to create awareness of their products. For example, a local software development company uses Twitter to keep people informed on the developments of their flagship product. New features and time lines for releases are regularly tweeted, and there are several thousand followers in place, including some celebrities like Arnold Schwarzenegger.

Twitter is the rising star of the social media platforms in South Africa. Its business and promotional value is rapidly being realized and is self-perpetuating by its very usage.

LinkedIn? Not Quite

LinkedIn, although quite popular with South African business professionals, has never achieved the same degree of popularity as Facebook or Twitter. LinkedIn is used as more of an informal online resume and seems to have made very little impact within South Africa. I am sure that some use this service to its full extent on a regular basis, but my experience has been that people create their profile, link to people they know, and "walk away," with little to no interaction thereafter. Unlike Facebook, LinkedIn offers very little in the way of real or meaningful interaction and its popularity has suffered as a result. Given the South African people's love of gadgets and interactivity, it is doubtful that LinkedIn will ever achieve the same degree of daily usage locally.

Rise of the Smart Device

With the advent of smart devices like the iPhone and Blackberry, social media has moved from being PC-based to mobile.

This phenomenon has subtly changed the nature and frequency of the usage. For example, I recently started using an iPhone and installed the apps for Twitter, Facebook, and LinkedIn. Having access to these facilities at any time or location has dramatically increased my usage (mostly of Facebook, which allows me to keep all my friends informed of my activities and opinions). For example, I regularly take pictures of things that amuse or impress me and immediately upload them to Facebook, which stimulates live debate or comment.

This also raises concerns as I have found that people are able to follow my movements throughout the day and I have on more than one occasion had friends "track me down" for a chat or coffee through nothing other than my Facebook posts.

As smart devices become more available and accessible, the integration of social media into the average South African's life will increase dramatically.

Nicholas Evans is the Lead Business Consultant with Airborne Consulting based in Cape Town, South Africa. Nicholas has sixteen years of working experience in the IT sector and has worked extensively within South Africa and abroad. He began his career as a technical consultant and gradually moved into the business consulting space. Nicholas is a skilled facilitator, program manager, and best practice, business process, and management consultant.

Nicholas Evans
nicholase@abg.co.za
http://www.airborneconsulting.co.za
+27-83-414-7421

Moving Forward

Starting Over In A 140-Character World

by

Michele Mattia

If you can succeed doing what you don't love, can you imagine the limitless possibilities when you discover and manifest your divine plan and life purpose? Starting over in an era of social media!

"I can't do this anymore," I shouted, as I sat up straight in bed from a sound sleep disrupted by a nightmare. "I can't! I can't! I won't!" The location was a romantic B&B in Venice, Italy, where the love of my life, Jim, and I were celebrating my 40th birthday.

"Can't do what anymore?" Jim mumbled with his eyes half opened. "Is this one of those 'we need to talk' conversations that will require me to be fully awake?"

Although the hairs on the back of my neck still stood on end from the nightmare that played like a documentary film of my current professional existence, I was able to find some humor in how my can't-and-won't tirade at 3 a.m. must have sounded. "We're good, handsome," I said while rubbing his back. "It's just time for me to step out of my comfort zone and take a leap of faith."

At the time of my revelation, I owned a successful technology-consulting firm in Manhattan for the past eleven years, with two other partners, specializing on the Macintosh platform. I had the opportunity to work with industries that ranged from PR and advertising, to film and television, to law and photography. Although the company was thriving and my clients were amazing, the partnership that on paper looked good at the beginning hadn't evolved into anything remotely cooperative, collaborative, or positive. There's much to be said about finding just the right people to enter into a business relationship with, but if you don't consider aligned interests, passions, and values, you are ignoring some key components. Even though I was unhappy with my partners, I was still in an extremely safe and secure situation. I was comfortable. My bills and extracurricular expenses were paid effortlessly with money left over for savings and investing. Yet, I was also comfortable with accepting and settling for less than who I was and what I was meant to do. We've all been there. The idea that we can do and be what we love seems so foreign.

For years I knew I should be doing something different, something bigger and something with purpose. It took a five-year-old little girl named Leila to point out what my heart had been trying to tell me. "Why are you scared of something you don't even know is gonna happen?" Leila asked, in all of her five-year-oldness, with clenched hands on her hips and a look of confusion on her face. It was the summer of 2006, and several of us had gathered at a friend's house for a barbeque. His backyard was expansive and housed many tall trees; however, the very best one of all had a tire swing. When Leila and her family arrived, she had zeroed in on that tire swing long before the door to her parents car slammed shut. Out of all the people she could have asked to push her in this swing, Leila came to me, which would normally be a wise choice, but on this occasion I said no with a long lists of whys. "The rope could snap, you could sail through the middle of the tire, and you could get hurt." She focused on my face for several minutes before throwing her hands up in the air and saying, "Oh well, I guess you're gonna be missing out on a lot of fun."

As you can imagine, Leila's words stuck with me. First, it was rather frustrating knowing a five-year-old was more connected to her spirit than I felt. Second, she was correct. I was no longer having fun in any areas of my life. Although at the time I was a successful business owner for close to a decade, lived in a fabulous Upper West Side apartment with views of Central Park, and traveled extensively, there was something missing. My divine plan and life purpose weren't anywhere to be found, but then again, up until that point I had not been looking very hard. It was right then that I embraced the importance of my "Life's Dash"—the precious time between arrival and departure from this world that many of us take for granted. I took a good hard look at mine and knew I was no longer doing or living what I loved. I knew my Dash was meant for something greater.

What happened next is, to date, the most anxiety-filled time in my life. I attended a silent retreat during a snowy February in Connecticut. Up until that point, the amount of silence I had experienced in my life could have fit into a thimble, but I knew if I didn't shut up and shut out my ego, I would not hear the still, small voice guiding me.

My unease was pretty high: I was not only putting my needs first, which was foreign to me, but I feared discovering something that would require leaving my comfortable, safe, and secure lifestyle.

While on retreat, I had many opportunities to participate in walking meditations—a serene and solitary thirty minutes of crunching through snow with the smell of crisp winter air and snowflakes tickling my eyelashes. Prior to one of those walks, I asked myself the question, "What would you do right now if you knew you could not fail?" Within minutes, I came across a magnificent tree. Her limbs branched outward as if waiting to receive a hug from me, and snow clung to tiny green leaves. It was the dead of winter and this was the only tree with foliage. For me it represented strength, growth, and limitless possibilities.

When I got back to the retreat center and sat in front of the fireplace, images of my tree and the words Life Design, transformation, growth, creativity, abundance, prosperity, and coaching swirled in my head. I wrote in my journal, "What are you thinking? Who leaves the success and security of an established company to start over based on a 30-minute walk?" But I knew I didn't love my current business and believed in my heart that we are not only meant to do what we love, but to live a life rich in joy, abundance, and prosperity while doing so.

By the end of the retreat, I had my company name, designed the logo, and wrote my mission statement: to inspire, co-create, and support all of the possibilities people are courageous enough to demand. I knew what I wanted and now it came time to figure out how I was going to get my message out to the world, become a part of the conversation, and make a difference. My Life Design coaching practice would be more than the creative strategies I formulated with individuals and companies. I wanted to provide value, give back, connect, and collaborate with others.

I was feeling delicious! I had said "yes" to my divine dream—but now what? For eleven years, my business "thinking" was on the back end of technology, where I created support solutions for brands; however, now I was the brand. Years of working in the technology industry gave me access, knowledge, and understanding of social media. But now it was time for me to come up with my own plan. It's an interesting process when we have the opportunity to focus on ourselves. The feeling isn't usually comfortable. We can't hide behind a client or a company logo.

Social media is not a tactic or a strategy. It's not about isolationism or the loss of the human connection. Social media is about expansion, engagement, connection, and conversation. It's about being a part of something bigger than ourselves, and the tremendous opportunity we have to learn from one another and affect change. More and more individuals and companies are employing the power behind social media (tweeting, blogging, posting) to become a part of the conversation and engage with a global community.

Now when I think about the concept behind social media, the butterfly effect comes to mind. When a butterfly flaps its wings, they say the movement will have an effect (albeit very small) on wind strength and weather systems throughout the world. When I blog, post to my Facebook professional page, retweet a news article, or upload a YouTube video of "Motivating Monday's with Michele" to my social network profiles, my thoughts and these actions have the potential to be read and viewed by thousands of people. Many of those individuals will be inspired to act and have their voices heard and could either forward my posts, tweets, and uploads, or create their own, which will have the potential to be read and viewed by thousands. In turn, those individuals will be inspired and so on and so on. Social networking has lead many to reach out via e-mail, which turns into a phone call, which turns into a meeting, which turns into networking, which turns into collaboration. This isn't the loss of the human connection. This is a gift!

As I wrote the business and marketing plans for my new endeavor, social media become a prominent component. Transparency, honesty, and sincerity were high on my list of concepts, as well as developing an authentic voice and generating a brand where people could see, feel, and understand my message even if they had not yet met me in person. I was interested in what others had to say about the world they lived in, and if sharing my observations, philosophies, and experiences inspired someone else to act or improve a situation, then my life purpose was on target. Additionally, it was important and imperative for me to incorporate my unique gifts, talents, and skills. I asked myself key questions like, "What comes naturally to you?" and "What makes your heart sing?" Knowing, honoring, and incorporating the "who" I was into my company made the process all the more exciting.

Aside from my Web site, I immediately planned on setting up a Twitter account, a Facebook Professional Page, a LinkedIn account, and a blog, which connected with my passion for writing. From a very young age, I knew my words, whether spoken or written, were meant to heal and motivate. Yet, to jump into any of the above social networking avenues without knowing the answer to why I was utilizing these powerful resources would have made the efforts challenging. While remaining centered on my desire for giving back, I began to work on my personal mission and life purpose statement. I posed questions that were imperative to my creation and implementation of a successful social media plan. "What specifically do I want to contribute to people? What causes/issues am I passionate about? What three gifts of wisdom about life would I give to those that follow me? What are the five most important lessons I have learned in this life? What do I want my life to stand for? What is unique about me?"

I'm a believer that there is more than enough for all of us and collaboration benefits us all. Instead of tackling all of the social networks at the same time, I started slow. My first venture was Twitter and I initiated my digital footprint with positive words, expressions, and affirmations—maybe two to three times a day. Like most of us, I first looked to find friends and former clients who had social media profiles, but eventually began to branch out toward those with similar backgrounds, goals, dreams, and aligned interests. Soon I got brave and began to retweet, and reply to tweets I liked and wanted to pass along to those who were following me. What I found interesting as my Twitter exposure grew is the realization that while I came from an industry where numbers mattered, I found myself being very selective with those I chose to follow and become fans of and of those who wanted to follow me. Social media is about quality versus quantity and providing value versus posting a sales pitch. My having thousands of followers was pointless if no one was talking. When I engaged with others, I never used auto replies. I took the time to look at their profiles and learned about what they do. To this day, people thank me for the personalized direct messages, thank yous, retweets, and yes, thanking me for thanking them. I don't do it for the recognition, but rather from wanting to get to learn about those who are interested in me. There's a reason why we connected and why not see where the online relationship naturally progresses.

While my use of Twitter increased, so did my connections with people all around the world. It's one thing to have your voice heard from this phenomenal outlet, but another to step out from behind your computer or laptop and meet people face to face. Many of my connections on Twitter have turned into relationships—both personal and professional. On many occasions we have collaborated on projects and events, as well as helping each other to spread our respective messages. I began to use third-party tools like Social Oomph and Twitterfeed to help manage and schedule my tweets, along with a more efficient manner for the release of my daily blog posts. It's extremely important to be mindful of your most ardent followers, as well as their geographic location. I made sure my daily affirmation, question of the day, daily challenge, and blog were scheduled to cover all time zones, including internationally.

Early on I had established who my target audience was and discovered where they spent their time both on and offline. This helped my social media plan to unfold organically. Not everyone looking for a life design coach or business and creative strategist was on Twitter or loved reading blogs. Some of my audience only gravitated toward Facebook as their social network preference, while others combined Twitter and Facebook, and then some were more visual and looking to connect with a face and video. Additionally, I discovered that with the social media platform preference my followers had, came a creative customization of each of my growing communities. My Facebook professional page is all about engagement. I found my groove when I realized that my most successful posts were when I posed questions and challenges that fostered engagement and communication. Receiving the "thumbs up" is great, but I want to know that what I'm sharing is making people move! What also developed were the connections, which stemmed from my followers beginning to follow one another on their respective Facebook pages. How fabulous!

As I did with Twitter, I utilized third-party software, tools, applications, and widgets to help manage and automate my Facebook professional page. Any post on Facebook automatically goes to Twitter, but not the reverse. I found that setting up my tweets to show up on Facebook didn't translate as well. What resulted in my seamless integration between Facebook and Twitter was a significant increase in those that were following my professional page, as well as comments that supported more than 140 characters. In addition, the hits and comments on my blog increased. The word was getting out!

One morning while meditating, the idea of an e-newsletter manifested. I named it "Michele's Daily Dash—words to inspire, support, and motivate the creation of your empowered and dynamic life design." It would incorporate the blog I wrote Monday through Friday, affirmations, quotes, daily challenges, questions of the day, and topics that cover life, career, and business. On more than one occasion I had people offering unsolicited commentary regarding my use of social networks and "giving away the farm without receiving compensation." Resolute in my absolute truth, the knowledge that I'm making a difference in the lives of others, word of mouth, and connecting like-minded people via my social networks in the hopes of their future collaboration was my compensation.

There are naysayers and opinionated individuals out there who are at the ready to inform us about the "rules" of social media. They point out their expertise within the technology and inform about what you should do and not do for each of the potential social networks. First of all, I am suspect of anyone who claims to be a social media expert. It is one of the fastest evolving technologies and there are numerous networks to choose from. Enthusiast and specialist I can accept. Second, how can any one of us know with 100% certainty what approach works for everyone? How many individual people out there can lay claim to knowing everyone? That's a lot of people! The only rules I follow are the ones that I apply to my life as a whole and they are based on my values. Please and thank you(s). If you don't have something positive or constructive to say, or the offering of a solution, or an attempt to act, then keep your mouth shut and your fingers from typing.

My being authentic and transparent means that I'm sharing parts of my life that are relevant and/or just plain fun. Because of how I decided to connect with others, I don't worry about tweeting my location at a 5Bucks (my slang for Starbucks), where I can't wait for my delicious venti soy, no water, no foam, chai latte. This information resulted in an actual connection within the company, as well as new business contacts and clients who happen to love Starbucks as much as I do.

When I started Life Design, my plan was that 70% of the practice would be devoted to life, career, and business strategy and coaching for individuals and small businesses, and 30% would be devoted to my writing and publishing articles, blogs, and books. Within three months of the official start date, the direction of my company was altered. Doing what I loved and becoming a part of a global community provided me with numerous occasions to meet and collaborate with people from all walks of life. Areas I had not thought to include in my practice showed up as opportunities, and instead of worrying about the "how" of the situation, I stepped out on faith and answered, "YES!" I was asked to speak publicly at events, conferences, and on radio, and realized that my heart sang when I engaged audiences and began conversations that challenged perceptions, centered on living our absolute truth, and created dynamic and delicious lives. I can assure you that it came as no surprise to teachers, professors, and my family that I am now paid to speak. Clearly I made an impression from an early age when the only thing that shut me up was a good book.

My social networks led me to an interview on New York City's NBC local evening news during sweeps week in February 2010, interviews with a production company who are in the development stages of a reality show focused on redesigning lives, a controversial article in the NY Post, a published book, and proposals for a radio show and product launch. This is where I found my core group that fostered and supported my inspirational and motivational speaking platform. I've been blessed to speak all around the country and am moved by the people I meet. They are the reason I do what I do, and I value what I learn from them. Michele's Daily Dash has grown from an e-newsletter to an e-zine, and I have close to 8,000 views a month. This success doesn't happen in a vacuum and I am forever grateful to those who believe in and support me.

What's the best part of a good rollercoaster? Not knowing when it's going to dip, turn, and flip! The best part of living is not knowing the "how," and being surprised by those opportunities that present themselves when we are open and receptive to the good we readily deserve. The experiences social media provides are limitless! As it turns out, Life Design wasn't my brand; it's a part of my philosophy and truth that we are all meant to live dynamic and delicious lives. This awareness and growth is a direct result of how people responded to my Twitter, Facebook, blog, and Daily Dash. In reality, my brand is me—Michele Mattia. Within a year and a half of starting my social media campaign, I am redesigning and expanding. I am focused on speaking and hosting workshops, events, and retreats to those who are courageous and empowered enough to affect change in their lives and the world, as well as a radio show that brings like-minded individuals together. When we have the courage to open our hearts toward new thoughts, ways to give back, and the promotion of good for all, grand shifts in consciousness occur and change in the world emerges. By living what I love, I have manifested my divine plan for becoming a part of the conversation and making a difference. Social media played a large role in it coming to fruition. I am grateful!

Michele Mattia, a life design coach, social media and creative strategist, popular blogger, author, writer, and inspirational speaker, motivates and assists others with designing delicious lives. Her mission is to inspire, support, and co-create all possibilities her clients are courageous enough to demand. To receive *Michele's Daily Dash,* an empowering e-zine and blog, go to www.lifes-dash.com or send an e-mail request to dailydash@MicheleMattia.com.

Social Media: What's Next?

By

Tonia Ries

The first iteration of Facebook launched in 2004, with a site open only to Harvard students. For most of us, however, Facebook first became accessible in September of 2006, when it became available to anyone age 13 and older with an e-mail address.

That was four years ago.

Today, Facebook has more than 500 million active users around the world[1]. In the U.S., it is the fourth-ranked site in terms of traffic and has surpassed Google in terms of total time spent on the site[2]. In the same time period, Twitter has gone from launch to nearly 150 million users[3], who send an estimated 85 million tweets a day[4].

Advertisers have taken notice, investing $1.68 billion in advertising on social networks in the U.S. alone[5]. And that figure does not include the untold hours of time businesses of all sizes are investing in developing and managing a social media strategy.

Social media has made a huge impact in a very short amount of time. But these numbers—and the case studies in this book—are only the very beginning of the story.

Social networks are rapidly adding new features and new ways for users to engage with each other, share content and make connections. Organizations are in the earliest stages of learning how to use these tools to engage with their customers and stakeholders.

---

[1] http://www.facebook.com/press/info.php?statistics.
[2] http://twtrcon.com/2010/09/11/u-s-internet-users-spent-41-1-billion-minutes-on-facebook-in-august/.
[3] http://blog.twitter.com/2010/09/evolving-ecosystem.html.
[4] http://royal.pingdom.com/2010/09/03/twitter-usage-up-33-over-the-summer/.
[5] http://www.emarketer.com/Article.aspx?R=1007869.

And the technology itself is evolving. In the coming months, there are some key trends to watch as you look for opportunities for your business and discover ways to enrich your own experience with social media technologies.

1. **Location-based services have checked in:** If you haven't yet experienced the joy of meeting a friend in a strange city because you noticed that they "checked in," you may not yet be sold on location-based networks. But millions of users are, and businesses, especially retail and entertainment firms, are creating campaigns designed to bring customers into their stores, and even to steer them to the right aisle. What if you could walk into the grocery store with your shopping list loaded on your phone and immediately receive information on specials, coupons related to the items on your list, and a map to guide you through the store to pick up your purchases most efficiently?

2. **Shopping gets social:** Swipely is a start-up that lets you share what you buy simply by tracking where you use your credit card. Foodspotting.com has thousands of users posting photos and reviews of food they encounter at restaurants around the world. Foursquare users leave "tips" and "to dos" wherever they check in. What if you could go to a new city and instantly build a program of restaurants, stores, and galleries to visit based on the ratings and recommendations of your friends or other users who share your interests?

3. **Influence becomes currency:** Bigger is better, and everybody wants more followers and Facebook fans. But the latest data from the emerging science of social media analytics indicates that popularity and influence are not the same thing. The exponential power of retweets, in which messages are passed from user to user, quickly adds up to far more impact than simply having a large number of followers. Reach will be replaced by metrics such as amplification and engagement, and marketers will pay more to reach users with high influence scores.

4. **Your social graph will include objects:** Since the early days of Twitter, hackers have devised ways of connecting physical objects to Twitter accounts. There's a London bakery that sends a tweet from its oven with every fresh tray of pastries (@AlbionsOven). A group of engineers built a machine that makes popcorn every time someone sends a tweet with the hashtag #popcorn in it. A company called stickybits recently created a service that lets users (or manufacturers) attach bar codes to physical objects, and then use the bar code to attach content to those objects. What if you could point your phone at that new assembly-required cabinet, and play a video of the instructions? What if you could instantly connect to a network of people who bought the same pair of shoes and share pictures they've posted of the outfits they created?

5. **Your social behavior will personalize your web experience:** You've probably noticed that many Web sites are littered with Facebook "Like" buttons. By recording your preferences, and those of your friends, these

buttons, in turn, will allow sites to create a personalized experience for you. Log in with your Facebook account, and a catalog, shopping site, or newspaper can offer products, entertainment, or articles targeted to your interests or based on content that your friends have recommended.

6. **The big social platforms will continue to become more horizontal:** In the race for users and traffic, all of the major social networks are building or acquiring new features to encourage their community to spend ever more of their online life inside the walls of their favorite network. Twitter is adding rich content to its Web site. LinkedIn is adding company profiles and reviews to its network of business contacts. Millions of users rely primarily on Facebook, not e-mail, to communicate and chat with their friends. Look for these and other networks to continue to add new widgets, e-commerce, games, app stores, and tools in an effort to be the primary gateway for their users' online activity.

7. **Marketers, social platforms, and users will struggle to capture, control, and integrate the data:** As social networks become broader and new social tools emerge to fill a variety of niches, the question of who owns the data—and the customer relationship—will become more contentious. Marketers will face a trade-off between the access and engagement offered by the large social networks, and the lack of direct control over their own customer relationships. One group of entrepreneurs is developing a social network that gives control over the data to the users themselves. Database and marketing vendors are rolling out tools to help companies capture information about their customers' social behavior and preferences, and then integrate that information into their existing customer relationship management strategies. Expect a lot of innovation, new services, and hype around topics such as Social CRM and integrated analytics.

If you're managing a social media strategy for your business, you may be wondering how you can create and manage an effective long-term social media strategy, when there are so many changes to keep up with. It's a natural question to ask, but it's the wrong question.

The most important question for businesses hasn't changed:

How are you engaging and building relationships with your customers and stakeholders?

Learn the basics. Develop a personal level of comfort with the tools, find out how your customers are using various social platforms, and then find ways to integrate them into your business and help you enhance your existing strategies.

What's critical is that you do get started. Don't wait until someone lets you know that an unhappy customer has launched a massive viral social media campaign before you create your first Twitter account.

If social media has irrevocably changed anything, it's that individual stakeholders, customers, voters, and community members, now have access to tools that let them make their voices heard and easily galvanize support from others. When it comes to getting the word out, social media has leveled the playing field between customer and advertiser, employee and big business, voter and political machine.

In this environment, the relationship between your organization and your stakeholders is based on a conversation among equals. If you are clear about your values, transparent about your motives, and treat everyone with respect, whether you're dealing with them in your store or on Facebook, it's an incredible opportunity for any organization to build long-term, valuable relationships.

Tonia Ries is the founder and host of TWTRCON, the Web site and conference for business in real time, and the CEO of Modern Media, an agency at the intersection of live, digital, and social media.

Tonia Ries
@tonia_ries
http://www.linkedin.com/in/toniaries
http://modernmediapartners.com/
http://twtrcon.com/